Half-Real

Half-Real

Video Games between Real Rules and Fictional Worlds

Jesper Juul

The MIT Press Cambridge, Massachusetts London, England

First MIT Press paperback edition, 2011

This book was set in Janson and Rotis sans serif on 3B2 by Asco Typesetters, Hong Kong. Printed and bound in the United States of America.

Library of Congress Cataloging-in-Publication Data

Juul, Jesper, 1970–
Half-real : video games between real rules and fictional worlds / Jesper Juul.
p. cm.
Includes bibliographical references and index.
ISBN-13 978-0-262-10110-3 (hc. : alk. paper)
ISBN-13 978-0-262-51651-8 (pb. : alk. paper)
1. Video games—Rules. 2. Video games—Psychological aspects. I. Title.
GV1469.3.J88 2005
794.8—dc22 2005047863

10 9 8

▶ Note on the Web Site

The book's Web site (http://www.half-real.net) provides a collection of resources about video games and video game theory. These include a continually updated dictionary of video game theory, a list of suggested readings, links to relevant Web sites, and several tools on which to base video game experiments.

Contents

Preface

It began on a slow summer afternoon, playing countless games of tic-tac-toe against a childhood friend. The contest was exhilarating, and we tracked the tally carefully until, to our surprise, every game began ending up as a draw. This was unexpected, but we had reached a point where we understood the game well enough to play it perfectly. We had exhausted the game, and we discussed its strategic patterns: If your opponent begins in the middle, *always* pick a corner.

Some time later, at the age of eleven, I created a racing game on an early computer terminal: I drew a racetrack made of Xs and moved the cursor around the track as quickly as I could (timing each lap with a digital watch), carefully making sure that my car (the cursor) did not collide with the barriers (the Xs). My game looked something like this:

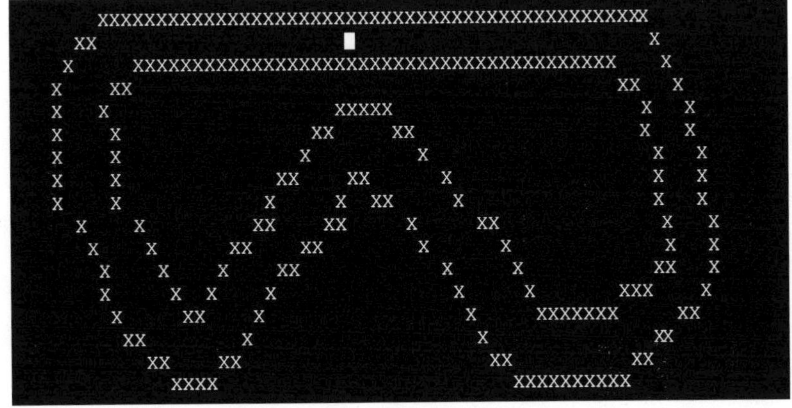

| **Figure P.1** |
Almost a video game.

What had I created? It was a game by most counts. But it was and it was not a *video game:* It took place on a screen, and though the terminal's processing power was modest, I had really designed a game *on* a computer. However, it was not a video game in the usual sense since it was me, and not the computer, that was upholding the rules.

In addition to setting up the rules of the game, I had also performed an act of imagination—I imagined the green characters on the black screen to be something else, a racetrack and a car, and I imagined that the movement of the cursor was the movement of a car. None of this required any cleverness: setting up a game with rules and goals was easy because I had at that time been exposed to hundreds or perhaps thousands of games, and imagining a rectangular cursor ▮ to be something else—a car—is easy for a child. I had also tried and thoroughly enjoyed a handful of computer and video games, and I sensed that there was a basic connection between computers and games. It was a connection that I urgently wanted to explore.

While the present book is the result of many twists and turns and changes of mind, it is also a book whose basic issues are clearly visible in the tic-tac-toe bout and in my crude video game of some twenty-three years ago: What does it take for something to be a video game, and when is a video game enjoyable? How do rules in games work, and how do they provide enjoyment for players? How and why does the player imagine the world of a game?

As for the first question, the object of this book is games played using computer power, where the computer upholds the rules of the game and where the game is played using a video display. I will be using *video games* as an umbrella term to describe all such PC, console, arcade, and other digital games.

I must thank the following bright minds for influencing me during the creation of this book: Susana Pajares Tosca, Lisbeth Klastrup, Espen Aarseth, Aki Järvinen, Gonzalo Frasca, Marie-Laure Ryan, Markku Eskelinen, Troels Degn Johansson, Henry Jenkins, Eric Zimmerman, Jill Walker, Mikkel Holm Sørensen, Simon Egenfeldt-Nielsen, Peter Bøgh Andersen, Lars Konzack, T. L. Taylor, Miguel Sicart Vila, Kim Forum Jacobsen, Noah Wardrip-Fruin, Clara Fernández-Vera, Chaim

Gingold, Anker Helms-Jørgensen, Rasmus Keldorff, and the people at MIT Press.

Thanks to Mads Rydahl for the line art and thanks to the tireless readers, Susana and Lisbeth.

The precursor of the book was produced on a Ph.D. grant at the IT University of Copenhagen between October 2000 and October 2003. Much of it was written between February and July 2003 during my stay at Comparative Media Studies, MIT, in Cambridge, Massachusetts.

Some parts of this book have previously been published:

- Most of chapter 2 was published as "The Game, the Player, the World: Looking for a Heart of Gameness," in *Level Up: Digital Games Research Conference Proceedings*, edited by Marinka Copier and Joost Raessens, 30–45. Utrecht: Utrecht University, 2003.
- Part of chapter 3's section on emergence and progression was published as "The Open and the Closed: Games of Emergence and Games of Progression," in *Computer Games and Digital Cultures Conference Proceedings*, edited by Frans Mäyra, 323–329. Tampere: Tampere University Press, 2002.
- An earlier version of chapter 4's section on time was published as "Introduction to Game Time," in *First Person: New Media as Story, Performance, and Game*, edited by Noah Wardrip-Fruin and Pat Harrigan, 131–142. Cambridge, Mass.: MIT Press, 2004.
- Parts of the conclusions were published as "Just What Is It That Makes Computer Games So Different, So Appealing?," *Ivory Tower* column for IGDA, April 2003. Available at ⟨http: www.idga.org/columns/ivorytower/ivory_Apr03.php⟩.
- Some of the notes on *Grand Theft Auto III* were taken from the article "Hvad Spillet Betyder" [What the Game Means], in *Digitale Verdener*, edited by Ida Engholm and Lisbeth Klastrup, 181–195. Copenhagen: Gyldendal, 2004.

| 1 |

INTRODUCTION

In the title, *Half-Real* refers to the fact that video games are two different things at the same time: video games are *real* in that they consist of real rules with which players actually interact, and in that winning or losing a game is a real event. However, when winning a game by slaying a dragon, the dragon is not a real dragon but a fictional one. To play a video game is therefore to interact with real rules while imagining a fictional world, and a video game is a set of rules as well as a fictional world.

Legend of Zelda: The Wind Waker (Nintendo 2003a) in figure 1.1 has been praised for its expressive graphics, lavish world, and detailed storyline. In the picture, the player's character has traveled far from his home island in search of his recently abducted little sister. In addition to the fictional world of the game, not only does a variety of on-screen displays provide the player with much information, there is also a curious arrow bouncing over the small girl in the flower field. The arrow indicates that we are playing a game with rules and a goal to work toward. It tells us that we can interact with the girl, and that she may help us progress in the game. It also illustrates that although the graphics depict an elaborate fictional world, only a small part of this world is actually implemented in the rules of the game; and the arrow indicates which part of the game fiction can also be found in these rules. Thereby *Legend of Zelda: The Wind Waker* points to a fictional world, and it points to the rules of the game. These are the two things that video games are made of: real rules and fictional worlds.

In having fictional worlds, video games deviate from traditional non-electronic games that are mostly abstract,[1] and this is part of the newness of video games. The interaction between game rules and game fiction is one of the most important features of video games, and it is a central

| **Figure 1.1** |
Legend of Zelda: The Wind Waker (Nintendo 2003a): The arrow points to what is important according to the rules of the game.

theme of this book. Their interaction is present in many aspects of games: in the design of the games themselves; in the way we perceive and use games; and in the way we discuss games. This interaction gives the player a choice between imagining the world of the game and seeing the representation as a mere placeholder for information about the rules of the game.

In addition, we face a choice between a focus on the game itself or on the player of the game: We can examine the rules as they are found mechanically in the game program or in the manual of a board game, or we can examine the rules as something that players negotiate and learn, and at which they gradually improve their skill. We can also treat the fictional world as a fixed set of signs that the game presents, and we can treat the fictional world as something that the game cues the player into imagining

| **Figure 1.2** |
Alan Kotok, Steve Russel, and J. M. Graetz playing *Spacewar!* Courtesy of the Computer History Museum.

and that players then imagine in their own ways. This book's intent is to integrate these disparate perspectives into a coherent theory of video games.

The Old and the New

The history of video games is both very brief and very long. The first video game was probably the 1961 *Spacewar!* (figure 1.2) (Russell 1961). The video game is thus a little more than forty years old, and it has been part of popular culture for around thirty years. Compare this to the roughly seventy-five years of television, a hundred years of film, and five hundred years of the printing press. Therefore, video games are a comparatively *new* cultural form, intimately linked to the appearance of computers, postdating literature, cinema, and television. However, if we think of video games as *games*, they are not successors of cinema, print

| **Figure 1.3** |

Queen Nefretiry playing senet. Ca. 1250 BC. *Egyptian Expedition of The Metropolitan Museum of Art, Rogers Fund, 1930. (30.4.145)* Photograph ©1978 The Metropolitan Museum of Art.

literature, or new media, but continuations of a history of games that predate these by millennia. The Egyptian board game, senet (figure 1.3), found in the 2686 BC tomb of Hesy-re is a precursor of contemporary backgammon and Parcheesi, games that are commonly played *using computers* today. Therefore, the question is not whether video games are old or new, but how video games are games, how they borrow from non-electronic games, and how they depart from traditional game forms.

But why do we even play games using computer power rather than using other recent inventions such as the telephone, microwave ovens, cars, or airplanes? There appears to be a basic affinity between games and computers: Like the printing press and cinema have historically promoted and enabled new kinds of storytelling, computers work as enablers of games, letting us play old games in new ways, and allowing for new types of games that would previously not have been possible.

Games as Rules

The rules of a game provide the player with challenges that the player cannot trivially overcome. It is a basic paradox of games that while the rules themselves are generally definite, unambiguous, and easy to use, the enjoyment of a game depends on these easy-to-use rules presenting challenges that *cannot* be easily overcome. Playing a game is an activity of improving skills in order to overcome these challenges, and playing a game is therefore fundamentally a learning experience. This takes different forms in different games, but we can outline two basic ways in which games are structured and provide challenges for players: that of *emergence* (a number of simple rules combining to form interesting variations) and that of *progression* (separate challenges presented serially).

Emergence is the primordial game structure, where a game is specified as a small number of rules that combine and yield large numbers of game variations for which the players must design strategies to handle. This is found in card and board games, in sports, and in most action and all strategy games.

Progression is the historically newer structure that became part of the video game through the adventure genre. In progression games, the player has to perform a predefined set of actions in order to complete the game. One feature of the progression game is that it yields strong control to the game designer: since the designer controls the sequence of events, progression games are also where we find most games with storytelling ambitions.

Though games may be different in structure, a player approaches every game with whatever repertoire of skills he or she has, and then improves these skills in the course of playing the game. To play a game is to improve your repertoire of skills, and the challenge of game design is to work with the skill set of the player through the game.

Games as Fiction

Most video games create fictional worlds, but games do this in their own special tentative and flickering way: the hero dies and is respawned moments later; the strategy game lets players "build" new people in a few seconds; the player dies and loads a *save game* in order to continue just before he or she died; in-game characters talk about the game controllers that the player is using. These things mean that the fictional worlds of many games are contradictory and incoherent, but the player may not experience this as such since the rules of the game can provide a sense of direction even when the fictional world has little credibility. In fact, the player's experience of the game fiction appears not to require much consistency—the world of a game is something that the player can often *choose* to imagine at will.

Fiction plays a different role in different games and game genres, and while some players may be thrilled by the fiction of a game, others may dismiss it as unimportant decoration of the game rules. Nevertheless, there is a general scale from the highly replayable multiplayer game (the emergence game) where the player can gradually begin to ignore the fiction to, at the other extreme, the "complete-once" adventure game (the progression game), where the player only faces each setting once and is therefore more likely to take the fictional world at face value.

What a Game Is

In this book, I have tried to examine what (if any) similarities can be found between the majority of the things we call "games," while at the same time being open to considerations of historical change and potential discussion about borderline cases. The *classic game model* presented in chapter 2 is a snapshot of a specific way of creating "games," a model that can be traced historically for thousands of years. The classic game model consists of six features that work on three different levels: the level of the game itself, as a set of rules; the level of the player's relation to the game; and the level of the relation between the activity of playing the game and the rest of the world. According to this model, a game is

1. a rule-based formal system;
2. with variable and quantifiable outcomes;
3. where different outcomes are assigned different values;

4. where the player exerts effort in order to influence the outcome;
5. the player feels emotionally attached to the outcome;
6. and the consequences of the activity are optional and negotiable.

The six features of the model are necessary and sufficient for something to be a game, meaning that all games have these six features, and that having these features is enough to constitute a game. While we can imagine any number of other phenomena that have only some of these features, this specific intersection is uniquely productive, allowing for the huge variation and creativity that we are witnessing in games.

This game model is the basis upon which games are constructed. It corresponds to the celluloid of movies; it is like the canvas of painting or the words of the novel. The game model does not mean that all games are the same, but that with these six features we can talk about how games are different from each other. Additionally, the model does not tie games to any specific medium, and games are therefore *transmedial* in the same way that storytelling is transmedial. Storytelling is a transmedial phenomenon since many different media can tell stories; games are a transmedial phenomenon since many different media (or tools) can be used for playing games.

While video games mostly conform to the classic game model, they also modify the conventions of the classic model. Games *have* changed. So while it makes sense to see games as a fairly well defined form, this book is also about how video games modify and supplement the classic game model; the history of video games is partly about breaking with the classic game model.

The Study of Video Games

This book was born from a brief and turbulent history of video game studies. It is a response to a number of questions that have been raised in numerous conferences, seminars, articles, and discussions over the past few years. It is also a book that does not rest easily with any one tradition, but neither did it appear out of thin air. Rather my work has consisted of collecting pieces from as many different fields and people as possible, while testing my ideas on as many different audiences as I could. As the history of the video game invokes a history of non-electronic games, video game studies must admit a debt to the study of non-electronic games.

Games for Other Purposes

For reasons that escape us, games have lingered under the cultural radar for thousands of years, and most of the commentaries that touch on games have been using *the idea* of games for other purposes.

Famously, the German philosopher Ludwig Wittgenstein used the concept of games[2] for building his philosophy of language, and games were singled out as an exemplary case of something that could not be defined or narrowed down. Games also inspired a theory that discusses a relation between rules and representation: Structuralists such as Vladímir Propp and Claude Lévi-Strauss claimed that meaning or narratives were based on formal structures (Pavel 1986; Propp 1968). Ferdinand de Saussure found chess to be inspirational for linguistics; as he wrote, "a state of the board in chess corresponds exactly to a state of the language. The value of the chess pieces depends on their position upon the chess board, just as in the language each term has its value through its contrast with all other terms" ([1916] 2000, 88). Therefore, the meaning of a chess piece stems from its relation to other pieces in the game, and is independent of its shape or makeup.

Games are usually well structured problems, and this has led to their being used in several other fields. John von Neumann and Oskar Morgenstern's 1944 book on game theory, *Theory of Games and Economic Behavior* (1953), deals primarily with economics, but in a way that has some relevance for the general study of games. Their economic *game theory* uses *games* as a general term for a specific type of problem. Game theory provides a generalized description of different types of *strategies*, and even though its focus is not on "games" that are meant to be enjoyed, it turns out that the formal game theoretical properties can yield important insights into games *and* game playing. For example, a game with a dominant strategy (a strategy that is better than all other strategies) is often *boring* because the player is not challenged in any way.

It is also the well structured character of games that have made them into a stable of artificial intelligence research. In 1950, Claude Shannon proposed using chess as a starting point for developing the modern "general purpose computer":

> The chess machine is an ideal one to start with, since: (1) the problem is sharply defined both in allowed operations (the moves) and in the ultimate

---

goal (checkmate); (2) it is neither so simple as to be trivial nor too difficult for satisfactory solution; (3) chess is generally considered to require "thinking" for skilful play; a solution of this problem will force us either to admit the possibility of a mechanized thinking or to further restrict our concept of "thinking"; (4) the discrete structure of chess fits well into the digital nature of modern computers. (Shannon 1950)

What the development of chess playing programs actually demonstrated was that humans play chess (and solve problems) in many different ways, and usually not as the early chess programs did, which was by considering as many chess positions as possible. In this way, the development of chess programs has been connected to cognitive science, where many studies have been conducted of how humans actually play games. Specifically, Adriaan D. De Groot's (1965) study of chess players looks into the psychology of play rather than the purely strategic aspect of play. Games and game-like problems have been commonly used for studying human problem solving—for example, in the work of Allen Newell and Herbert A. Simon (1972).

Finally, as Marcel Danesi has explored, games and puzzle solving have yielded many mathematical insights and methods. For example, the field of graph theory originates from the mathematician Leonhard Euler's study of the *Königsberg Bridge Problem:* whether seven bridges in the city of Königsberg could be traversed without crossing any bridge more than once (Danesi 2002, 19–22; Weisstein 2004). All of this demonstrates that game-related research has historically mostly been concerned with using games for studying other matters, and the insights reached concerning games have mostly been incidental to this research.

Games for Their Own Sake

In the study of games for their own sake, the field has been widely scattered historically. It probably flourished first in the late nineteenth century around folklore studies, for example in the work of Stewart Culin's 1907 *Games of the North American Indians* (1992), an 800-page collection and categorization of the games of Native Americans. Game studies also flourished around 1970. For example, E. M. Avedon and Brian Sutton-Smith's anthology *The Study of Games*[3] (1971) is an excellent overview of theory on non-electronic games, collecting articles into sections on the history of

---

games, the usage of games, and the structure and function of games. *The Study of Games* demonstrates that the narrow history of game research has mostly been sociological, anthropological, or philosophical, but not very well developed as an aesthetic field. That is, while much space has been devoted to the study of people (other than the researcher) playing games, very little has been said about the first-person experience of playing a game.

The two classic texts of game studies are Johan Huizinga's *Homo Ludens* (1950) and Roger Caillois's *Man, Play, and Games* (1961). For my purposes here, they suffer from the same problem of covering a broader area than *games* in that both discuss rule-based games as well as free-form play. Johan Huizinga focuses on *play* as a central component of all culture, but provides only sketchy discussions about games as such. Caillois is best known for his categorization of games (and play) into *agôn* (competition), *alea* (chance), *mimicry* (simulation or make-believe), and *ilinx* (vertigo). If anything, Caillois demonstrates that categorizations need to clearly reflect their goals and presuppositions, since in actuality games are not choices *between* chance and competition, or even placed on a scale between them, but rather almost all games are competitive *and* contain varying amounts of chance. It seems more reasonable to describe chance as one single example of a multitude of game design principles (as discussed in chapter 3) on the same level as showing or hiding information, mutual or contradictory goals, etc. Likewise, while *ilinx* (vertigo) is certainly a part of many physical game activities and of many video games, it is but a single example of the infinite number of different types of experiences that a game can give.

A complementary examination of games is provided by Bernard Suits's philosophically oriented dialogue *The Grasshopper* (1978), where a series of game definitions are proposed and discussed. Suits is best known for his description of games as letting the player reach the goal using only the *less efficient means* available. Suits belongs to a tradition of sports philosophy that has grown largely around the *Journal of the Philosophy of Sport*. This book is intended to be less purely philosophical than sports philosophy, but on the other hand more aesthetically oriented than play studies, a field that is often oriented toward the play of children. R. E. Herron and Brian Sutton-Smith's *Child's Play* (1971) provides a good overview of the field, as does Sutton-Smith's *The Ambiguity of Play* (1997).

Video Game Studies

The relatively short history of video games is complemented by an even shorter history of research. It is only around the turn of the millennium that video game studies began to come together as a field with its own conferences, journals, and organizations. This brief history has been something of a gold rush and a race toward being the first to point out special aspects of games, to format the field, to define words, and to point to similarities and dissimilarities between games and other cultural forms. This is not the place for an exhaustive review of the field so far; I will simply relate the discussions to which this book responds.

Video game studies have so far been a jumble of disagreements and discussions with no clear outcomes, but this need not be a problem. The discussions have often taken the form of simple dichotomies, and though they are unresolved, they remain focal points in the study of games. The most important conflicts here are games versus players, rules versus fiction, games versus stories, games versus the broader culture, and game ontology versus game aesthetics.

Games or Players

A basic dichotomy concerns whether we study the games themselves or the players who play them. Economic game theory is arguably originally the study of games as objects unrelated to players, but game theory does not rule out discussion of player experiences—it is just outside the scope of game theory. Still it would be perfectly possible to propose that we look exclusively at the games "themselves," while ignoring the fact that they are played by people. We can then at least imagine the reverse argument that declares the rules of a game unimportant compared to the way they are actually used. Linda Hughes has examined how a group of girls played Foursquare.[4] This turns out to be a combination of official and unofficial rules, conflicting success criteria, and rule negotiations. According to Hughes, "Game rules can be interpreted and reinterpreted toward preferred meanings and purposes, selectively invoked or ignored, challenged or defended, changed or enforced to suit the collective goals of different groups of players. In short, players can take the same game and collectively make of it strikingly different experiences" (1999, 94). This is a convincing argument, and part of a larger point that children's games cannot be meaningfully described only as the rules that make them up. If we took this argument to a logical extreme, we could claim that the game rules do not matter at all. This argument would unfortunately imply that the children might as well be fencing, playing poker, or playing rugby! A more detailed analysis of Foursquare reveals that the protracted structure of the game, with no clear termination, no final winner, and no clear score count *allows* the players to play while having many other considerations than simply perfecting their own performance. Moreover, the unclearness of some rules such as the rule against slamming[5] makes room for all kinds of social power play. At the same time, the players have *chosen* to play this game rather than other games, and players change the rules because they want to play *this game*, with specific rules. We cannot ignore the role of the rules without ignoring a basic aspect of the player experience: that different games yield different kinds of experiences.

Rules or *Fiction*

The main argument of this book, that video games are rules *and* fiction, is a response to a long history of discussions of whether games were one *or* the other. As in Saussure's observations about chess, it has often been noted that in a board game the actual shape of a piece appears unimportant in relation to the rules. Erving Goffman has proposed a principle called *rules of irrelevance*, meaning that the specific shape of a piece in a game is not important:

> [Games] illustrate how participants are willing to forswear for the duration of the play any apparent interest in the aesthetic, sentimental, or monetary value of the equipment employed, adhering to what might be called *rules of irrelevance*. For example, it appears that whether checkers are played with bottle tops on a piece of squared linoleum, with gold figurines on inlaid marble, or with uniformed men standing on colored flagstones in a specially arranged court square, the pairs of players can start with the 'same' positions, employ the same sequence of strategic moves and countermoves, and generate the same contour of excitement. (Goffman 1972, 19)

Roger Caillois does not deny that games can have fiction, but surprisingly states that games are rules *or* fiction, that rule-based games *do not* have a make-believe element:

Despite the assertion's paradoxical character, I will state that in this instance the fiction, the sentiment of *as if* replaces and performs the same function as do rules. Rules themselves create fictions. The one who plays chess, prisoner's base, polo, or baccara, by the very fact of complying with their respective rules, is separated from real life where there is no activity that literally corresponds to any of these games. That is why chess, prisoner's base, polo, and baccara are played *for real. As if* is not necessary.... Thus games are not ruled and make-believe. Rather, they are ruled *or* make-believe. (Caillois 1961, 8–9)

The division is, however, contradicted by most modern board games and video games. Most video games are ruled *and* make-believe.

In video game studies, the denial of fiction is an alluring position that I have also previously taken (Juul 1998). It is based on a simple recurring argument that tends to follow this pattern:

1. Rules are what makes a game a game.
2. Fiction is incidental to whether something is a game.
3. A game can be interesting without fiction.
4. A game with an interesting fictional world can be a terrible game.
5. Therefore, fiction in games is unimportant.

Though the conclusion is tempting, it is also false. Compare these two games based on identical rules (and programming), but with different graphics. In the first game (figure 1.4), the player controls a spaceship in a battle against the heads of the hosts of a television program. In the second game (figure 1.5), the player controls a spaceship in a battle against various theories, in this case a narratological model.

In a 1998 paper, I compared two games based on this program, and my conclusion was as follows: "As you can see, the symbolical or metaphorical meaning of the game is not connected to the program or the gameplay. The relationship is, in a word, *arbitrary*" (Juul 1998).

This idea that the representation of a game is irrelevant appears to have a constant allure, but it also break down upon further scrutiny. The game designer Frank Lantz has provided a similar argument based on design experiences:

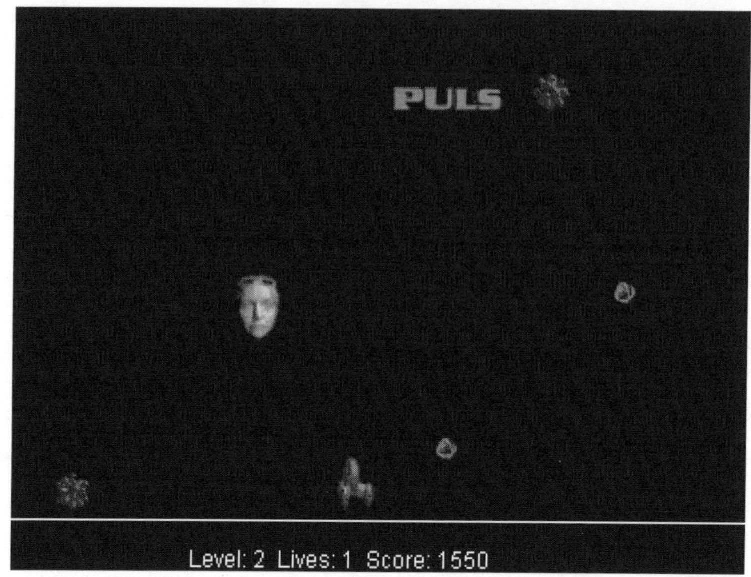

| **Figure 1.4** |
Puls in Space (Juul 1998a).

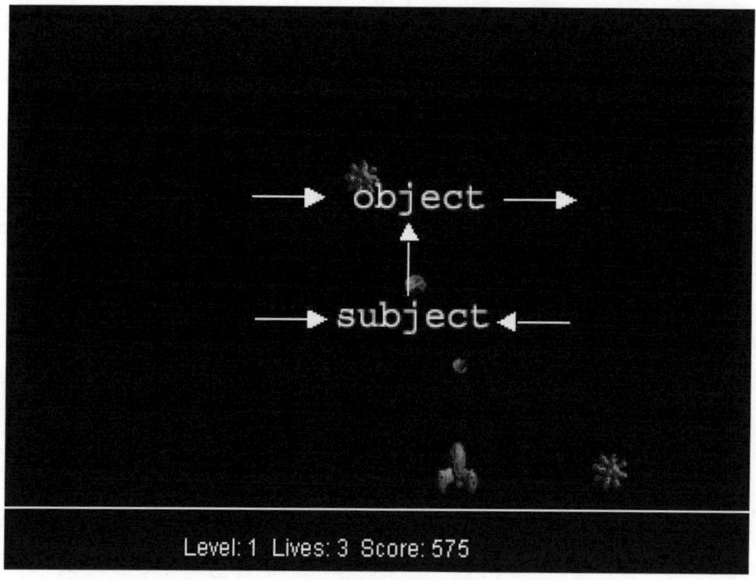

| **Figure 1.5** |
Game Liberation (Juul 2000).

I began to think about how structure and representation work in games. There was a notion buried in my original idea, the idea of a fundamental separation between a game's structure and whatever subject matter or activity or setting the game represents. The implication was that you could take any number of different structures and match them up with various themes for different effects, but there wasn't any *deep, essential* relationship between any particular theme and any particular game mechanic. . . .

After a couple of months of banging my head against it, this notion seemed less certain, or at least less interesting. . . .

There are, of course, many relationships between theme and structure in a game. Whether or not any of those relationships are *essential,* they are complex and vital enough to resist my attempt to lightly shuffle them around. (Lantz 2004, 310)

This strongly suggests that the relation between rules and fiction in the games in figure 1.4 and 1.5 is *not* arbitrary. Rather, these two games are *satirical.* In the first case they stage the love/hate relationship that viewers may have with television personalities as a deep-space battle. In the second case they stage an academic discussion—defending games against theoretical imperialism—as a deep space battle. Both are based on a background of some existing antagonism—and that is why they work, because the rules fit the representation—in an allegorical way.

Games Telling Stories

The early years of video game studies were often conceived as a discussion between *narratology* (games as stories) versus *ludology* (games as something unique). This discussion tended to alternate between being a superficial battle of words and an earnest exploration of meaningful issues (Murray 1997; Frasca 1999; Juul 1999; Eskelinen 2001b; King and Krzywinska 2002b; Atkins 2003; Aarseth 2004a; Jenkins 2004). Video game studies did not appear in a vacuum, so we need to remember the history that led up to this discussion. While *narratology* originated from Aristotle's *Poetics* and the study of storytelling media such as drama, novels, and films, the concept of *narrative* is today commonly used in a much broader sense. We can speak of a *narrative turn* after which it has become common to see narrative as the primary way in which we make sense of and structure the world. From this perspective, such different things as scientific discourse, the ideology of a nation, and our understanding of our personal lives are structured in the same way, using narratives. Espen Aarseth (2004a) has criticized this for being an unproductive ideology of *narrativism*. Outside game studies, Thomas Pavel (1986) has called this *mythocentrism*. The description of games as storytelling systems often overlaps with the prescriptive idea that video games (or "interactive narratives") would be *better* if they were more like stories. Building on Aristotle, Brenda Laurel (1986) has proposed a system for generating well formed plots. In this system, the computer program must take on the role of an author while the game progresses and make sure that regardless of the player's actions, every game session becomes well formed. Janet Murray's book *Hamlet on the Holodeck* (1997) describes the similar utopia of a *holodeck*—a completely immersive and transparent environment in which a user/player can engage in a well formed story. While this is in itself an overwhelming technical challenge, the logical problem is that there is no compelling argument demonstrating that a well formed "narrative" would be a more interesting *player* experience.[6]

Ludology is broadly taken to mean "the study of games." The history of the word itself is something of a mystery—its earliest known usage is from 1982 (Csikszentmihalyi 1982). *Ludology* was probably popularized by Gonzalo Frasca's 1999 article "Ludology Meets Narratology." I first used it in my paper "What Computer Games Can and Can't Do" (Juul 2000). From the outset, ludology has often been perceived as focused on distancing itself from narratology, and as trying to carve out video game studies as a separate academic field.

Some more recent theory has tried to stake something of a middle ground where the unique qualities of games are not denied, but the function of fiction or story in a game can still be discussed. In Rune Klevjer's paper "In Defense of Cutscenes" (2002), he criticizes "radical ludology" for completely dismissing cut-scenes (cinematic intermissions in games), and argues that cut-scenes serve several positive functions: they provide a unifying logic for the game and rewards for the player's actions. Additionally, Wibroe, Nygaard, and Andersen's article "Games and Stories" (2001) offers a nuanced discussion of game-story relations.

From the other end of the spectrum, Geoff King and Tanya Krzywinska (2002a) have discussed the relationship between games and cinema as a complex relationship with synergy and mutual inspiration as well as some notable differences. As an attempt at bridge-building between the open structure of games and the closed structure of stories, the concept of *quests* has been proposed by Ragnhild Tronstad (2001), Espen Aarseth (2004b), and Susana Tosca (2003). Quests in games can actually provide an interesting type of bridge between game rules and game fiction in that the game can contain a predefined sequence of events that the player then has to actualize or enact. This is discussed as a *progression* structure in chapter 3, and the relation between games and stories is discussed at the end of chapter 4.

Games or the Broader Culture

In a broader perspective, Henry Jenkins (2003) sees video games as part of a bigger complex of *transmedia storytelling*, where content can move between different media. In this broad sense of storytelling, video games *are* part of a general ecology of transmedia storytelling, but on a level that is often closer to the level of toys and merchandising than to the level of movies or novels. Realistically, video games are to some degree part of a general *storytelling ecology*, incorporating at least some elements of popular stories.

Just as we can choose to discuss games or players, we can also choose between studying a specific game for its role in the general media ecology or focusing on the game itself and the playing of the game. There is no reason to commit ourselves to one side of the discussion.

The added perspective in this book is that video games are also part of a general *game ecology*, where the video game incorporates other kinds of games and inspires other types of games.

Game Ontology or Game Aesthetics

We can also choose to discuss what video games *are* (ontology) or what they *should be* and what makes them enjoyable (aesthetics). In practice, this can be quite muddled: The video game researcher is usually (and arguably should be) a big fan of video games, and hence the game researcher enters the field with preferences for specific types of games, and the selection of games influences the researcher's arguments.

The extreme version of this is the game review, written with the explicit purpose of evaluating the quality of a game. I will be quoting reviews from several sources in order to discuss the relative merits of different games and different ways of structuring games. Game reviews provide documentation about the informal vocabulary that is used in the video game community. It is worth remembering that terminology is continually developed and discussed outside academia, and that this, too, is worthy of attention.

One issue is to what extent game research should deal with game design. The game development community has in recent years produced a large body of interesting books and articles. Chris Crawford's seminal *The Art of Computer Game Design* (1982) is an early discussion of video game design, but for the purpose of this book, more relevant discussions can be found in Richard Rouse's *Game Design—Theory and Practice* (2001) and Andrew Rollings and Dave Morris's *Game Architecture and Design* (2000). Game development writings cover a variety of different subjects including programming, artificial intelligence, 3-D graphics modeling, 3-D texturing, sound, music, team building, team management, as well as what is closest to my focus, game design. I will refer to a number of articles and presentations from *Game Developer Magazine*, *Gamasutra*, and the annual Game Developers' Conference.

If game design and game research often fall into separate camps, Katie Salen and Eric Zimmerman's book *Rules of Play* (2004) is a good example of how they can overlap. Working on the three levels of rules, play, and culture, Salen and Zimmerman describe games from a multitude of perspectives using examples of many games commissioned for the book. For various historical reasons, it is tempting to choose between being theoretical or practical, and while the present book is primarily theoretical, it is meant to be at least compatible with practical work on games.

Fun in Theory

When we are theorizing about games, it can seem that games contain a built-in contradiction: Since play is normally assumed to be a free-form activity devoid of constraints, it appears illogical that we would choose to limit our options by playing games with fixed rules. Why be limited when we can be free? The answer to this is basically that games provide context for actions: moving an avatar is much more meaningful in a game environment than in an empty space; throwing a ball has more interesting implications on the playing field than off the playing field; a rush attack is only possible if there are rules specifying how attacks work; winning the game requires that the winning condition has been specified; without rules in chess, there are no checkmates, end games, or Sicilian openings. The rules of a game add *meaning* and *enable actions* by setting up *differences* between potential moves and events.

Likewise, a game for multiple players is nominally a *limitation* of what the players are allowed to do, but it is a limitation that provides an occasion for interesting social interaction. When it is sometimes suggested to be a problem that games are competitive, it is a basic misunderstanding of how a game works: The conflict of a game is not antisocial; rather it provides a context for human interaction. Controlling a character that hits a character controlled by another player does not mean that one wants to attack that other person in real life: It means that one enters a complex world of symbolic interactions where attacking someone in a game can be an invitation to friendship, and helping someone in the same game can be a condescending rejection. In a game, things are not what they seem. Humans are not always literal in their interactions, and we cannot take human games at face value. Competitive games are social affairs, and much more so than the rarely played non-competitive games that have been proposed.[7]

Why are video games fun? One idea states that the all-important quality factor of a game is its *gameplay*, the pure interactivity of the game. In other words, that the quality of a game hinges on its rules, on the game-as-rules rather than on the game-as-fiction. In the words of Sid Meier, designer of *Civilization* and other classics, a *game is a series of interesting choices* (Rollings and Morris 2000, 38), by which Meier means that high-quality games are the ones whose choices provide high-quality mental challenges for players. While this is a compelling idea, a closer examination reveals many games that are considered enjoyable even though they do not provide any mental challenges. I believe that there is ultimately no one-sentence description of what makes all games fun; different games emphasize different types of enjoyment and different players may even enjoy the same game for entirely different reasons.

By analogy, James Cameron's movie *Titanic* (1997) contains a historical element, the spectacle of a big ship crashing into an iceberg, political commentary on class societies and gender roles, dramatic action where we follow an escape from the ship as it sinks, a hit title song, and, of course, a love story. Different viewers may enjoy the film for different reasons, and one viewer may enjoy the action sequence while disliking the hit song, while another viewer may like the love story and the hit song, but dislike the action sequence. Part of the audience may simply be in the theater because the people they were with wanted to go. Any popular cultural object or pastime can be popular for several different reasons at the same time.

Fortunately, this does not prevent us from discussing game enjoyment in more detail. The idea of what makes a game enjoyable may change over time and things that were once considered dull obstacles to the player's enjoyment can be foregrounded and become the central focus of a new game. Arguing about the rules of a game is often considered a problem, but it can also be enjoyable in its own right. Though a game generally maintains some consistency in the kinds of challenges it presents to a player, it is also possible to enjoy a game because the challenges it presents are inconsistent. And even though games usually let players perform actions that they can not perform in real life, it is, for example, possible to make a popular game like *The Sims* (Maxis 2000) that involves mundane tasks such as cleaning a house.

The Cultural Status of Games

Video games are notoriously considered lowbrow catalogues of geek and adolescent male culture. While this is not the whole picture, there is some extent to which the settings of many games can be somewhat unimaginative and where the actions that the players can perform tend to be simple. Video games generally focus on manipulating and moving objects, and less commonly address the more complex interactions between humans such as friendships, love, and deceit. We can suggest many reasons why this is so—we can blame unimaginative game designers; we can blame a conservative game audience; we can blame a risk-averse game industry; and finally we can look at game design and see that the game form lends itself more easily to some things than to others—it is *hard* to create a game about emotions because emotions are hard to implement in rules.

While games are regularly considered lowbrow, this is often due to some very naïve notions of what is highbrow or what is *art*. In a very simple view of art, art is what is ambiguous, whereas most games tend to have clear rules and goals. As Immanuel Kant would have it, art is *without inter-*

est, whereas game players clearly play with *much* interest and probably send the wrong signals simply because they *look* completely unlike visitors to an art gallery. We cannot reasonably use such claims as checklists, and we should avoid thinking about art, and games, in a limited and unimaginative way.

It should also be clear that playing a game does not imply literally endorsing the actions in the game or wanting to perform them in real life. This book is not about violence in games, but followers of the discussion may find it interesting to consider what a game is or what role the fictional world of a game plays. There are certainly strong arguments in favor of seeing the fictional worlds of games as just that, *fiction*. In a historical perspective, the current preoccupation with the assumed dangers of video games is a clear continuation of a long history of regulation of *games* as such: For example, in 1457 golf was banned in Scotland because it was felt that it kept young men from practicing archery (Avedon and Sutton-Smith 1971, 24). Pinball machines were banned in New York City from the late 1930s to 1976 (Kent 2000, 72). The Australian Office of Film and Literature Classification refused to classify *Grand Theft Auto III* (Rockstar Games 2001), making it illegal to sell it in Australia (IGN.com 2001). Video games were accused of being the reason for the Columbine high school shootings in the United States (Jenkins 1999). Perhaps games have always had the appearance of an uncontrollable activity with unclear and double meanings, and this is why they continue to be targets of regulation.

I do not see any particular contradiction between enjoying an action game and enjoying the poetry of Rainer Maria Rilke. There are a number of historical reasons why we might be tempted to see these things as incompatible, but they are basically misunderstandings. There is nothing inherent in video games that prevents them from ultimately becoming and being accepted as high art, even if this may take some time.

About This Book

The methods chosen in this book are intended to be non-exclusive. A method can easily preclude other methods of investigations, but the present investigation is meant to be at least *compatible* with empirical studies, game design, sociology, film theory, and more. I have attempted to be open about the status of different discussions and definitions, and I have tried to avoid preference for any specific type of conclusion.

In addition to this introduction, the book has five parts.

Chapter 2 presents a *classic game model;* this model was inspired by a number of previous writers on games. The model describes how games have been constructed in a specific historical period, while allowing for the possibility that video games have developed beyond this older model.

Chapter 3, on rules, attempts to combine a former understanding of game rules with a focus on the experience of playing games. In order to describe games as rule-based systems, I draw on computer science and the sciences of complexity. To describe the player's use and experience of the rules of a game, I draw on Marcel Danesi's writings on puzzles (2002), some game design theory, and some cognitive science.

The goal of chapter 4, on fiction, is to provide an account of the fictional aspect of games, an account that covers the spectrum from abstract games to games with incoherent fictional worlds to games with detailed fictional worlds. To be able to discuss this spectrum, the theory of *fictional worlds* is employed.

Chapter 5, on rules and fiction, is the synthesis of the two perspectives of rules and fiction and discusses their interactions using multiple examples.

Chapter 6 sums up the points of the book and provides some further perspectives.

2
VIDEO GAMES AND THE CLASSIC GAME MODEL

The eight games in figures 2.1–2.8 look to be quite different: One might be tempted to conclude that they have nothing in common and that their sharing the term "games" is an insignificant linguistic coincidence. In the words of Ludwig Wittgenstein, "What is common to them all?—Don't say: 'There *must* be something common, or else they would not be all called "games"'—but *look* and *see* whether there is anything common to all" ([1953] 2001, 27). Indeed, this is the subject of this chapter. Building on seven game definitions by previous writers, I create a new game definition that I call the *classic game model.*[1] The model is *classic* in the sense that it is the way games have *traditionally* been constructed. It is also a model that applies to at least a 5,000-year history of games. Although it is unusual to claim that any aspect of human culture has remained unchanged for millennia, there are strong arguments for this. In the introduction, I mentioned the Egyptian board game of senet, which appears to be a precursor of contemporary games such as backgammon and Parcheesi (Piccione 1980). Additionally, the board and card games developed during the past few thousand years commonly have a shared European-African-Asian history, and the American anthropologist Stewart Culin has documented the games of the North American Indians (Culin 1907). This means that games following the classic game model have been known in the vast majority of human cultures.[2] While many definitions of games have been attempted, the one I will propose here has the goal of explaining what relates video games to other games and what happens on the borders of games. What should the definition look like? We are probably interested in understanding the properties of the games themselves (the artifact designed by the game developers), how the player interacts with them, and what it means to be playing rather than, say, working. So let

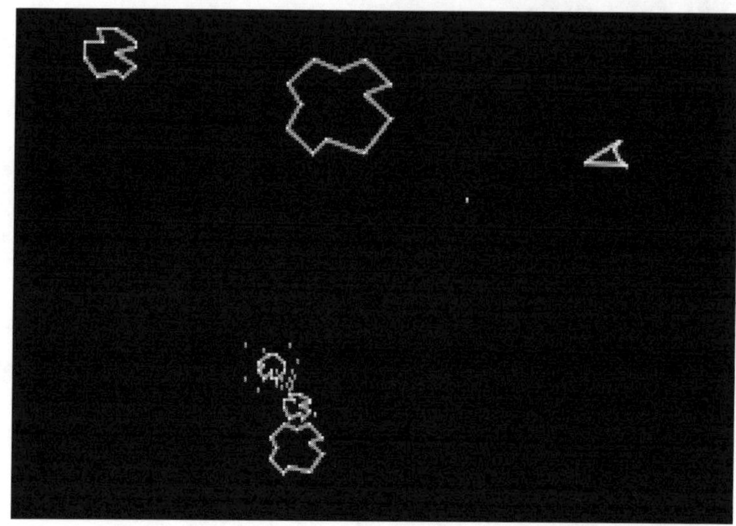

| **Figure 2.1** |
Asteroids (Atari 1979).

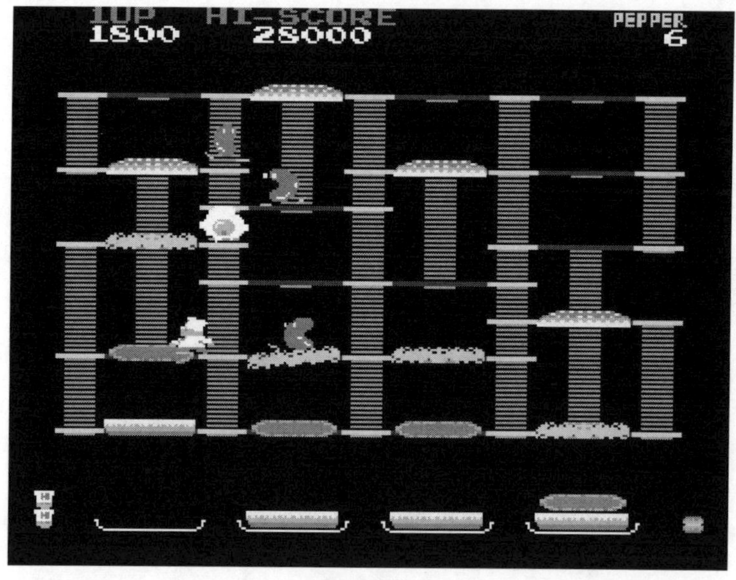

| **Figure 2.2** |
Burger Time (Data East 1982).

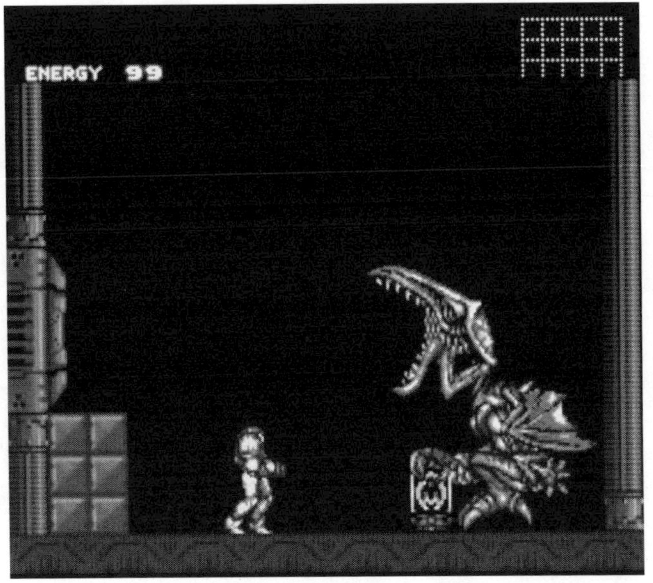

| **Figure 2.3** |
Super Metroid (Nintendo 1993).

| **Figure 2.4** |
Counter-Strike (The Counter-Strike Team 2000).

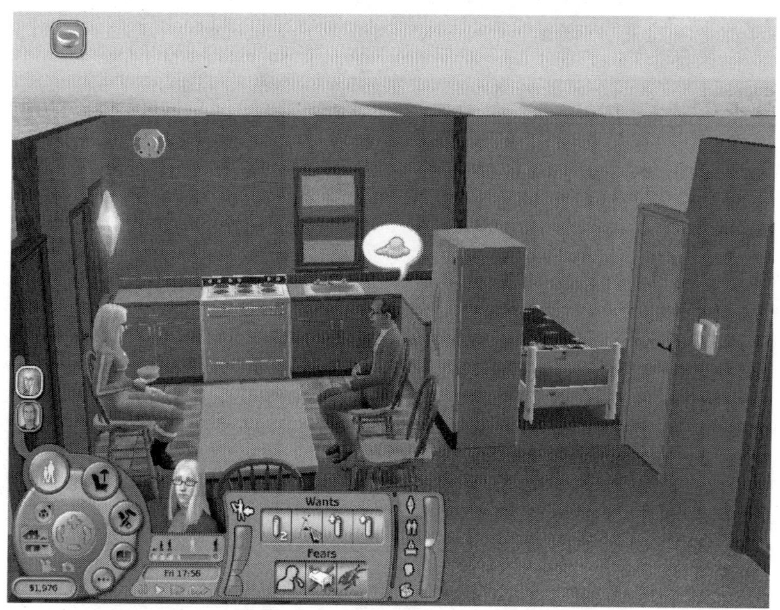

| **Figure 2.5** |
The Sims 2 (Maxis 2004).

| **Figure 2.6** |
Super Monkey Ball 2 (Amusement Vision 2002).

| **Figure 2.7** |
Grand Theft Auto III (Rockstar Games 2001).

| **Figure 2.8** |
Legend of Zelda: The Wind Waker (Nintendo 2003a).

us assume that a good definition should describe these three things: (1) the system set up by the rules of a game, (2) the relation between the game and the player of the game, and (3) the relation between the playing of the game and the rest of the world.

As demonstrated by Bernard Suits (1978), the simplest way to test a game definition is to test it for being either too broad or too narrow. To set up the test before the definition, I will assume that *Quake III Arena* (ID Software 1999), *Dance Dance Revolution* (Konami 2001), checkers, chess, soccer, tennis, and Hearts are games; that open-ended games such as *The Sims* (Maxis 2000) and *SimCity* (Maxis 1989), gambling, and games of pure chance are borderline cases; and that traffic, war, hypertext fiction, free-form play, and ring-a-ring o' roses[3] are not games. The definition should be able to determine what falls inside from what falls outside the set of games, but also to explain in detail why and how some things are on the border of the definition. The existence of borderline cases is not a problem for the definition as long as we are able to understand *why* and *how* something is a borderline case.

In the big perspective, practically every single game found in any compilation of traditional card games, board games, or sports falls squarely within the classic game model I describe here. It appears that it is only during the last third of the twentieth century that new game forms have challenged the classic model.

Like the fact that mentioning the rules of a game can make it sound dull, the idea of a definition may sound limiting but it is really the opposite. In fact, to define games is to create what Douglas Hofstadter (1985) has termed a *productive set*. An example of a productive set is the set of all shapes that represent the letter *A*, where the mere description of the properties of the set help show how the set can be expanded. Having described all possible *A*'s makes it much easier to come up with new typographical designs for the letter *A*. Having a definition of games also points to how we can create new kinds of "games" that try new things that games have not tried before. It is easier to break the rules once you are aware of them.

The Language Issue

The first thing to note is that it may be easy to accept that there is a difference as well as a close relation between *play* and *game*.[4] *Play* is mostly taken to be a free-form activity, whereas *game* is a rule-based activity.

The problem is that this distinction is very dependent on the language used, and much confused by the fact that in French, Spanish, or German, neither *jeux*, *juego*, or *Spiel* has such a distinction. In English, this is also a bit muddled since "play" is both a noun and a verb (you play a game), whereas "game" is mostly a noun. In English, it is common to see *games* as subset of *play*. Scandinavian languages have a stronger distinction with *leg* = play and *spil* = game with verbs for both—you can play play ("*lege en leg*") and game game ("*spille et spil*"), so to speak. When writing about games in Danish, it is therefore not self-evident that games are a subset of play, whereas while writing about *Spiel* in German, it is not obvious that one should distinguish between games and play from the outset. This manifests itself with the English translations of writers such as Ludwig Wittgenstein and Roger Caillois who write in languages with no clear play/game distinctions.[5] At the same time, even within the English language, our focus is not on the letter sequence g-a-m-e, since we probably consider big *game* hunting to be a slightly different thing. To clarify, the focus here is on the set of games that we can describe as *rule-based games*.

Some Previous Definitions

Let us go through some previous definitions of games, focus on their similarities and point to any modifications or clarifications needed for our current purpose. First, we should note that the definitions do not necessarily try to describe the same aspect of games: Some concentrate purely on the game as such, some on the activity of playing a game. Additionally, it turns out that many things can be expressed in different ways. When one writer talks about goals and another discusses conflict, it is possible to translate between them: conflict entails (conflicting) goals; the notion of goals entails the possibility of not reaching the goal, and thereby a conflict. We will get back to this, but let us simply list seven game definitions, which we will categorize afterward (table 2.1).

There are more similarities than differences in these definitions. If we want to look at games on three different levels, we can sort the points of the individual definitions according to what they describe. For example, "rules" describes games as formal systems. That a game is "outside ordinary life" describes the relationship between the game and the rest of the world. That a game has an "object to be obtained" describes the game as a

Table 2.1
Seven game definitions

Source	Definition
Johan Huizinga 1950, 13.	[. . .] a free activity standing quite consciously outside "ordinary" life as being "not serious," but at the same time absorbing the player intensely and utterly. It is an activity connected with no material interest, and no profit can be gained by it. It proceeds within its own proper boundaries of time and space according to fixed rules and in an orderly manner. It promotes the formation of social groupings which tend to surround themselves with secrecy and to stress their difference from the common world by disguise or other means.
Roger Caillois 1961, 10–11.	[. . .] an activity which is essentially: free (voluntary), separate [in time and space], uncertain, unproductive, governed by rules, make-believe.
Bernard Suits 1978, 34.	To play a game is to engage in activity directed towards bringing about a specific state of affairs, using only means permitted by rules, where the rules prohibit more efficient in favor of less efficient means, and where such rules are accepted just because they make possible such activity.
E. M. Avedon and Brian Sutton-Smith 1971, 7.	At its most elementary level then we can define a game as an exercise of voluntary control systems in which there is an opposition between forces, confined by a procedure and rules in order to produce a disequilibrial outcome.
Chris Crawford 1982, chapter 2.	I perceive four common factors: representation ["a closed formal system that subjectively represents a subset of reality"], interaction, conflict, and safety ["the results of a game are always less harsh than the situations the game models"].
David Kelley 1988, 50.	[. . .] a game is a form of recreation constituted by a set of rules that specify an object to be attained and the permissible means of attaining it.
Katie Salen and Eric Zimmerman 2004, 96.	A game is a system in which players engage in an artificial conflict, defined by rules, that results in a quantifiable outcome.

formal system *and* the relationship between the player and the game. If we allow ourselves to translate between different points, seeing for example "goals" and "conflict" as different ways of expressing the same concept, we can group all the points of the definitions according to the level(s) they describe: the game as a formal system, the player and the game, and the game and the rest of the world (table 2.2).[6]

The definitions have many overlaps, but with some work, it is possible to separate the actual disagreements from mere differences in wording.

Rules and Outcomes

All writers agree that games are rule-based (Crawford calls this a "formal system"). While there are many things to say about rules (see chapter 3), let us for the time being focus on the fact that rules are designed to be above discussion—it is supposed to be clear whether a given action is or isn't allowed by the rules of a game.

The question of outcomes is more interesting: It is a salient feature of games that they have variable outcomes—if the outcome is the same every time, it does not qualify as a game. The variability of the outcome follows from Crawford's mention of conflict (only one side can succeed).

Salen and Zimmerman's contribution (2004) here is to point out that the outcome of a game shares some features with the rules of the game: the outcome of a game is quantifiable, meaning that it—like the rules—is designed to be above discussion.

Goals and Conflict

Only Bernhard Suits talks explicitly about goals (a specific state of affairs to be brought about) but goals are implicit in Salen and Zimmerman and Crawford's *conflict*—a conflict presupposes mutually contradicting goals between two entities or, in a broader sense, between a player and the difficulty of reaching a goal. As we will see later, a game without a goal is a borderline case.

Voluntary

Roger Caillois claims that games are voluntary. The problem is that it is quite unclear what this means. Is it not a game if social pressure forces the player to play? Because human motivation is too complex to be simply explained in terms of its being voluntary/involuntary, I believe that it is

Table 2.2
Game definitions compared

	The game as formal system	The player and the game	The game and the rest of the world
Rules Fixed rules (Huizinga) Rules (Caillois) Rules (Suits) Procedure and rules (Avedon and Sutton-Smith) Formal system (Crawford) Rules (Kelley) Rules (Salen and Zimmerman)			
Outcome Uncertain (Caillois) Disequilibrial outcome (Avedon and Sutton-Smith) Changing Course (Kelley) Quantifiable outcome (Salen and Zimmerman)			
"Goals" Bringing about a state of affairs (Suits) Opposition (Avedon and Sutton-Smith) Conflict (Crawford) Object to be obtained (Kelley)			
Interaction Interaction (Crawford)			
Goals, rules, and the world Artificial conflict (Salen and Zimmerman)			
"Separate" Outside ordinary life/proper boundaries (Huizinga) Separate (Caillois) No material interest (Huizinga) Unproductive (Caillois)			

Table 2.2
(continued)

	The game as formal system	The player and the game	The game and the rest of the world
"Not work" Free/voluntary (Caillois) Voluntary control systems (Avedon and Sutton-Smith) Recreation (Kelley)			
Less efficient means Less efficient means (Suits)			
Social groupings Promotes social groupings (Huizinga)			

not possible to meaningfully describe whether games are voluntary or not. However, it could be said that games are primarily autotelic; that is, they are mostly used for their own sake rather than for an external purpose. It is very hard to set this up as a clear criterion—the game definition I am proposing at least partly explains *why* games are such that this issue cannot be settled.

Separate and Unproductive

In Johan Huizinga's description, play is an activity that has "no material interest, and no profit can be gained from it" (1950, 13). Roger Caillois points out that this leaves no place for gambling and suggests that in games, "Property is exchanged, but no goods are produced" (1961, 5).

Both Huizinga and Caillois describe games as being outside "normal" life: They are assigned a separate space and separate time. In Huizinga's description, games take place inside a *magic circle*, outside which the game does not apply. There are some obvious objections and counterexamples to this description—I will return to this.

Less Efficient Means

Bernard Suits famously describes games as permitting players to use only the "less efficient means" in order to reach the goal (Suits 1978, 34). I will contend that this description is interesting but ultimately misleading. Suits's argument hinges on the fact that it is (mostly) possible to describe a game as the effort to reach what he calls a *pre-lusory goal,* a goal which can be said to exist independently of the game, and that there is always an optimal but disallowed way of reaching this goal. This idea is in itself quite problematic.[7] The concept of inefficient means makes sense in Suits's prime examples of the race where it is not allowed to cut across the infield and the high jump where using a ladder is disallowed. The problem is that it would always be possible to set up a game using the *most* efficient means possible: a racing game where cutting over the infield was allowed; a race to climb a ladder, etc. And the concept of less efficient means completely breaks down in the case of video games. In *FIFA 2002* (a soccer game) (Electronic Arts 2002) and *Virtua Tennis* (Hitmaker 2000), the video games are much easier to master than their real-life professional counterparts are—namely, soccer and tennis. If we look at *any* video game, how can we say that the player is using less efficient means? Would this be compared to making the game yourself? Hacking the game? Using a cheat code?

Bernard Suits's definition is exemplary in that it shows how a feature of a definition can be alluring, in this case not because "less efficient means" is actually part of what makes a game a game, but because it *entails* some other features that are important, namely some player effort, some kind of separation of the game from the rest of the world, and some element of acceptance of the rules—in a way, Suits hints at the characteristic of games being *voluntary*.

Fiction

As already discussed, the issue of fiction depends much on the games discussed. *Some* games have a fictional element, but this is not universal to games. I discuss fiction in chapter 4 of this book.

Social Groupings

Since some games are solitary, social groupings are not a universal aspect of games, but game rules and social groupings interplay—a group may form around the playing of a specific game, and an existing group may decide to play a game. The way a game can build community is discussed in chapter 3.

The Game and the Player: A Second Look at Goals

The list of examples gives us two border case examples of the concept of goals: *The Sims* and *SimCity* are often labeled games even though they do not have explicit goals. While the game designer, Will Wright, claims that they are not games but toys (Costikyan 1994), they are nevertheless often categorized as "video games." The proposal here is to be more explicit about the player's relation to the game by dividing the concept of *goals* into three distinct components, namely:

1. Valorization of the possible outcomes: Some outcomes are described as positive, some as negative.
2. Player effort: The player has to *do* something.
3. Attachment of the player to an aspect of the outcome: The player agrees to be happy if he or she wins the game, unhappy if he or she loses.

Separate and Unproductive: Negotiable Consequences

In Roger Caillois's definition, games are *separate* in time and space from the rest of the world and *unproductive*. It is fairly easy to find examples of games that transgress the first aspect: It is after all possible to play chess by mail, in which case the game overlaps with daily life, both in the sense that the time span of the game overlaps a non-game part of life and in the sense that it is possible to consider the moves one wants to play while going about one's daily business. Likewise, many Internet-based strategy games stretch over months or even years. The second feature, *unproductive*, is dubious if productivity can mean something other than the production of physical goods. Caillois's suggestion is that gambling does not *produce* anything. From an economic viewpoint, this is problematic since gambling is a huge industry. Also note that it is possible to bet on the outcome of any game,[8] and that many people do make a living playing games.

Separation is a special issue in live action role-playing games (games where players typically dress up as characters to play the game), where the games may be played in spaces also used for "normal life." In these cases, specific descriptions have to be made as to what interactions are allowed between non-playing people and players.[9]

Taking a step back, we can see that the notions of games being *separate* and *unproductive* are quite similar in two respects. Both specify what interactions are possible (and allowed) between the game activity and the rest of the world, and neither are perfect boundaries, but rather fuzzy areas under constant negotiation.

When Caillois claims that a game played involuntarily is not a game, there is a distinction between a given game and a given playing of a game. All copies of a given title do not suddenly cease to be games because someone is making money playing them. Since all games are potential targets for betting and professional playing, I suggest that games are characterized as activities with *negotiable consequences*. A specific playing of a game may have assigned consequences, but games are characterized by the fact that they can be assigned consequences on a per-play basis. That games carry a degree of separation from the rest of the world is entailed in their consequences being negotiable.

A New Definition: Six Game Features

From this, the game definition I propose has six features:

1. *Rules:* Games are rule-based.
2. *Variable, quantifiable outcome:* Games have variable, quantifiable outcomes.
3. *Valorization of outcome:* The different potential outcomes of the game are assigned different values, some positive and some negative.
4. *Player effort:* The player exerts effort in order to influence the outcome. (Games are challenging.)
5. *Player attached to outcome:* The player is emotionally attached to the outcome of the game in the sense that a player will be winner and "happy" in case of a positive outcome, but a loser and "unhappy" in case of a negative outcome.
6. *Negotiable consequences:* The same game [set of rules] can be played with or without real-life consequences.

In short form:

A game is a rule-based system with a variable and quantifiable outcome, where different outcomes are assigned different values, the player exerts effort in order to influence the outcome, the player feels emotionally attached to the outcome, and the consequences of the activity are negotiable.

Table 2.3
The classic game model and the game, the player, the world

	The game as formal system	The player and the game	The game and the rest of the world
1. Rules			
2. Variable and quantifiable outcome			
3. Value assigned to possible outcomes			
4. Player effort			
5. Player attached to outcome			
6. Negotiable consequences			

In diagram form, the new definition can be visualized as six features, spanning the three categories of the game, the player, and the world (table 2.3). Features 1, 2, and 4 describe the properties of the game as a formal system; 3 describes the values assigned to the possible outcomes of the system—the goal that the player must strive for; 4 and 5 describe the relation between the system and the player (feature 4 describes both the fact that the game system can be influenced by player input and that the player does something); 6 describes the relation between the game activity and the rest of the world. Each of these features can be elaborated.

1. Rules

Games have rules. The rules of games have to be sufficiently well defined that they can be either programmed on a computer or that players do not have to argue about them every time they play. The playing of a non-electronic game is an activity that in itself involves trying to remove any lack of clarity in the game rules: If there is disagreement about the rules of a game, the game must be paused until the disagreement has been solved. In a commercial non-electronic game, the developer will (hopefully) have made sure that the rules are unambiguous, but what about non-commercial games? A non-electronic and "folk" (non-commercial) game tends to drift toward becoming unambiguous. This explains some of the affinity between games and computers—and the fact that a several thousand-year-old non-electronic game is easily implementable in a computer program: The drive toward definiteness in the rules makes the game ripe for implementation in a programming language.

The rules of any given game can be compared to a piece of *software* that then needs *hardware* to actually be played. In the case of games, the hardware can be a computer, mechanical devices, the laws of physics, or even the human brain.

Even if the rules are unambiguous, the game activity still requires that the players *respect* the rules. Bernard Suits has described this as *lusory attitude* (1978, 38–40)—the player accepts the rules because they make the game activity possible. Even a cheater depends on the rules to be able to play.

2. *Variable, Quantifiable Outcome*

For something to work as a game, the rules of the game must provide different possible outcomes. This is straightforward, but for a game to work as a game *activity*, the game must also match the skill of the player(s). Consider the game of tic-tac-toe in figure 2.9.

This is a general property of tic-tac-toe: if your opponent begins by placing a piece in the middle, you must *always* place your first piece in the corner, otherwise you will lose to a reasonably intelligent opponent. This explains why tic-tac-toe is a children's game, and this is where we find that there is a subjective aspect to games. Tic-tac-toe remains interesting as long as it is mentally challenging, but once the players figure out a perfect strategy, they will achieve a draw every time they play. Variable outcome therefore depends on who plays the game. If players always achieve a draw or if a master player continually wins against a beginner, it is still a game, but the players are unable to use it as a game *activity*.

Many games have features for ensuring a variable outcome. Go, golf, or fighting games like *Tekken 3 Tag Tournament* (Namco 2000), allow for handicaps for the players in order to even out skill differences. A few racing games cheat to even out the skill differences between players: In *Gran Turismo 3: A-Spec* (Polyphony Digital 2001), players who are trailing be-

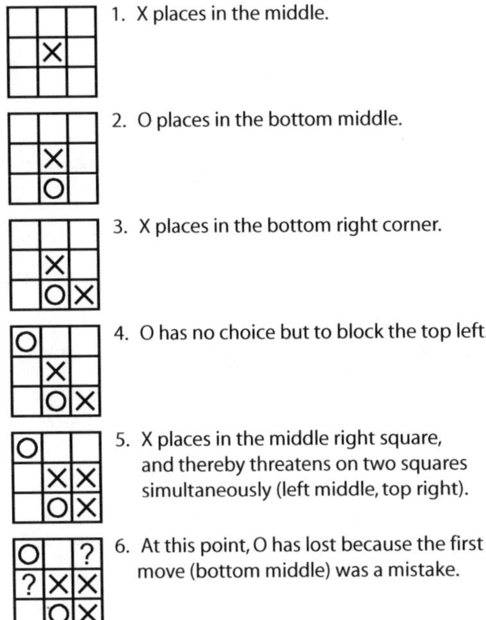

| **Figure 2.9** |
A game of tic-tac-toe.

hind on the racetrack automatically drive faster than the leading players, allowing them to catch up.

Likewise, players themselves may feign ineptitude in order to bring some uncertainty to the outcome—the *Tekken 3* player may play slightly unfocused; the race game player may simply drive slowly or even reverse the car, the chess player may try especially daring strategies. We may term this *player-organized criticality*—in the same way that players try to uphold the rules, players may also try to ensure suspense about the outcome of the game.

Finally, quantifiable outcome means that the outcome of a game is designed to be beyond discussion, meaning that the goal of *Pac-Man* (Namco 1980) is to get a high score, rather than to "move in a pretty way."[10] Since playing a game where the participants disagree about the outcome is rather problematic, the specification of the outcome develops like the rules of a game, toward becoming unambiguous.

3. Valorization of Outcome

Valorization means that some of the possible outcomes of the game are *better* than others. In a multiplayer game, the individual players are usually assigned conflicting positive outcomes (this is what creates the conflict in a game).

The values of the different outcomes of the game can be assigned in different ways: by a statement on the box ("Defend the Earth"); by instructions of the game; by the fact that some actions give a higher score than others; by virtue of there being only one way of progressing and making something happen; or it can be implicit from the setup—being attacked by hostile monsters usually means that the player has to defend himself or herself against them.

Positive outcomes are usually harder to reach than negative outcomes—this is what makes a game challenging. A game where it is easier to reach the positive outcome than to not reach it would likely not be played much.

4. Player Effort

Player effort is another way of stating that games are challenging, or that games contain a conflict. It is a part of the rules of most games (except in games of pure chance) that the players' actions can influence the state of the game and the game's outcome. The investment of player effort *tends* to lead to an attachment of the player to the outcome, since the investment of energy into the game makes the player (partly) responsible for the outcome. The challenge of games and the player's effort are examined in chapter 3.

5. Player Attached to Outcome

The emotional attachment of the player to the outcome is a psychological feature of the game activity. A player may feel genuinely happy if he or she wins, and unhappy if he or she loses. Curiously, this is not just related to player effort: a player may still feel happy when winning a game of pure chance. As such, attachment of the player to the outcome is a less formal category than the previous ones in that it depends on the player's attitude toward the game. The spoilsport is one who refuses to seek enjoyment in winning, or refuses to become unhappy by losing.

6. *Negotiable Consequences*

A game is characterized by the fact that it can *optionally* be assigned real-life consequences. The actual assignment can be negotiated on a play-by-play, location-by-location, and person-to-person basis. So while it is possible to bet on the outcome of any normally "for-fun" game, it is impossible to enter a casino in Las Vegas and play without betting money.

If a player loses a game and faces horrible consequences from this, conforming to the negotiated outcome is then a question of honor. In the work *Germania*, the Roman historian Tacitus (ca. AD 56–ca. AD 120) is surprised at how absolutely the Germanic people respect this: "Gambling, one may be surprised to find, they practise in all seriousness in their sober hours, with such recklessness in winning or losing that, when all else has failed, they stake personal liberty on the last and final throw: the loser faces voluntary slavery: though he be the younger and stronger man, he suffers himself to be bound and sold" (Tacitus [AD 98] 1914, 297–299).

There is an important difference between the actual operations of the game and the outcome of the game. The only way for a game to have negotiable consequences is if the operations and moves needed to play the game are mostly harmless. Any game involving actual weapons has strong *non-negotiable* consequences. This is in itself a point of contention, since many sports can lead to injury and even death. Arguably, part of the fascination with some sports such as boxing or motor sports lies in the fact that they are dangerous. Nevertheless, it is a convention of these games that injuries are to be avoided. Public outrage is likely if a motor sports event has poor security precautions.

The consequences of a game have a special status in that they are under continued negotiation, probably both in general societal terms—what is permissible for any game—and on a per-game basis, where the participants may openly or implicitly discuss the range of permissible reactions that the game can elicit.

Even so, all games have some officially sanctioned non-optional consequences, namely in that they may take the time and energy of the players and, more prominently, as described in point 5, that games can make the players happy or unhappy, hurt or boost their pride. But, again, this can happen only within certain negotiable limits, since there are several well known transgressions, such as excessive sulking (being a poor loser), excessive boasting, or leaving the game prematurely if one is losing. The amount of permissible teasing and provoking of other players is not set in stone; there is a continuous breaking of ideals: Friendships may end over negotiations in *Monopoly* (Parker Brothers 1936), or players may get angry that their loved ones did not protect them in a game of *Counter-Strike* (The Counter-Strike Team 2000). However, *ideally* in game playing, this should not occur. The explicitly negotiated consequences concern what the players can consciously control, such as the exchange of goods or money, but the involuntary and less controllable reactions such as joy or sorrow are less clearly defined.

Since much of human interaction is symbolic rather than physical, this raises a question about the boundaries between games and non-games. For example, for any given country, we could in theory take the complete set of regulations regarding parliamentary elections and perform them as games in which contestants would perform actual rallies and speeches in order to make the public vote for the contestant who might then receive a cash prize rather than public office. This sounds much like a game and, in fact, it would be. Elections are not games since the consequences of the outcome are defined and not subject to negotiation, but the rules governing the execution of the election are potentially usable for game purposes. Many human activities can in principle be performed as games. Examples could include politics, courtship, and academia. Note that these are activities that are occasionally metaphorically described as being "games": the game of politics, the game of love, the game of getting tenure at universities.

Professional sports is a special case. According to Roger Caillois, the professional player or athlete is working rather than playing (1961, 6). This quickly becomes counterintuitive since a contest such as a marathon may include professional athletes as well as amateurs who are running "for the fun of it." This logically means that the marathon is and is not a game at the same time. A better explanation is that even professional players are *playing* a *game*, but that in this specific *game session*, the consequences have been negotiated to be financial and career-determining. Perhaps the reason it can be discussed whether professional sports are games or not is that we associate a game with the context in which it usually appears; that is, we tend to not think of something as a game if we have only seen it performed with serious consequences. So, even though the rules governing the stock market or elections could be used for game purposes, we do not consider them games, and even though soccer is played professionally, we consider it a game because it is also played in non-professional settings and we are aware that its consequences are negotiable.

On the Borders of Games

In diagram form, we can visualize the game model as two concentric circles, where things considered games have all six previously defined features and therefore belong within the inner circle; borderline cases can be placed between the two circles; and decidedly non-game cases are placed outside the outer circle (figure 2.10).

If we begin with the borderline cases: pen and paper role-playing games are not classic games because, having a human game master, their rules are not fixed beyond discussion.[11] Open-ended simulations like *SimCity* are not classic games since they have no explicit *goals*—that is, no explicit values are assigned to the possible outcomes of the game, but what happens in the game is still attached to the player and the player invests effort in playing the game.

Outside the set of games, free-form play has variable rules; structured play like ring-a-ring o' roses has fixed rules but also fixed outcome. Storytelling has fixed outcome, the player does not exert effort in order to influence the outcome, and the player is not personally attached to the outcome. Watching Conway's game of life or watching a fireplace is to experience a system with rules and outcomes, but there are no values assigned to the outcomes, the player is not attached to the outcome, and no player effort is required.

Traffic shares most of the game features, namely rules (traffic laws), variable outcome (you either arrive or you do not arrive safely), value attached to outcome (arriving safely is better), player effort, and players attached to the outcome (you actually arrive or do not), but the consequences of traffic are *not* optional—moving in traffic *always* has real-life consequences. The same applies to the concept of noble war such as war waged respecting the Geneva Convention.

Games as Objects and Games as Activities

Even with this definition, "game" can mean two things: A static object or artifact or an activity or event that players perform. Chess is a game (a static object), but we can also play a game of chess (an activity).

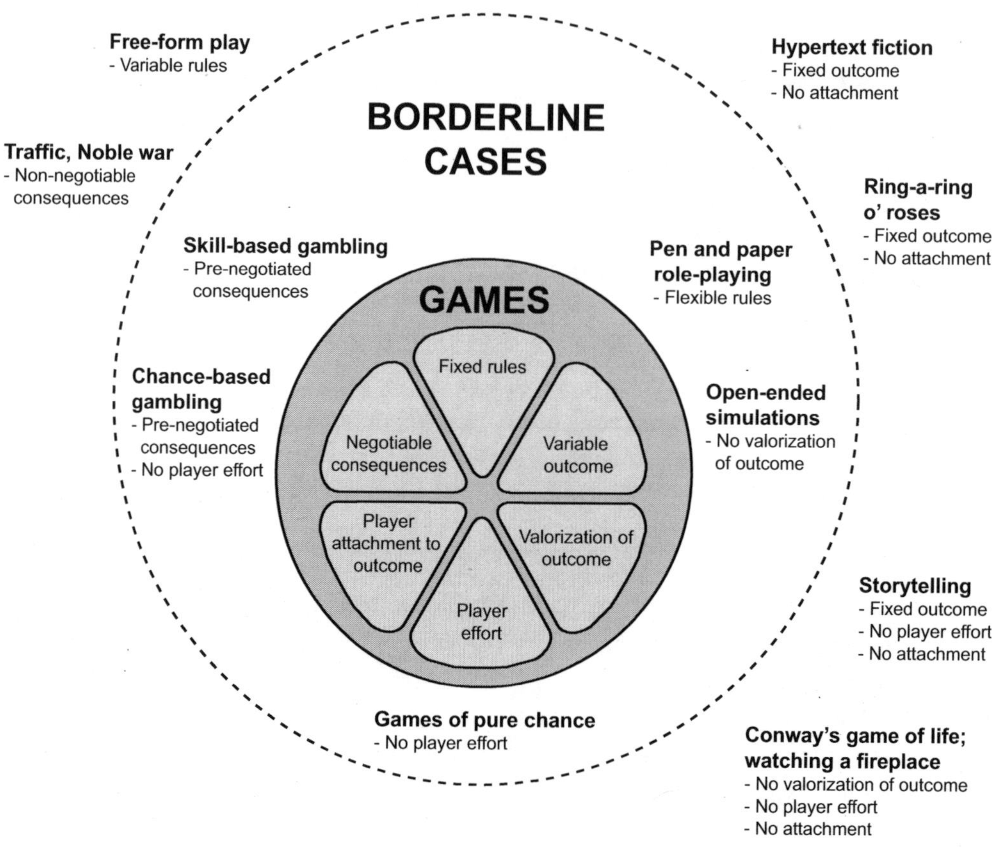

| **Figure 2.10** |
On the borders of the classic game model.

According to this game definition, the game *as an object* is a list of rules with the property that a computer or a group of players can implement unambiguously: the rules must—if implemented—produce variable and quantifiable outcomes and describe how the player(s) can exert effort. The game must provide a description of which outcomes are positive and which are negative. The game must explicitly or by convention signal to players that it is an activity with an outcome to which they *should* feel emotionally attached. Finally, the activity that the game describes must have consequences that are negotiable.

As an *activity*, a game is a system that changes state according to a set of rules that are implemented by humans, computers, or natural laws. The game is such that its outcome is undetermined, variable, and quantifiable. The players are aware that some outcomes are more desirable than others. The players are able to exert effort in order to influence the outcome. The players feel attached to the eventual outcome. Finally, the consequences of the game *have been* negotiated, ideally before the beginning of the game.

In practice, this distinction is mostly straightforward. Concepts such as rules and state machines statically describe dynamic objects. The more difficult distinctions concern the psychological aspects of games. It is possible to take anything with rules, variable outcomes, player effort, and negotiable consequences and turn it into a game by simply assigning values to the outcomes between players. For example, two people walking down the street can decide to turn it into a race by describing it as *better* to reach the destination first. A single person performing a mundane task such as sweeping the floor can decide to make it into a game by timing him or herself, trying to beat a personal record. Drawing on a piece of paper can be assigned simple rules and turned into a game. This can then become a convention—the two people who originally raced down the street can for a time permanently agree to race when turning a specific corner. The activity of doodling according to rules may feel sufficiently entertaining that the players tell others of their doodling game. Most of the things described as games are sufficiently well defined that they can be played again. This indicates that there is a loose idea that games are repeatable. When we speak of a specific game, we generally speak of it as being a repeatable event. Salen and Zimmerman explicitly write that "rules are repeatable" (2004, 139).

Game Examples

The game model does not mean that all games are the same, but it provides a way of describing what distinguishes different games from each other. The game model is implemented differently in various games:

Checkers

Let us look at an example game, checkers (or draughts):

1. Rules: In short form, the rules state that two players, white and black, each have twelve pieces that can move diagonally across the board, jump over opponent pieces and capture them.
2. Outcome: Defined as one player having lost all his or her pieces.
3. Value: Better to be the one with pieces left.
4. Effort: Consider moves.
5. Attachment: *You* win.
6. Negotiable consequences: Generally, a harmless pastime, but it is possible to play for money. Tournaments exist.

Soccer

1. Rules: Two teams with eleven players each, one of whom is a goalkeeper. Each team has a goal, which are at opposite ends of the playing field. Players can kick the ball but not touch it with their hands (goalkeepers can touch it with their hands). If the ball leaves the boundary of the playing field, the ball is given to the opposite team of the team that last touched it. Putting a ball in the opponent's goal scores a point. The game takes place within two halves of 45 minutes each.
2. Outcome: Defined as the goals scored within the time allotted to a game.
3. Value: The team with most goals wins.
4. Effort: Moving about, strategies, tactics, general skill in handling of the ball, communication.
5. Attachment: *Team* wins; the individual player can be *informally* judged on the basis of his or her achievements in the game.
6. Negotiable consequences: Social consequences in doing well for the team versus doing badly. Injuries non-negotiable; there are many professional leagues; betting is common.

Battlefield 1942

This refers to the "Conquest" game mode of *Battlefield 1942* (Digital Illusions 2002).

---

1. Rules: Two teams play against each other. There are rules regarding the movement of players, weapons, vehicles, level design, counting of points for having taken a base, respawning, etc. Some rules are explicit (counting of points); some rules are likely to be inferred by the player from the environment (guns kill); some rules, such as the way in which vehicles handle, have to be learned by the players.
2. Outcome: Defined as the accumulated time important locations on the map were held.
3. Value: More points (for time locations were held) win. Potentially one team can kill more players than the other team, but still lose the game.
4. Effort: Moving, shooting, strategies, communication.
5. Attachment: *Team* wins.
6. Negotiable consequences: Harmless, but some tournaments are being played. Social consequences in doing well for the team versus doing badly.

Borderline Case: SimCity

As previously mentioned, *SimCity* is considered a borderline case.

1. Rules: Rules regarding economy, buildings, assumptions about how the city works, transport. Some rules are explicit, some are inferred by the player from the setting, some contradict the setting—a power plant can be built in a few months in the game, unlike in real life.
2. Outcome: Few specified outcomes.
3. Value assigned to outcome: No outcomes are assigned values, though the player may feel that building a city is better than not building one, but the game conversely accommodates players who want to destroy their creations. Players may assign their own personal values to the different outcomes.
4. Effort: Building, planning.
5. Attachment: Whatever happens is to some extent the players *fault*, but this is loosely defined.
6. Consequences: Not a prime candidate for betting since the outcome is not clearly defined.

Transmedial Games

The definition of games proposed here does not tie games to any specific medium[12] or any specific set of tools or objects. Furthermore, we know that many games actually move between media: card games are played on computers, sports continue to be a popular video game genre, and video games occasionally become board games. Since this has not, to my knowledge, been explored in any systematic way, we can take a cue from narratology: stories cannot be examined independently but only through a medium such as oral storytelling, novels, and movies. Seymour Chatman has argued that narratives exist since they can be translated from one medium to another. "This transposability of the story is the strongest reason for arguing that narratives are indeed structures independent of any medium" (1978, 20). While it is clear that stories can be passed between a novel and a movie and back, it is also clear that not everything passes equally well. For example, novels are strong in creating inner voices and thoughts, while movies are better at conveying movement.

We can view games from a similar perspective: While there is no single medium or set of props that is the ideal game medium, games do exist, and do contain recognizable features, whether as card games, board games, video games, sports, or even mind games. There is no set of equipment or *material support* common to all games. What is common, however, is a specific sort of *immaterial support*, namely the upholding of the rules, the determination of what moves and actions are permissible and what they will lead to. Upholding the rules is in actuality provided by human beings (in board games or card games), computers, or physical laws (in sports).

The card game hearts can be transferred to a computer because the computer can uphold and *compute* the rules that would normally be upheld by humans, and because the computer has the *memory* capacity to remember the *game state*. The adaptation of board and card games to computers is possible due to the fact that computers are capable of performing the operations defined in the rules of the games, operations that are normally performed by humans, as well as keeping track of the game state, something normally done by using cards and board pieces. What we have is therefore an ecology of game media that support games, but do so differently. Thus games can move between different media—sometimes with ease, sometimes with great difficulty.

Chess qualifies as one of the most broadly implemented games, since chess is available as a board game, on computers, and even played *blind*, where the players keep track of the game state in their head. Sports are somewhat special in that the properties of the individual human body are part of the game state. This means that the rules of sports are less clearly defined than the rules of other games (hence the need for a referee). It is very hard to realistically implement the physics of something like pool, soccer, or bowling in video games. At the time of writing, there are several companies (e.g., Havok and Mathengine) dedicated exclusively to providing simulation of physics in video games.

Game Implementations and Game Adaptations

There are big differences in the ways that games move between media. Card games on computers should be considered *implementations* since it is possible to unambiguously map one-to-one correspondences between all the possible game states in the computer version and in the physical card game. Sports games on computers are better described as *adaptations*, since much detail is lost in the physics model of the computer program because it is a simplification of the real world, and in the interface because the video game player's body is *not* part of the game state. Adapting soccer to computers is therefore a highly selective adaptation. Game media support games in two distinct ways:

1. *Computation:* how the game medium upholds the rules and decides what happens in response to player input.
2. *Game state:* how the game medium keeps track of the current game state.

The distinction between computation and game state is necessary in order to explain the differences between some of the game media mentioned here (table 2.4). In technical terms, it corresponds to the low-level distinction in the computer between CPU (computation) and the RAM (memory).

- Generally speaking, video games are a superset of board games and card games; most card and board games are immediately implementable in computer programs. The physical setting around the game does not translate well.

Table 2.4
Games moving between media

	Rules/computation	Game state
Card games	Human brain	Cards
Board games	Human brain	Game pieces
Blind chess	Human brain	Human brain
Competitive sports	Physics + human brain	Players' bodies/ game objects
Video games	Computer (CPU)	Computer (RAM)
Card/board games on computer	Computer (CPU)	Computer (RAM)
Sports on computer	Computer (CPU)	Computer (RAM)

- Board games implemented on computers include *Axis & Allies* (Hasbro Interactive 1998), *Risk* (BlueSky Software 1997), chess, checkers, and backgammon.
- The feasibility of adaptation from video game to board or card game depends on the game. In the 1980s, many popular arcade games were used for selling poor quality board games: this befell (among others) *Pac-Man* (Milton Bradley 1982), *Berzerk* (Milton Bradley 1983), and *Frogger* (Milton Bradley 1981).
- One of the most popular adaptations is from sports to video games. These adaptations are imperfect due to both lack of fidelity in the physics simulations and the low amount of information that the player can input, but they are also extremely popular, probably because they allow players to imagine that they are doing something they could not normally do.[13]
- Video game to sport adaptations are almost nonexistent. A notable exception is that some players of paintball games have adopted the rules of *Counter-Strike*.
- Card decks are good at keeping track of possessions, and resources and at hiding information.
- Board games provide possessions and spatial gameplay well, but are most immediately suited to games of perfect information (where all players have access to all information in the game). This is easily implemented on computers.

- Dance and rhythm games like *Dance Dance Revolution* (Konami 2001) are special in that the amount of information transferred between the player and the game state is very low, but the body is nevertheless heavily involved since the physical layout of the dance mat requires you to move your body in order to play.
- Sports allow for many things that video games cannot, mostly because of the importance of bodily capabilities in the world and the depth of the "interface." More information is transferred to the game state—in fact, the player's body is part of the game state.

Game Implementations: Mapping between Domains

The distinction between an implementation and an adaptation concerns whether there is an unambiguous correspondence between the possible game states in the two game versions. Nevertheless, two games that appear completely unrelated can turn out to be equivalent on a game state to game state basis. For example, a spatial game may be converted into a non-spatial game.[14] Consider the following game:

Two players take turns picking a number between 1 and 9. Each number can only be picked once. The first player to have 3 numbers that add up to 15 has won. If all numbers are picked without a winner, the game is drawn.[15]

As an example game between player A and player B:

1. A picks 5.
2. B picks 9.
3. A picks 2.
4. B has no choice but to pick 8 (otherwise, A could get 5+2+8=15).
5. A picks 7, and thereby threatens to win by either picking 3 (5+7+3=15) or 6 (2+7+6=15).
6. At this point, B has lost because the first pick (9) was a mistake.

If this sequence seems familiar, it is because it can be completely mapped to the example game of tic-tac-toe earlier in this chapter: If we lay out the numbers 1 to 9 in a 3 × 3 grid, the game is an implementation of tic-tac-toe (figure 2.11).

Picking the numbers 6, 7, and 2 is therefore identical to placing three pieces in the rightmost column; if your opponent has picked 5 and 2, it is a

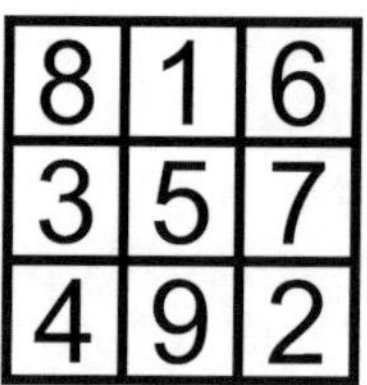

| **Figure 2.11** |
Tic-tac-toe as a mathematical game: Pick three numbers that add up to 15.

good idea to pick 8 in order to prevent him or her from getting a sum of 15. This works because the numbers above are laid out in a *magic square* where the sum of each vertical, horizontal, and diagonal line adds up to 15. (For the history of magic squares, see Danesi 2002, 147–151.) Compare the two games (figure 2.12).

This mathematical game is *equivalent to* tic-tac-toe in the sense that there is an unambiguous mapping between every possible position in tic-tac-toe and every possible position of the mathematical game. The two games are, however, probably not *experienced* identically by players—in tic-tac-toe, players will think of the game as a spatial problem; in the mathematical game, players will think of the game as a game of adding numbers. Anecdotal evidence suggests that most players find tic-tac-toe *much* easier. *This means that games that are formally equivalent can be experienced completely differently.*

The Limits of the Classic Game Model

While some writers have claimed that games are forever indefinable or ungraspable, a review of David Parlett's two books *The Oxford History of Board Games* (1999) and *The Penguin Encyclopedia of Card Games* (2000) indicates that all of the hundreds of games described fall within the *classic game model.* The vast majority of things called "games" are found in the intersection of the six features of the game model. It is an intersection that can be traced historically for at least a few thousand years and through most human cultures.

Why is there an affinity between computers and games? Because games are a transmedial phenomenon, and the material support needed

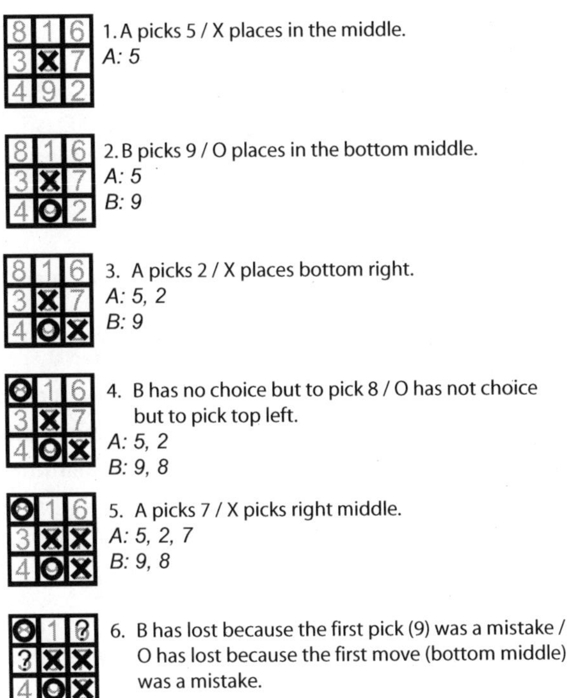

| **Figure 2.12** |
Equivalence between tic-tac-toe and a mathematical game.

to play a game (like the projector and the screen in cinema) is *immaterial*, since games are not tied to a specific set of material devices, but to the processing of rules. This fits computers well because the well defined character of game rules means that they can be implemented on computers.

The classic game model is no longer all there is to games. With the appearance of role-playing games, where a game can have rules interpreted by a game master, and with the appearance of video games, the game model is being modified in many ways.

1. *Rules:* While video games are just as rule-based as other games, they modify the classic game model in that it is now the *computer* that upholds the rules. This gives video games much flexibility, allowing for rules more complex than humans can handle; freeing the player(s) from

having to enforce the rules; and allowing for games where the player does not know the rules from the outset.

2. *Variable outcome:* In many cases, the computer can act as a referee in order to determine the outcome of a game on the basis of events that would not be immediately discernible to a human.

In persistent online games, the player never reaches a final outcome but only a temporary one when logging out of the game.

3. *Valorization of outcome:* Open-ended simulation games such as *The Sims* change the basic game model by removing the goals, or more specifically, by *not* describing some possible outcome as better than others.

4. *Player effort:* The non-physical nature of video games means that player effort can work in new ways. For example, the player can control a large number of automatic units in a real-time strategy game, which would not be possible in a non-electronic game.

5. *Attachment to outcome:* Because an open-ended simulation game does not have a specific win or lose state, it gives the player a less well defined relation to the game outcome.

6. *Negotiable consequences:* It is perhaps implicit in the classic game model that a game is bounded in time and space; the game has a specific duration and a specific location. Pervasive games, location-based games, and some live-action role-playing games break this, as do games such as *Majestic* (Anim-X 2001) where actual phone calls are part of the playing of the game.

Let us consider what the classic game model does: It provides a barebones description of the field of games; it explains why computers and games work well together; it explains why games are transmedial; and it points to some recent developments in games. The game model by itself does not provide much explanation of the variations between games, or of why games are enjoyable. It is an abstract platform upon which games are built, a platform that games use in different ways.

Games *do* have something in common; we *can* talk about the borders between games and what is not a game—video games are the latest development in a history of games that spans millennia.

3
RULES

Game rules are paradoxical: Rules and enjoyment may sound like quite different things, but rules are the most consistent source of player enjoyment in games. We may associate rules with being barred from doing something we really want, but in games, we voluntarily submit to rules. Game rules are designed to be easy to learn, to work without requiring any ingenuity from the players, but they also provide challenges that *require* ingenuity to overcome. Finally, the rules of a game tend to add up to more than the sum of their parts: For most games, the strategies needed to play are more complex than the rules themselves.

Fixed rules are a core feature of games, but rules do not appear out of nowhere; they are created by players in folk games and by game designers in commercial games. Many games are played using either playing cards or computers, but the rules appear to *be the same*, even if it is the players that uphold the rules when played with cards, but the computer that upholds the rules in the video game version. As a game can move between different media, so can the rules that make up the game. But then what are rules made of and what function do game rules serve?

Let us assume that games are enjoyable in part because players *enjoy* the sense of accomplishment that solving a challenge gives them. In a multiplayer game, the enjoyment may also come from the interaction with other players, the contest or the teamwork involved in playing the game. These are not the only enjoyable aspects of games, but they are surely among the most universal ones.

In short, rules work like this.

1. *Rules* are designed to be above discussion in the sense that a specific rule should be sufficiently clear that players can agree about how to use it. Rules describe what players can and cannot do, and what should

happen in response to player actions. Rules should be implementable without any ingenuity.

2. The rules of the game construct a *state machine*, a "machine" that responds to player action (regardless of whether the game is played using computer power or not).

3. The state machine of the game can be visualized as a landscape of possibilities or a branching *game tree* of possibilities from moment to moment during the playing of the game. To play a game is to interact with the state machine and to explore the game tree.

4. Since a game has multiple outcomes, the player must expend effort trying to reach as positive an outcome as possible. It is usually harder to reach a positive outcome than a negative one—harder to win than to lose. If the player works toward the positive outcome, the player therefore faces a *challenge*.

5. The way the game is actually played when the player tries to overcome its challenges is its *gameplay*. The gameplay is an interaction between the rules and the player's attempt at playing the game as well as possible.

6. Games are learning experiences, where the player improves his or her skills at playing the game. At any given point, the player will have a specific *repertoire* of skills and methods for overcoming the challenges of the game. Part of the attraction of a good game is that it continually challenges and makes new demands on the player's repertoire.

7. Any specific game can be more or less challenging, emphasize specific types of challenges, or even serve as a pretext for a social event. This is a way in which rules can give players *enjoyable experiences*, and different games can give different experiences.

There are two extreme ways of creating challenges for players: that of *emergence* (rules combining to provide variation) and *progression* (challenges presented serially by way of special-case rules). Emergence games are the historically dominant game form. Progression games are a historically new game form where the game designer explicitly determines the possible ways in which the game can progress. Rules in games of emergence present a paradox contained in the sentence *easy to learn but difficult to master*. This is a common description of the type of game with nominally simple rules where it nevertheless requires immense amounts of effort to gain proficiency in playing the game. The apparent paradox here is that the simplicity of the rules of a game may lead to very complex gameplay. Emergence in games comes in many different forms, and it explains many interesting aspects of games such as the fact that a game can be played for hundreds of years without being exhausted; how the actual playing of a game can be unpredictable even to its designer. The element of surprise in emergent games is special in that it is an interaction between the rules of the game and the fuzzy ways in which humans understand games.

What makes an enjoyable challenge? Using a combination of Marcel Danesi's discussion of puzzles (2002) and discussions from the game development community about what Sid Meier has coined *interesting choices* (Rollings and Morris 2000, 38) I will examine what *kinds of* challenges games provide and how. Rules are not the only source of game enjoyment; I discuss the enjoyment of games as fictional worlds in chapter 4.

What Are Rules?

There is generally a clear-cut split between the fiction and rules of a game: The rules of chess govern the movement of the pieces; the representation fiction of chess is the shape and color of the pieces. No matter how the pieces are shaped, the rules, gameplay, and strategies remain identical.

What are rules? One school of thought describes rules as primarily being *limitations*. In the previous chapter, I rejected Bernard Suits's definition of games as being based on allowing the player to reach a goal by only using the *less efficient means* available (1978, 34). In Suits's view, games limit the options of a player: in high jump, using a ladder is disallowed; in a track race, the player may not run across the midfield. My objection was that it made some sense in the choice of examples, but that it is not a general feature of games. In sports, we generally have the option of finding a more efficient way of reaching the game goal. On a basic level, this is because the human body and the laws of physics exist *before* the game, but in a game, they are appropriated for the game's purposes, and some limitations are added to how they can be used. This is similar to my racing game mentioned in the preface, where the movement of the cursor on a terminal was an existing system that was used to signify the movement of a car; the game then imposed additional rules on that system, disallowing the movement of the cursor into the characters that signified the racetrack. Likewise, Katie Salen and Eric Zimmerman describe rules as *limiting player action* with the following argument: "**Rules limit player action**. The chief way that rules operate is to limit the activities of the player. If you are playing the game Yatzee, think of all the things you could do with the dice in that game: you could light them on fire, eat them, juggle them, or make jewelry out of them.... Rules are 'sets of instructions,' and following those instructions means doing what the rules require and not doing something else instead" (2004, 122). This is technically true, but the limitation view of rules only paints half the picture: you *could* make jewelry of the dice, but it would be meaningless within the Yatzee game. The rules of a game also *set up potential actions*, actions that are meaningful inside the game but meaningless outside. It is the rules of chess that allow the player to perform a checkmate—without the rules, there is no checkmate, only meaningless moving of pieces across a board. Rules specify *limitations* and *affordances*. They prohibit players from performing actions such as making jewelry out of dice, but they also add meaning to the allowed actions and this *affords* players meaningful actions that were not otherwise available; rules give games *structure*. The board game needs rules that let the players move their pieces as well as preventing them from making illegal moves; the video game needs rules that let the characters move as well as rules that prevent the character from reaching the goal immediately.

Sports and other physical games require an extra note here: Though the explicit rules of soccer only state the dimensions of the playing field, the ball's specifications, what the players can and cannot do, and the conditions for winning, the game of soccer is also governed by the laws of physics—the air resistance of the ball, gravity, the condition of the grass, and the limits of human anatomy. If we compare the physical sport of soccer with a video game version of soccer such as *FIFA 2002*, the video game adaptation requires that the laws of physics and the human anatomy be explicitly implemented in the programming *on the same level as the explicit rules of the game:* A computer-based soccer game needs to implement the physics of the players and the soccer pitch as well as the rules of the game. Gravity existed prior to the invention of soccer, and the human body existed prior to the invention of the foot race, so including them in a game is a choice that the creators of the game make. It therefore makes sense to see the laws of physics on the same level as the conventional rules in soccer: The main difference between the rules of a video game and the rules of a sport is that sports use the preexisting systems of the physical world in the game.

Strategies and State Machines

As explained in *game theory* by Neumann and Morgenstern, there is an important distinction between rules and strategies: "Finally, the *rules* of the game should not be confused with the *strategies* of the players.... Each player selects his strategy—i.e. the general principles governing his choices—freely. While any particular strategy may be good or bad—provided that these concepts can be interpreted in an exact sense—it is within the player's discretion to use or to reject it. The rules of the game, however, are absolute commands" (1953, 49). In game theory, a strategy is an overall plan for how to act in the variety of different states that the game may be in. A *complete strategy* is one that specifies unambiguously what the player should do for every possible game state. In actuality, humans tend to play games with incomplete and loosely defined strategies: A player may have a strategy that applies to only a small subset of the possible ways in which the game can be played, and will subsequently have to invent a new strategy if the game turns out differently than expected.[1] Actual strategies tend to group many possible game states into clusters in order to reduce the large number of potential game states to a manageable set of more generalized situations (Holland 1998, 41). A *dominant strategy* is one that is always better than all other strategies, regardless of the actions of any opponent.[2] A given game allows for any number of different strategies, some of which will be more effective than others. While the strategies of a game are different from the rules of the game, the relative effectiveness of a potential strategy is *a consequence* of the game rules.

Game theory also distinguishes between games of *perfect information* and games of *imperfect information:* In the former case, all players have complete knowledge of the game state at any given moment (Neumann and Morgenstern 1953, 30). In the latter case, players only have partial knowledge of the game state. Games of perfect information include many traditional board games and a few video games such as *Space Invaders* (Taito 1977), *Tetris* (Pazhitnov 1985), *ChuChu Rocket* (Sonic Team 2000), and *Tekken 3 Tag Tournament*.[3] Games of imperfect information include most card games (since the hands of the other players are hidden) and the majority of video games including all three-dimensional games (3-D graphics hide things from the player's view).

To borrow from computer science, the rules of a game provide a *state machine*. Briefly stated, a state machine is a machine that has an *initial state*, accepts a specific amount of *input events*, changes state in response to inputs using a *state transition function* (i.e., rules), and produces specific outputs using an *output function*.[4] In a literal sense, a game is a state machine: A game is a machine that can be in different states, it responds differently to the same input at different times, it contains input and output functions and definitions of what state and what input will lead to what following state (e.g., the piece can move from E2 to E4, but not to E5; if you are hit with the rocket launcher, you lose energy; if your base is taken, you have lost). When you play a game, you are interacting with the state machine that is the game. In a board game, this state is stored in the position of the pieces on the board; in sports, the game state is the score *and* the players; in computer-based games, the state is stored in memory and then represented on screen. Henceforth, I will be referring to the state of a game as the *game state*. If you cannot influence the game state in any way (as opposed to being unable to influence the game state in the *right* way), you are not playing a game.[5]

The game state only refers to the game, and not to the minds of the players. For example, in a game of perfect information, the players will not know in any detail the plans and thoughts of opponents; these are considered external to the game state. What happens in the mind of the players will be discussed later in the chapter. We can visualize the state machine of the game as a *game tree* where each game state can lead to a number of other game states, which can lead to other game states, until the game ends. Figure 3.1 is a small part of the game tree of tic-tac-toe.

It is often impractical to draw the complete game tree of a game, so the game tree is most useful as a way of understanding the large number of possibilities that a few simple rules can establish. In fact, a tic-tac-toe program I have written shows that there are 211,568 possible tic-tac-toe games—211,568 paths through the game tree of this simple game. The game tree visualizes the dynamic possibilities of a game as a map that players travel through when playing the game.

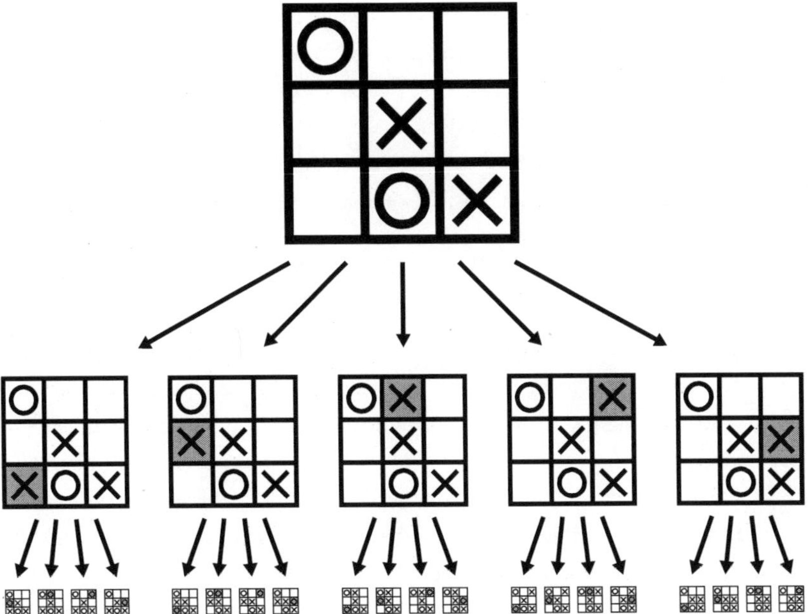

| **Figure 3.1** |
A partial game tree of tic-tac-toe.

► To see the complete listing of possible tic-tac-toe games, visit the book's Web site at http://www.half-real.net/tictactoe.

Even though it is easier to illustrate the game tree of a turn-based game, action games can also be seen as game trees, but with a much larger number of branches from moment to moment.

Algorithmic Rules

Is there anything special about game rules? Rules are limitations as well as affordances, but is there a limit to what can be a rule in a game? The rules in games are designed to be above discussion, not in the sense that it is above discussion *what* rules to use, nor in the sense that rules are never subject to disagreement, but in the sense that the *application* of a specific rule *should* be above discussion. If we think exclusively in terms of games played using computers, the question of what kinds of rules can be implemented in a computer program has already been specified in computer science with the concept of an *algorithm*. In Donald Knuth's classic computer science textbook, *The Art of Computer Programming*, he lists five important features for an algorithm:

1. **Finiteness.** An algorithm must always terminate after a finite number of steps. . . .
2. **Definiteness.** Each step of an algorithm must be precisely defined; the actions to be carried out must be rigorously and unambiguously specified for each case. . . .
3. **Input.** An algorithm has zero or more inputs . . .
4. **Output.** An algorithm has one or more outputs . . .
5. **Effectiveness.** An algorithm is also generally expected to be *effective*. This means that all of the operations to be performed in the algorithm must be sufficiently basic that they can in principle be done exactly and in a finite length of time. (Knuth 1968, 4–6)

For our purposes, *definiteness* corresponds to the description of rules as being unambiguous; *finiteness* and *effectiveness* imply that the rules of a game have to be practically usable; *input* and *output* relate to the input and output of the state machine described earlier. Knuth explains how a cookbook recipe *does not* qualify as an algorithm:

Let us try to compare the concept of an algorithm with that of a cookbook recipe: A recipe presumably has the qualities of finiteness (although it is said that a watched pot never boils), input (eggs, flour, etc.) and output (TV dinner, etc.) but notoriously lacks definiteness. There are frequent cases in which the definiteness is missing, e.g., "Add a dash of salt." A "dash" is defined as "less than $\frac{1}{8}$ teaspoon"; salt is perhaps well enough defined; but where should the salt be added (on top, side, etc.)? Instructions like "toss lightly until mixture is crumbly," "warm cognac in small saucepan," etc., are quite adequate as explanations to a trained cook, perhaps, but an algorithm must be specified to such a degree that even a computer can follow the directions. (Knuth 1968, 6)

Students of contemporary literary theory may find the demand for *definiteness* daring since it is well known that any piece of text or information can potentially be understood in any number of ways, but in actuality, algorithms can be definite because of the way they are constructed. In the recipe example, Knuth points to the fact that the recipe can be understood by a trained cook, but not by someone who has not cooked before. The recipe presupposes knowledge about the problem domain—in this case cooking. For something to be an algorithm, it has to be usable *without an understanding* of the domain. As such, what can qualify as an algorithm—and therefore what can be made a rule in a game—hinges on a *decontextualization:* an algorithm can work *because* it requires no understanding of the domain and because it only reacts to very selected aspects of the world—the state of the system; the well defined inputs; but generally *not* the weather,[6] the color of the computer case, the personality of the computer operators, or the current political climate.

This leads back to Goffman's notion of *rules of irrelevance:* playing a game involves ignoring many aspects of the current context: "any apparent interest in the aesthetic, sentimental, or monetary value of the equipment employed" (1972, 19). As such, *all game rules relate only to selected parts of the context in which they are played.* In state machine terms, this is because a game has a predefined number of *input events*—the state of the game does not change because the sky becomes overcast or because someone coughs; it only changes when someone performs a permissible move: *Game rules relate to selected and easily measurable aspects of the game context.* To rephrase Goffman's description, every game rule also has a *rule of relevance:* A rule includes a specification of what aspects of the game and game context are relevant to the rule. The rules of relevance are a place where rules and fiction meet in that learning a game also means learning to ignore the purely decorative aspects of that game. This is part of the process of *information reduction,* discussed later.

Compare two different possible versions of the checkmate rule in chess:

1. A player is in checkmate when his or her king is in a hopeless position.
2. A player is in checkmate when the king is checked [can be captured in the next move] and he or she is unable to bring the king into an unchecked position in one move.

The actual rule for checkmate is of course the second one, and it works because the aspects of the game situation that are relevant to the rule are well defined—only the positions of the pieces. Rule #1 would immediately lead to long discussions about what constituted a hopeless position; whether a position was hopeless would depend on how skilled the player was, which could then be subject to discussion and so on. Rule #1 fails to work because it does not specify what aspects of the context are relevant—in Knuth's terms, it lacks *definiteness*. Rule #2 works because it does specify what is relevant. Furthermore, even when the relevant aspects of the context are specified, rules still need to be specified in such a way that we can easily decide whether a condition is met or not. Imagine two rules in soccer:

1. The ball is out of play when it is far away.
2. The ball is out of play when it crosses the white line drawn on the grass.

Both rules specify what aspect of the game context is relevant—in this case the position of the ball—but the first one fails to specify it in sufficient detail to be of any use. Again, rule #1 would likely lead to much discussion because it is not easily decidable.[7] In a video game, the distinction is more likely to be between what *can* be an enforceable rule (since the computer keeps track of the game state, everything in the game is already measured) and what players find to be an *acceptable* rule (players tend to become frustrated if they cannot tell exactly what happened).

Making Rules, Changing Rules

How are the rules of a game determined? In a video game, the rules are explicitly designed by the game developers, and usually developed through play-testing. In a folk game, the rules of a game are developed, passed on, and changed by thousands or even millions of independent players. In the 1894 report "Mancala, the National Game of Africa" (Culin [1894] 1971), the American anthropologist Stewart Culin examined the diffusion and variations of the game of mancala (also known as kalaha) around Africa and the Middle East, and found considerable variations in the way the game was played. Given the historical and geographical spread of the game, this makes sense. Perhaps more surprising is that a game can undergo a considerable amount of development and variation within a confined area and time period. Jean Piaget has offered a more local and detailed description of the negotiations about the rules of a "folk" game among children, a marble game called "the square game":

> As we had occasion to verify, the rules of the Square game are not the same in four of the communes of Neuchâtel situated at two to three kilometers from each other. They are not the same in Geneva or Neuchâtel. They differ, on certain points, from one district to another, from one school to another in the same town. In addition to this, as through our collaborator's kindness we were able to establish, variations occur from one generation to another. A student of twenty assured us that in his village the game is no longer played as it was 'in his days'. These variations according to time and place are important, because children are often aware of their existence.
>
> Finally, and clearly as a result of the convergence of these local or historical currents, it will happen that one and the same game (like the Square game) played in the playground of one and the same school admits on certain points of several different rules. Children of 11 to 13 are familiar with these variants, and they generally agree before or during the game to choose a given usage to the exclusion of others. (Piaget 1976, 414–415)

This suggests that it is a common experience to discuss the variations in the rules of a game, changing them at will, and being aware of a number of different variations. Piaget documents that children are well versed in the art of discussing the rules of games, and he confirms what I postulated in chapter 2, that games generally require that the rules be agreed upon *before* the game starts.

The Joy of Arguing about Rules

The description of rules having to be defined before a game starts makes it sounds like disagreement about rules is *always* a problem, something that stands in the way of the enjoyment of playing a game. But any aspect of the enjoyment of games can potentially be placed in the background in favor of something else that was previously considered a dull obstacle, and discussing rules can in fact be enjoyable: In her article "Sex Differences in the Games Children Play," Janet Lever compared the play of some eight hundred children and concluded that the boys *enjoyed* discussing the rules of a game: "During the course of this study, boys were seen quarrelling all the time, but not once was a game terminated because of a quarrel and no game was interrupted for more than seven minutes. In the gravest debates, the final word was always, to 'repeat the play,' generally followed by a chorus of 'cheater's proof.' In fact, it seemed that the boys enjoyed the legal debates as much as they did the game itself" (1976, 482). I am not sure how far we can extend the gender-specific aspects of this research, and we must be wary of extending this description to cover all game players of all games, but it certainly points to the possibility that the emphasis of a game can be shifted so as to place the enjoyment somewhere else. Additionally, a few games exist that are in themselves about the discussion of rules—Peter Suber's game *Nomic* (1982) is a game *about* changing rules.[8] This does not challenge the main point here, that the dominant way of playing games is to agree on the rules *before* the game starts, and that arguing about rules is *usually* considered an impediment to game play.

Other Rules: Gaming, Sportsmanship, Gravity

Still, the explicit rules are not the only rules in a game. The most obvious example is the notion of sportsmanship: sports, especially, tend to have associated with them a number of ideas of how the noble player should perform. These ideas or conventions are loosely defined guidelines open to interpretation that *tend* to be followed by players. I can see three main kinds of sportsmanship:

1. *Preventing bodily harm:* Even if the rules would actually allow it, players try to prevent injury.

2. *Maintaining fairness in case of force majeure:* In tournament soccer, if one team has an injured player on the field, it is quite common for the other team to kick the ball out of the playing field, in effect pausing play, letting the injured player be treated, and giving the ball to the injured player's team. In a real-time strategy game, this corresponds to letting another player pause the game when they have to answer the phone.[9]

3. *Keeping the game interesting:* In some situations, a specific strategy may increase the player's chance of winning, but make the game a dull affair. In the game of *Counter-Strike*, violent discussion often breaks out around the issue of *camping:* This is a strategy where a player simply stays hidden most of the game waiting for unsuspecting players to walk by in order to promptly shoot them (Wright, Boria, and Breidenbach 2002). This is not explicitly disallowed by game, but players may agree not to

camp. The problem is that it is hard to describe camping in unambiguous terms—players do not move all the time, so for how long is a player allowed to stay still? Furthermore, a player that walks into a room and is immediately killed may feel that camping was involved—even if the other player entered the room just a few seconds earlier.

Sportsmanship is not strictly a rule according to my previous definition since its ambiguity makes it subject to continued discussion and social regulation.

Generally, to play a game also requires competence in initiating or terminating game sessions and managing the interplay between the game and the context in which the game is played. This has been called *gaming* and *gaming rules*, and these are not rules as much as they are "rules for rules" in games (Hughes 1999, 195). This is a worthwhile study in its own right, but generally falls outside the scope of this book. Finally, many aspects of physical games are specified by preexisting systems such as the laws of physics, which are used as *objets trouvés* or *found objects*, appropriated for game purposes.

As such, the explicit game rules are not all there is to a game and games do not appear in a void. Games have an undetermined relationship to what is outside the game, and this is also part of the classic game model: the *negotiable consequences* of the game. Games often incorporate many things that are not specified in the rules.

Rule Structures: Games of Emergence and Games of Progression

In the beginning of this chapter I discussed how games can present players with challenges. This can be done in several different ways, but the two most important ways are *games of progression* that directly set up each consecutive challenge in a game, and *games of emergence* that set up challenges indirectly because the rules of the game interact. To understand this, compare two old video games, the simple table-tennis game of *Pong* (figure 3.2) (Atari 1973) and the adventure game *The Hobbit* (figure 3.3) (Melbourne's House 1984), where the object of the game is to complete the travels of Bilbo as described in J. R. R. Tolkien's novel.

The Hobbit is a text-graphics hybrid adventure game where some of the world is represented in graphics and most is represented in text. The player interacts with the game exclusively through text input. To complete

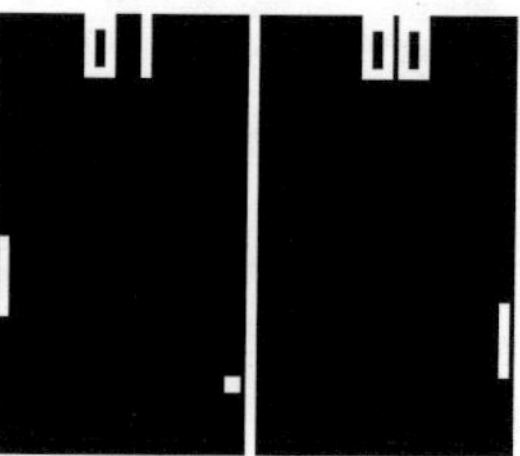

| **Figure 3.2** |
Pong (Atari 1973).

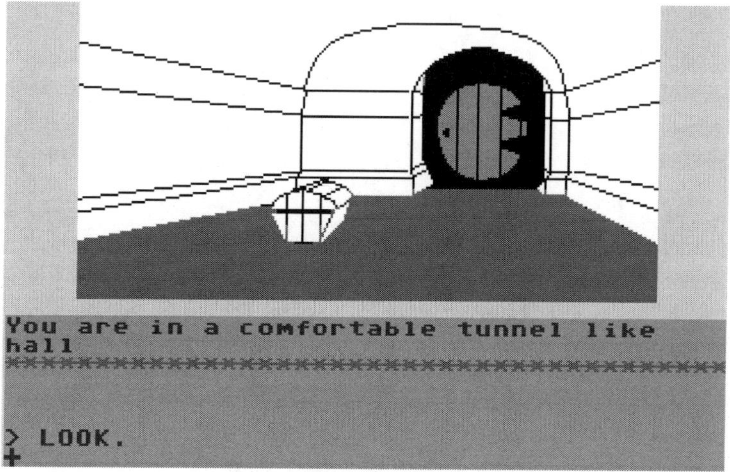

| **Figure 3.3** |
The Hobbit (Melbourne House 1984).

the game, the player has to overcome a number of challenges such as getting a key from some trolls without being eaten, escaping from a goblin, sailing a river on a barrel, slaying a dragon using a helper, and finally getting back home again. On the surface of things, *The Hobbit* is the more complex game, having large amounts of graphics, dialogue, and a quite varied setting. *Pong,* on the other hand is as simple as can possibly be. Katie Salen and Eric Zimmerman have discussed how it can be difficult to understand why *Pong* became a popular game:

People love pong.
They do. But why?
Really. What's to love? There isn't much to the game; a pair of paddles moves to blunt white lines on either side of a black screen, a blocky excuse for a ball bounces between them, and if you miss the ball, your opponent scores a point. The first player to score fifteen points win. (Salen and Zimmerman 2004, 13)

They then list six reasons for playing *Pong*, the second one being the following: "*Every game is unique*. Because the ball can travel anywhere on the screen, Pong is an open-ended game with endless possibilities. Pong rewards dedicated play: it is easy to learn, but difficult to master" (Salen and Zimmerman 2004, 15). Therefore, *Pong* gives us a very rudimentary example of how a game with very simple rules can provide variation and replayability. *The Hobbit*, on the other hand, contains a wider range of possible actions that the player can perform (picking up things, talking to people, using objects to manipulate the world). Even so, the complete solution to *The Hobbit* fits on a sheet of paper (figure 3.4).

When actually playing the game, the player will at first fail to find the sequence of commands needed to complete the game. Having completed *The Hobbit*, he or she finds little reason to play the game again; the possibilities of the game are exhausted once it has been completed. This is not to cast a value judgment on the two games, but simply to point out the difference in the economy of their rules. A shorthand description of the rules of *Pong* is as follows:

Pong: Players control a bat each (at the left and right side of the screen) using a paddle. A ball is served by the computer; it bounces off two lines at the top and bottom of the screen and off the player bats. Players can direct the direction of the ball by hitting the ball with different parts of their bats. The ball accelerates until a player fails to block the ball with his or her bat, whereupon the other player scores a point. The first player to gain 15 points wins.[10]

Pong has very few rules, yet it provides the players with a large possibility space. A shorthand version of the rules of *The Hobbit* would follow the general structure of the walkthrough above, first describing where Bilbo starts, where the different players are, and what the conditions are for the solution of each task in the game. In fact, the rules of *The Hobbit* are quite

(You start in your Hobbit Hole, a "comfortable tunnel like hall")

- READ MAP
- EAST
- EAST
- NORTH
- WAIT (until day dawns)
- SOUTH
- GET KEY
- NORTH
- UNLOCK DOOR
- OPEN DOOR
- NORTH
- GET ROPE AND SWORD
- SOUTH
- SOUTH
- GET MAP
- SOUTH EAST
- GIVE MAP TO ELROND
- SAY TO ELROND "HELLO"
- SAY TO ELROND "READ MAP"
- WAIT (until Elrond gives you some lunch)
- EAT LUNCH
- SAY TO ELROND "GIVE ME MAP"
- EAST
- SOUTH
- EAST
- NORTH
- NORTHWEST
- NORTH
- SOUTHEAST
- DOWN
- DOWN
- DOWN
- DOWN
- EAST
- GET GOLDEN KEY
- UP
- NORTH
- WEST
- SOUTH
- EAST
- NORTH
- WAIT (you should be by a crack in a wall, WAIT until it opens and you get captured and thrown in the goblin dungeon!)
- DIG
- SMASH TRAP DOOR (keep doing it until it breaks, there is a CURIOUS KEY underneath. Thorin will take the Key)
- SAY TO THORIN "OPEN WINDOW"
- SAY TO THORIN "PICK ME UP"
- SAY TO THORIN "WEST"
- SOUTHWEST
- WAIT (until a goblin appears)
- NORTH
- SOUTHEAST
- EAST
- GET RING
- NORTH
- SOUTH
- NORTHWEST
- EAST
- OPEN DOOR
- UP
- CLOSE DOOR
- EAST
- EAST
- OPEN CURTAIN
- OPEN CUPBOARD
- GET FOOD
- EAT FOOD
- NORTHEAST
- EAST
- EAST
- LOOK ACROSS RIVER (you should see a boat)
- THROW ROPE ACROSS RIVER (may need to try more than once)
- PULL ROPE
- SAY TO THORIN "CLIMB INTO BOAT"
- CLIMB OUT
- EAST
- SMASH WEB (until it breaks)
- NORTHEAST
- SMASH WEB
- NORTH
- WEAR RING
- EXAMINE DOOR
- WAIT (until the door opens)
- NORTHEAST
- SOUTH
- KILL BUTLER WITH SWORD
- GET RED KEY
- UNLOCK RED DOOR WITH RED KEY
- OPEN DOOR (if Thorin got captured earlier, he'll reappear now)
- OPEN BARREL
- OPEN TRAP DOOR
- GET BARREL
- THROW BARREL THROUGH TRAP DOOR
- SAY TO THORIN "JUMP ONTO BARREL"
- GET BARREL
- THROW BARREL THROUGH TRAP DOOR
- JUMP ONTO BARREL
- EAST
- PICK UP BARD
- WEST
- NORTH
- UP
- NORTH
- NORTHWEST
- NORTH
- WEST
- EAST
- NORTHWEST
- NORTH
- WAIT (keep waiting until sun shines on the rock and opens the SECRET DOOR)
- SAY TO THORIN "UNLOCK DOOR WITH CURIOUS KEY"
- DROP BARD
- EAST
- SAY TO THORIN "WEST"
- WEAR RING
- EAST
- GET TREASURE
- EAST
- WEST
- PICK UP BARD
- UP
- DROP BARD
- SAY TO BARD "GET STRONG ARROW FROM QUIVER"
- WAIT (until Smaug the Dragon shows up)
- SAY TO BARD "SHOOT THE DRAGON"
- SOUTH x 3
- DOWN
- SOUTH x 3
- WEAR RING
- WEST
- WAIT
- WAIT
- WEST
- WAIT
- WAIT
- WEST
- NORTH
- SOUTHWEST
- WEST x 4
- SOUTHWEST
- WEST
- OPEN CHEST
- PUT TREASURE IN CHEST

(You're back in your Hobbit Hole and rich, rich, rich. Congratulations!)
(Chesire 2001)

Figure 3.4

Complete solution to *The Hobbit*.

similar to the preceding walkthrough. *The Hobbit* provides challenges via many rules, but even so, the possibility space of *The Hobbit* is quite small.

I have chosen these old examples to point to the dual origins of the video game. The history of video games can be seen as the product of two basic game structures, the *emergence* structure of *Pong* and the *progression* structure of adventure games. Though games of emergence are theoretically much more interesting, I emphasize that the distinction is purely descriptive. Chris Crawford has described a similar but not identical[11] normative distinction between information-rich and process-intensive games (1982, 46). Crawford argues that since the computer is a data-processing device, a game should take advantage of the computer's strengths by emphasizing processing over data storage.[12] The distinction is also present in Harvey Smith's call for systemic level design over special-case level design (2001), which will be discussed later.

Before I describe these two game types in more detail, I suggest the reader performs the *game guide test of emergence* on a number of games:

The game guide test of progression and emergence

Search for a guide to the game on the Internet. If the game guide is a walkthrough (describing step by step what to do), it is a game of progression. If the game guide is a strategy guide (describing rules of thumb for how to play), it is a game of emergence.

Many games can be found on a scale between emergence and progression, and their game guides are consequently a combination of step-by-step descriptions ("get the red key, walk north, and open the third door") and strategy guides ("in the large room, the best way of reaching the exit is to work your way around the side while keeping all enemies at a distance using the laser rifle"). There are two extremes of this scale and two primary ways of creating hybrids:

- *Pure progression games:* The traditional adventure game is the purest example of a progression game.
- *Pure emergence games:* The multiplayer board, card, action, or strategy games are the purest examples of emergence games.
- *Progression games with emergent components:* The single-player action game is usually a hybrid in that the player has to traverse a number of

areas each of which can be negotiated in a number of ways and are therefore emergence structures.

- *Emergence games with progression components:* Multiplayer role-playing games like *EverQuest* (Verant Interactive 1999) are hybrids where the overall game structure is emergent but contains a number of small *quests* where the player has to perform a sequence of events to complete the quest.[13]

Games of Progression

Progression is the historically newer structure that entered the computer game through the adventure genre. Most clear-cut progression games are adventure games. The first adventure game is the text-based *Adventure* (Crowther and Woods 1976). A typical start of *Adventure* looks like this (">" marks what the player types.)

Welcome to Adventure!

. . .

At End Of Road
You are standing at the end of a road before a small brick building. Around you is a forest. A small stream flows out of the building and down a gully.

>enter building

Inside Building
You are inside a building, a well house for a large spring.
There are some keys on the ground here.
There is tasty food here.
There is a shiny brass lamp nearby.
There is an empty bottle here.

>get lamp

Taken.

The traditional adventure game was based loosely on the fantasy genre inspired by Tolkien: a world of elves, trolls, dragons, caves, and treasures. During the 1980s, the genre changed from being text-based to being primarily graphical.[14] In *The Longest Journey* (Funcom 2000) the game protagonist, April Ryan, is on board a ship threatened by a storm. To save

| **Figure 3.5** |
The Longest Journey (Funcom 2000): Go to the cargo bay.

her, the player must perform a predefined sequence of events (figure 3.5–3.8). If the player does not perform the right actions, the game is over. It is characteristic of progression games that there are more ways to fail than to succeed (figure 3.9). The progression structure yields strong control to the game designer: Since the designer controls the sequence of events, this is also where we find the games with cinematic or storytelling ambitions.

Games of Emergence

Emergence is the primordial game structure where a game is specified as a small number of rules that combine and yield a large game tree, that is, a large number of game variations that the players deal with by designing strategies. Emergence is found in card and board games, most action, and all strategy games. Almost all multiplayer games are games of emergence. Games of emergence exhibit a *basic asymmetry* between the relative simplicity of the game rules and the relative complexity of the actual playing

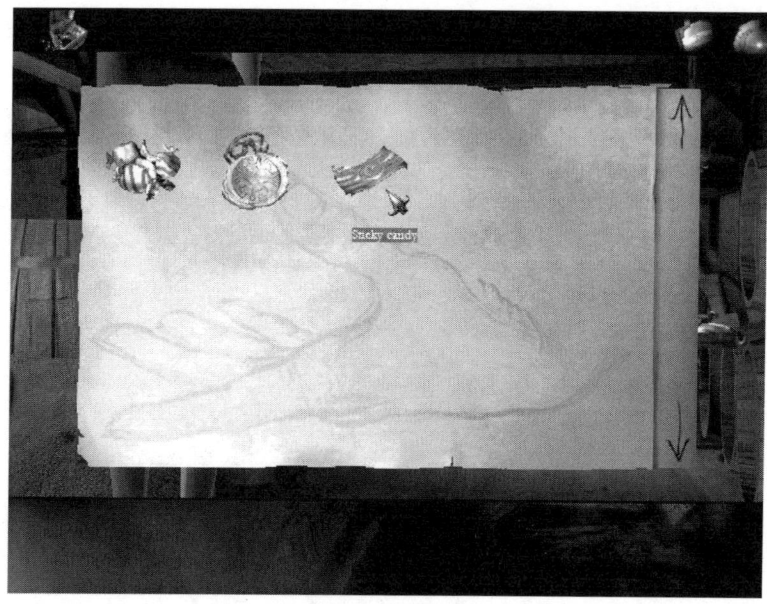

| **Figure 3.6** |
Eat some candy, leaving a candy wrapper.

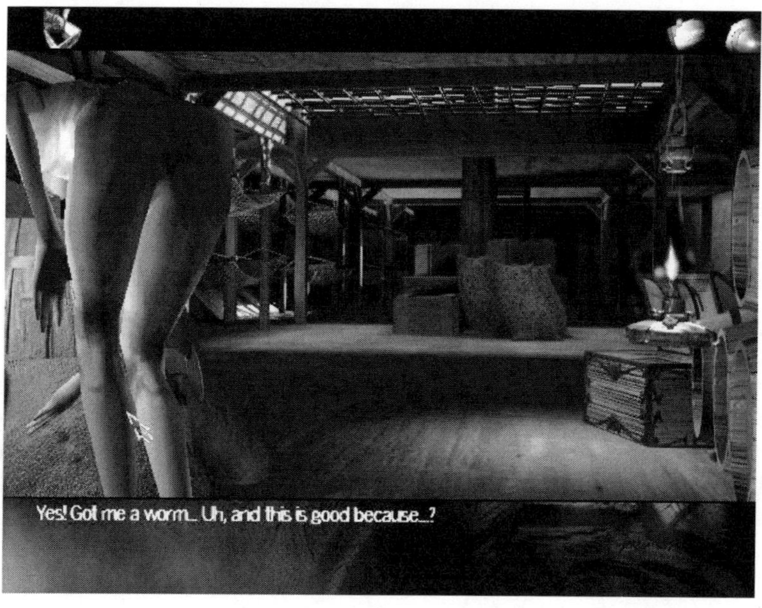

| **Figure 3.7** |
Stop a hole with the wrapper and catch a worm.

| **Figure 3.8** |
A storm appears.

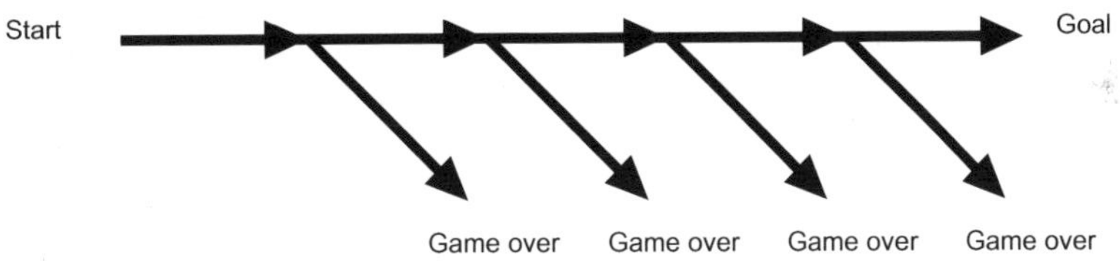

| **Figure 3.9** |
Progression games: to complete the game, the player has to perform exactly the actions that the game designer planned or the game ends.

of the game. To give a non-electronic example, the rules of chess can be described on a sheet of paper, but a well stocked bookstore carries shelf after shelf of books on specific openings, gambits, endgames, and so on; there is more to playing such games than simply memorizing the rules. In a game of emergence, the game is therefore not as much a straight line as an open landscape of possibilities: In chess you win by checkmating your opponent—but there is a myriad of end positions in chess that qualify as checkmate, and each of these positions can be reached in an immense number of different ways. A game of emergence has a broadly defined goal—there are many game states that qualify as the goal—and a large number of ways to reach these states.

A terminological caveat about *emergence:* The term is commonly used very loosely, and even scientific literature on emergence is often contradictory. My goal here is not to write a treatise on the general phenomenon of emergence, but to understand game rules. At a most basic level, the question is whether emergence is a feature of the game systems themselves or a feature of human cognition. There are good arguments for both positions, and I will therefore borrow from a number of different descriptions of emergence in order to distinguish between different types of emergence in games.

Emergence in games has recently received much attention under the heading of *emergent gameplay*. Emergent gameplay is usually taken to be situations where a game is played in a way that the game designer did not predict. The game designer Harvey Smith has argued extensively for *systemic level design;* game design that allows for emergent gameplay. He makes the distinction between *desirable* emergence, where the interaction between the different elements of the game leads to interesting gameplay, and *undesirable* emergence, where players find ways to exploit the rules in ways that make the game less enjoyable. The best-known example of the latter is the *proximity mine* problem in *Deus Ex* (Ion Storm 2000), illustrated in figure 3.10:

> Some clever players figured out that they could attach a proximity mine to the wall and hop up onto it (because it was physically solid and therefore became a small ledge, essentially). So then these players would attach a second mine a bit higher, hop up onto the prox[imity] mine, reach back and remove the first proximity mine, replace it higher on the wall, hop up one step higher, and then repeat, thus climbing any wall in the game, escaping our carefully predefined boundaries. (Smith 2001)

Smith's distinction corresponds closely to the distinction between emergence and progression games. Harvey Smith's aesthetic argument for systemic level design is that it allows for more *self-expression* on the

| **Figure 3.10** |
Deus Ex (Ion Storm 2000): Climbing the wall using mines (from Smith 2001).

players' part; the players can solve problems the way they want to solve them rather than in the way the game designers planned. The *practical* argument is that it allows content to be created faster, which mirrors the basic asymmetry mentioned.

That rules and gameplay are asymmetrical, and that emergence games give the player freedom to play a game using different strategies, are in many ways flip sides of the same coin. This can be understood by way of what is broadly called "the sciences of complexity" (cf. Waldrop 1994), the study of systems (biological, economical, or otherwise) that exhibit an asymmetry between the simplicity of some basic rules and the complexity of the system. As Stephen Wolfram puts it: "Whenever you look at very complicated systems in physics or biology . . . you generally find that the basic components and the basic laws are quite simple; the complexity arises because you have a great many of these simple components interacting simultaneously. The complexity is actually in the organization—the myriad of possible ways that the components of the system can interact" (qtd. in Waldrop 1994, 86).

This corresponds quite well to the asymmetry between rules and gameplay in most games. What the sciences of complexity can provide is a framework for understanding how this happens. As for the term *emergence*, this is often taken to mean a higher-level pattern that is the result of interaction between many lower-level entities. Classical examples of emergence are life (life is molecules), consciousness (the result of interactions between brain cells), anthills (there is no central command in an anthill), bird flocks (there is no leader in a bird flock) (cf. Johnson 2001). As you read this, no cell in your brain is the one that is *really conscious;* your consciousness is an emergent property of the interactions between all your brain cells. In John Holland's description: "Emergence, in the sense used here, occurs only when the activities of the parts do *not* simply sum to give activity of the whole. For emergence, the whole is indeed more than the sum of its parts. To see this, let us look again at chess. We *cannot* get a representative picture of a game in progress by simply adding the values of the pieces on the board. The pieces interact to support one another and to control various parts of the board" (1998, 14).

A more concrete example of how something complex can arise from something simple is John Conway's *Game of Life* (Holland 1998, 136–142). Note that this is not a game, but an example of the emergent properties of some simple rules. Conway's *Game of Life* takes place on a grid of squares, each of which can be *on* (white) or *off* (black). The grid goes through a number of steps, in each of which the following rules are applied:

- If a square is on, it dies with less than two neighbors (from loneliness) or more than three neighbors (overcrowding).
- If a square is off, it is turned on if it has exactly three neighbors.

This may not sound very interesting, but it turns out to be a simple system that generates a large number of different patterns (figure 3.11).

▶ It is hard to do justice to the *Game of Life* on paper; an online version is available at http://www.half-real.net/gameoflife.

———

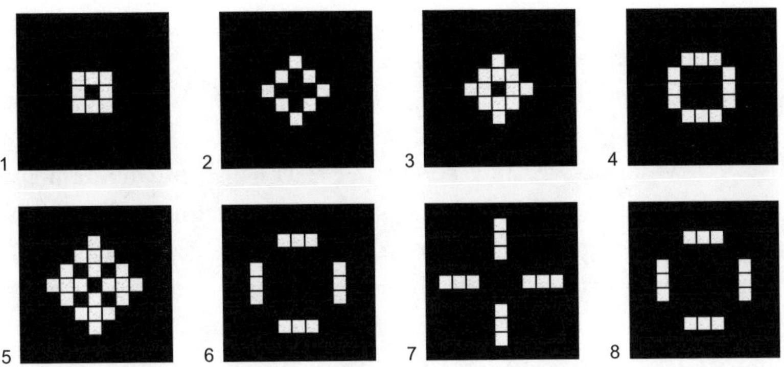

| **Figure 3.11** |

Game of Life: eight steps of a pattern generated by simple rules. It eventually cycles between steps seven and eight.

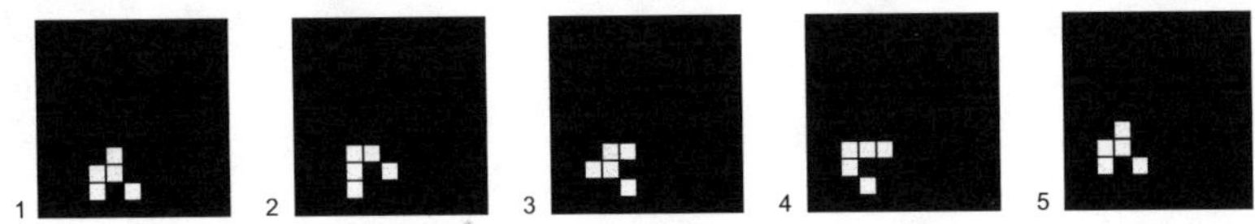

| **Figure 3.12** |

The glider: A pattern that moves across the grid in four steps.

All emergent systems are heavily *connected*. Their separate elements can all potentially influence each other in due time. The *Game of Life* has interesting properties because all its elements can interact with each other. Much effort has been dedicated to the study of the *Game of Life* and the more generalized field of *cellular automata* (for an example, see Wolfram 2002). One of the discoveries is that the *Game of Life* can support a number of regular patterns, the most famous of which is the *glider* (figure 3.12). The glider is a pattern that changes over the course of four steps, and finally reappears shifted one position on the grid (position five is identical to position one except it is shifted one position left and up). An animated version of the *Game of Life* shows the glider crawling (or gliding) across the computer screen. Patterns that are much more complex exist, such as the *glider gun*, a pattern that regularly creates new gliders.

What Emergence Can Teach Us about Games

There is some disagreement about whether emergence is a property of a system (Holland 1998, 5) or simply situations in which a game surprises its designer (Johnson 2001, 179–180; Rouse 2001, 124–125), but as we are interested in the human experience of playing games, we certainly can not afford to leave out the psychological aspects of games. The original question was how game rules provide challenges for players, and the ability of a game system to surprise players is important for games. We can distinguish between different variations of emergence in games: emergence as *variation*, as *patterns*, as *irreducibility*, and as *novelty* or surprise.

1. *Emergence as variation* is the variety of possible states and game sessions that a game's rules allow. *Pong* is an instance of *variation* coming from the interaction between some very simple rules. This is *not* emergence as surprise: It should be obvious that a large number of different games can be played by having simple rules describing, for example, the movement of a ball and some bats.

2. *Emergence as patterns:* These are patterns that players cannot immediately deduce from the rules of the game.

- All game strategies. (Since a strategy requires regularity to work, strategies require some kind of pattern in the gameplay of a game.)
- The team play required in *Counter-Strike* or the advantage of working in groups in *EverQuest*. (Specific higher-level patterns.)

3. *Emergence as irreducibility*. In his article "Guidelines for Developing Successful Games," game designer Bruce Shelley emphasizes the importance of play-testing in game development: "Prototyping is not only useful from a technology standpoint, but is also critical for testing gameplay. Designers are usually left guessing until their games can be played. There are always surprises when a game is first played, some good and some bad. Prototyping for gameplay testing is especially useful for strategy and other empty map games that do not depend on pre-planned or linear story lines" (2001).

It is striking to compare Shelley's guideline for game design to what Stephen Wolfram has written on the complexity of cellular automata: "This complexity implies limitations of principle on analyses which can be made of such systems.... The behaviour of the system can thus be found effectively only by explicit simulation. No computational short cut is possible. The system must be considered 'computationally irreducible'" (1988). Most games are irreducible; there is no shortcut to actually playing the game. And the reason why Shelley puts less emphasis on play-testing for pre-planned or linear (progression) games is, of course, that they are not emergent games because their rules and game objects have very few potential ways of being combined.

If commercial games require play-testing to develop, where does this leave "folk" (non-commercial) games? Folk games are developed over long periods of time. Since most traditional games are strongly emergent, no one can predict from the rules how they will be played. Whenever changes are made to the rules of a folk game (by deliberate design or simply by misremembering), nobody can deduce whether this will lead to good game sessions is by playing the game. What happens then is that rule changes that lead to interesting game sessions survive by word of mouth, but the rule changes that lead to boring game sessions die out.

4. *Emergence as novelty or surprise:* This is in its simplest form when several rules or objects in a game are combined in a hitherto unseen way and surprise a human player or designer.

- In the game of *Quake III Arena*, this includes *rocket-jumping*, which is the tactic of jumping into the air, firing a rocket into the ground below, and flying on the shockwave of the blast. (This is a way of jumping further than you would otherwise be able.)
- Harvey Smith's example (2001) of proximity mine climbing in *Deus Ex* is also emergence as novelty.

Designing a game with many connections between different objects and rules certainly increases the likelihood that players will find unpredicted rule combinations.

Emergence and the Player

All emergent systems contain a high number of interactions between the different parts of the system. This observation provides a more precise way of differentiating between games of emergence and games of progression: In a game of emergence, a large percentage of the rules and objects in the game can potentially influence each other; in a game of progression, most rules and objects are localized. Strategy games are highly emergent and have a large degree of connectedness, since every move and unit can potentially matter to every other move and unit in the game. On the other hand, many games of exploration contain large areas that the player has to traverse, where the exact path the player follows is inconsequential—in a strategy game, the exact path of each piece always potentially matters to every other piece.

I mentioned the question of whether emergence is in the game itself or just in the mind of the player. Harvey Smith's examples (2001) describe situations where the game designer was *surprised* by what happened in the game, but he concludes that to promote emergent gameplay, games should be designed in a specific "systemic" way where the objects in the game can interact in many different ways. The experience of surprise occurs because the player and designer do not imagine the entire game tree and all possible game sessions. Emergence as novelty is therefore an interaction between the game system and human cognition. A game with many objects that interact according to well-defined rules can surprise a player in a way where the player can afterwards understand what *did* happen because the game proceeded according to clear rules.

Games between Emergence and Progression

Progression and emergence are the two extreme ways of creating games. In practice, most games fall somewhere between these poles.

To give a high-profile example, in *Grand Theft Auto III* the player is free to drive around the city and to take on the missions that various dubious characters offer. "Deal Steal" is a typical mission that takes place about one-third of the way through the game (figure 3.13–3.19). *Grand Theft Auto III* is structured in two different ways: In the big picture, the game is a linear sequence that the player has to complete, from being betrayed in the beginning of the game to finally getting revenge. There are a few optional missions and a few missions that can be completed in different order, but overall *Grand Theft Auto III* is a game of progression. Nonetheless, "Deal Steal" shows how the goals do not specify how they are to be achieved. It is up to the player to complete the mission in the way he or she wants. In diagram form, this is illustrated in figure 3.20. The advantage of structuring a game like this is that the player experiences a predefined story by completing the missions, *while* having freedom

| **Figure 3.13** |

Grand Theft Auto III (Rockstar Games 2001). An indicator on the map (lower left corner) shows where to receive a mission.

to solve the tasks in different ways. Even though the player is in principle free to ignore the missions, most players will try to complete them *because they want to*, because it is more interesting to undertake the missions than not to. So even figure 3.20 does not quite express the flexibility of the game.

Gameplay: Rules in Action

While we can, in principle, list all the rules that govern any game and then proceed to draw the game tree of the game, this does not tell us how the game will be played. The term *gameplay* is commonly used to describe this dynamic aspect of a game. It is important to understand that the gameplay is not the rules themselves, the game tree, or the game's fiction, but the way the game is actually played. Richard Rouse's discussion of gameplay focuses primarily on gameplay as a property of the game:

(a)

(b)

(c)

| Figure 3.14 |

Kenji explains that we should help him by getting rid of a gang.

| **Figure 3.15** |
Leaving Kenji, the mission is explained in detail: The player has to steal a specific car, a yardie.

| **Figure 3.16** |
Once in the car, the map indicates where to drive to.

| **Figure 3.17** |
It turns out to be an ambush.

| **Figure 3.18** |
Having disposed of all the enemies, pick up a suitcase and return it to Kenji's casino.

| **Figure 3.19** |
Fulfilling the mission, a $25,000 reward.

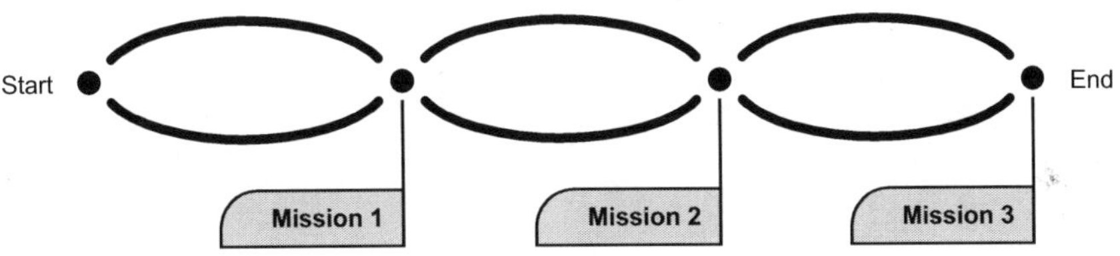

| **Figure 3.20** |
Grand Theft Auto III is a series of missions, each of which can be solved in many ways.

A game's gameplay is the degree and nature of the interactivity that the game includes, i.e., how the player is able to interact with the game-world and how that game-world reacts to the choices the player makes. (Rouse 2001, xviii)

All the glitz and glitter poured into games these days, such as expensive art, animation, real actors, or the best musicians, cannot cover up for poor gameplay. (Saltzman 1999, 16)

| **Figure 3.21** |
Quake III Arena (ID Software 1999)

The Rouse quotation describes gameplay as the purely dynamic aspect of games: the interactivity, the way the player can interact with the game world, and the way in which the game world reacts. The Saltzman passage is the archetypal statement about the *importance* of gameplay—gameplay as the fun factor of games, the secret ingredient that makes them worth playing.[15]

Where does gameplay come from? I believe that gameplay is not a mirror of the rules of a game, but a consequence of the game rules and the dispositions of the game players. For example, the two games of *Quake III Arena* (figure 3.21) and *Counter-Strike* (figure 3.22) have mostly similar rules, but are considered very different gameplay experiences: "*Counter-Strike* is a game of kill or be killed. But unlike *Quake III Arena* or *Unreal Tournament*, it's not a mindless action game that involves nothing more than twitch-shooting" (Ajami and Campanaro 2001). It is a general trait of emergent systems that a small change can have big ramifications throughout the system, and this is also the case with games: *Quake III*

| **Figure 3.22** |
Counter-Strike (The Counter-Strike Team 2000)

Arena is a fast-paced first-person shooter. When players die, they respawn within a few seconds. Even when playing multiplayer team games, the game tends to be fairly individual.

Unlike *Quake III Arena*, *Counter-Strike* is famous for its team-oriented gameplay, but since there are no rules in *Counter-Strike* that tell the players to "play team-oriented," the question is, what makes *Counter-Strike* a team-oriented game? *Counter-Strike* only adds a few variations on the team-based modes of *Quake III Arena:* Players do not respawn during a round, there are goals that can win an entire round for a team, and players move more slowly and are much more vulnerable. As it turns out, these variations completely change the game to be more oriented toward team play. Since the player has only one life per round, death becomes something to be avoided at all costs. This makes it very important for players to work together. In even a simple skirmish, being in a group is much better than being alone. Having your back covered becomes important. Communication therefore becomes important. In this way, very simple rule changes can completely change the gameplay of a game. This is how *Counter-Strike* can be team-oriented even though it does not say so anywhere in its rules.

As has now been discussed, emergence allows for variation and improvisation that was not anticipated by the game designer, variation that is not easily derivable from the rules of the game. However, this does not mean that players are free to do what they like or that their behavior is devoid of patterns or regularity. Even in an emergent system, some events can still be determined or at least be very likely to happen. This can be a property of the system—some games tend to drift toward certain outcomes no matter what the players do—as well as a psychological effect. The psychological effect is straightforward: Especially in multiplayer games, players tend to accept the rules and agree to pursue the game goal. This means that players will tend to do certain things. Since players pursue the game goal, they will search for a good strategy. If the game allows for a good strategy that leads to interesting interaction, it is a good game. If the optimal strategy for playing the game leads to dull game sessions, the game will be considered uninteresting.

Games of *Counter-Strike* usually lead to skirmishes between the two teams. Neither the *Counter-Strike* instructions nor the *Counter-Strike* programming state that fights *will* take place, but they take place because the players try to win, and because winning is best achieved by subduing the other team. To give a non-electronic example, a game of *Monopoly* usually ends with a player going bankrupt. There is no rule in *Monopoly* stating, "a player will go bankrupt," but this nevertheless almost always happens as a *result* of the rules and the players' desire to win. Viewed as a game tree, Monopoly ends with a player going bankrupt because the players explore specific parts of the game tree in order to win. Gameplay therefore results from the interaction between three different things:

1. The rules of the game.
2. The player(s)' pursuit of the goal. The player seeks strategies that work due to the emergent properties of the game.
3. The player's competence and repertoire of strategies and playing methods.

As such, game design is about designing rules so that the actual strategies used by the players are enjoyable to execute.

Since gameplay is in many ways unpredictable, the actual playing of a game may reveal unanticipated dominant or plainly uninteresting strategies. When game companies issue patches, they often address not only technical bugs or incompatibilities with specific hardware, but also modify the rules of a game in order to prevent uninteresting gameplay.[16]

Gameplay and the Social

In the *Counter-Strike* example, the small modification of the rules compared to *Quake III Arena* changed the best strategies from being mostly individual to being mostly team-oriented. In the case of multiplayer games, rules are generally designed to make sure that the best strategies require interaction between the players. It would be very easy to design a multiplayer game where the optimal strategy was to avoid other players at all time. This would, however, not be a very interesting game. In the board game of Ludo/Parcheesi, the rule for capturing makes it pay off to seek out other players and interact with them (since it sends their pieces back to square one). The rule could be reversed so that the player who lands on an opponent's piece is the one that is sent back to square one. In this case, it would not pay off to seek out other players on the board, and player-to-player interaction would generally be *discouraged* by the game. *Counter-Strike* is more than just team play for a single game session: *Counter-Strike* has a large community of players who form clans, meet for tournaments to compete, and discuss strategy tips on web sites. The fact that communication and strategic planning is important for victory in *Counter-Strike* is an important incentive to build community—being part of a community will make you a better player. Similarly *EverQuest* promotes playing in groups and guilds simply because this is the best strategy (and in many cases the only working strategy) for fighting higher-level monsters.

This explains Johan Huizinga's observation that play/games can produce social groupings (1950, 3). The rules, the player's skills and the resultant gameplay can encourage community-building around a given game. The gameplay of a game is the basis for the building of player-driven communities.[17]

Enjoyable Rules: Interesting Choices and Aesthetics of Mind

If games are enjoyable, and enjoyment partially comes from the gameplay of the game, the question is then, what is quality gameplay? The most famous one-line description of game quality describes it as hinging on challenging choices: "A game is a series of interesting choices" (Sid Meier, in Rollings and Morris 2000, 38).

What is an interesting choice? Elsewhere, Sid Meier has described three criteria for interesting choices:

1. No single option should be the best.
2. The options should not be equally good.
3. The player must be able to make an informed choice. (Rouse 2001, 27–28)

In Sid Meier's description, an "interesting choice" is one that is mentally challenging (strategic rather than skill-oriented). A simple game such as rock-paper-scissors does meet the first criterion since there is no single option that is the best—scissors beat paper, paper beats rock, rock beats scissors. If we played an alternative version where the scissors were made of kryptonite and could cut through rock, all players would choose scissors and the game would cease to hold interest. Rock-paper-scissors fails the second criterion—it does not really matter which one we choose. According to the third criterion, it is not sufficient for a game to contain a choice that *is* slightly better than the other choices if the player does not understand it.

Our example of the tic-tac-toe example in chapter 2 can also be viewed in this new perspective: Tic-tac-toe ceases to be enjoyable over time. Once you figure out a complete strategy, the game ceases to provide you with any interesting choices—and tic-tac-toe remains a children's game.

Marcel Danesi's book on puzzles, *The Puzzle Instinct* (2002), provides another starting point for considering the quality of gameplay. Though puzzles are just a small subset of games, being usually considered the kind of single-solution tasks that constitutes a step in an adventure game, Danesi has some relevant opinions on the quality of a challenge. In Danesi's view,

> Puzzles are pleasurable in themselves. The suspense that accompanies an attempt to find a solution to a challenging puzzle, or the anxiety that develops from not finding one right away, is a significant part of what makes the puzzle so fascinating and engaging.... The peculiar kind of pleasure that puzzles produce can be called an *aesthetics of mind*.... Poetry and music, for instance, evoke a cathartic response that imparts a sense of meaningfulness to existence. This can be called, more specifically, an *aesthetics of emotion*....
>
> Needless to say, some puzzles are more intellectually pleasurable than others are. The *aesthetic index* of a puzzle, as it may be called, seems to be inversely proportional to the complexity of its solution or to the obviousness of the pattern, trap, or trick it hides. (Danesi 2002, 226–227)

From a game perspective, puzzles hold a unique place in that they usually conceal their own solution or even lead the player down the wrong path in the quest for a solution: "A man was watching his son pick apples, noticing that the number of apples in his basket doubled every minute and that it was full at precisely 12 noon. At what time was the basket half full?" (Danesi 2002, 29).

The reader should consider this puzzle before continuing. The solution is here.[18] This puzzle, as is common, tries to trick the reader into believing that the solution is much more complex than it is.

An emergent game will generally not present challenges that have been *designed* to be misleading, but the player may in actuality be lead to attempt to solve a challenge in a wrong way. What is shared between puzzles and most games is the mode of reasoning needed in order to play the game: Danesi distinguishes between puzzles that can be solved using straightforward *reckoning* and puzzles that require *insight thinking*. This is the difference between challenges that can be solved using a simple routine and therefore do not require any ingenuity, and the more interesting (or actual) puzzles that require some thinking "outside the box."

According to an anecdote from Danesi, John von Neumann, the co-creator of economic game theory, was present at a cocktail party where the following riddle was told:

Two children, a boy and a girl, were out riding their bikes yesterday, coming at each other from opposite directions. When they were exactly 20 miles apart, they began racing toward each other. The instant they started, a fly on the handlebar of the girl's bike also started flying toward the boy. As soon as it reached the handlebar of his bike, it turned and started back toward the girl. The fly flew back and forth in this way, from handlebar to handlebar, until the two bicycles met. Each bike moved at a constant speed of 10 miles an hour, and the swifter fly flew at a constant speed of 15 miles an hour. How much distance did the fly cover? (Danesi 2002, 33–34)

Please try to solve the riddle before proceeding.

In the story, Neumann rushed into an adjacent room, and the teller of the riddle explained the simple solution to the audience: Since the two children are 20 miles apart and bike at 10 miles per hour, they will meet in one hour. Moreover, since the fly flies at 15 miles per hour, the fly will cover 15 miles during that time. Neumann then rejoined the party and exclaimed the solution to be "15 miles!" The teller of the riddle commented that this was interesting since most mathematicians usually failed to see the simple solution and instead tried to solve the problem as the sum of an infinite series of ever-smaller numbers, to which Neumann exclaimed, "Well, that's how I solved it!" (Danesi 2002, 33–34).

We can extend Danesi's ideas to focus on the player of games and puzzles: (1) Different people have different tools available for the solving of problems. (2) For Neumann, a brilliant mathematician, the preceding riddle did not work as a riddle since he had the tools to solve it using straightforward reckoning. In general terms, *a given task will not be equally challenging to all players*. Tic-tac-toe is only challenging up to a certain point in life after which it becomes trivial. This also means that there is no guarantee that a puzzle works as a puzzle: The player may simply be too smart, and the tools for solving, for example, a mathematical puzzle can improve over time, rendering it too easy for the general public.

Improving with Practice: The Player Repertoire

If games are challenging, they are also challenging in a way that players often learn to surmount. To play a game is essentially a learning experience where the player acquires the skills needed to overcome the challenges of the game. Cognitive scientists Allen Newell and Paul S. Rosenbloom have noted that—for any task—practice *almost always* brings improvement in performance: "*Practice makes perfect.* Correcting the overstatement of a maxim: Almost, always, practice brings improvement, and more practice brings more improvement" (1981, 1). In other words, players improve their skills at playing a game over time. If a game has to be challenging to be enjoyable, it means that the game must match the current skill level of the player.

But how do players improve their playing? In a 1996 article, Hilde Haider and Peter Frensch list four types of theories of skill acquisition: "Existing theories of skill acquisition generally assume that the effects of practice on task performance are due to either (a) qualitative changes in the effective task structure . . . (b) an increased efficiency of performing *individual* task components . . . (c) an increased efficiency in performing *sequences* of task components, or (d) some combination of these mechanisms" (1996, 305). For our purposes, we need not settle on one specific theory. We can focus on the larger picture, that players improve their skills over time, and on two theories of skill acquisition that are undoubtedly not exhaustive but can tell us something about game playing. In their article, Haider and Frensch present a theory of type (a), according to which performance improvement stems from learning to process only information that is relevant to completing a task:

> We argue that people learn, over the course of practice, to separate task-relevant from task-redundant information and to limit their processing to relevant aspects of the task. Thus, the information processed early in skill acquisition may be qualitatively different from the information processed late in skill acquisition. [Performance improvement] may at least partially reflect systematic reductions in the amount of information that is processed, rather than changes in the efficiency with which task components can be performed. (Haider and Frensch 1996, 305)

This theory will especially be useful in chapter 4, for understanding how the fictional aspect of a game can lose importance over time as the player learns to ignore elements of the fictional world that are not implemented in the rules.

For a general understanding of challenges, Newell and Rosenbloom present the better-known theory of *chunking* (a theory of type (c) according to Haider and Frensch), which states that people improve at processing information (and completing tasks) by combining a number of primitive elements of the environment into high-level chunks, which are then processed faster than it would be to process every primitive element: "The performance program of the system is coded in terms of high-level chunks, with the time to process a chunk being less than that time to process its constituent chunks" (1981, 42). For example, a master chess player can memorize and understand chess positions at great speed because he or she has a large collection of chunks.

According to Newell and Rosenbloom, "The master has acquired an immense memory for chess positions, organized as a collection of chunks. His ability for immediate perception and short-term memory of chess positions depends directly on how many chunks are used to encode a position.... By implication, master players must spend an immense amount of time with the game, in order to acquire the large number of chunks; this seems to be well supported by historical data" (1981, 50).

The theory of chunking is just one of many theories on skill acquisition, but it can serve as a starting point. Let us think about games not specifically in terms of chunking, but in terms of *methods:* a game will demand a specific repertoire of methods (or skills) that the player has to master in order to overcome its challenges. Having mastered or completed a game, the player will have expanded his or her repertoire to include the repertoire demanded by the game. This is, I think, a quite overlooked aspect of playing games, that *a game changes the player that plays it*. The negotiation of the challenges of a game can be described in general terms:

- A player will, at any given time, have a repertoire of methods to use for playing a game. Improving skills at playing a game involves expanding and refining the repertoire.
- A quality game must present the player with challenges, continually letting the player develop a better repertoire for methods for playing the

game, while continually preventing the player from playing the game just using a well defined routine.

Progression: Working with the Player's Repertoire

Different games provide challenges in different ways. This is apparent in the distinction between games of progression that are only completed once, and games of emergence that can be played to their conclusion many times. In the progression game, the challenges presented can be explicitly designed on a case-by-case basis, and the designer can work with the player's current expectations and current repertoire. In the emergence game, the rules of the game must keep producing new challenges by way of their design.

In the elegant puzzle game, *ChuChu Rocket*, the player must guide a number of mice to a number of spaceships. The player cannot directly control the mice, but only place a limited number of directional arrows and then the mice start. Mice change direction according to the arrows they encounter. If the player has placed the arrows correctly, the mice eventually end up in the spaceships. On some stages, the mice are threatened by cats that need to be avoided. The first stage is, as in any good game, very simple (figure 3.23). The mice are simple creatures and move according to the very simple rules stipulated here. On the first stage, the player has one "up" arrow to use, and has to bring the mice to the six spaceships on the top of the screen. This is easily done by placing the arrow anywhere in the path of the mice (figure 3.24). The game makes the player build a repertoire of methods for moving the mice. The first method is the straightforward one: Place an arrow pointing in the direction of the spaceships. Soon, however the player finds that this does not suffice: on stage 5, only an up arrow is available, but since the only spaceship is placed on the bottom row, the first method will not solve the problem (figure 3.25). It turns out that the up arrow can be used to send the mice on a major detour that will eventually bring them to the spaceship. The player's understanding of the game is challenged because the goal at this level cannot be attained using the method learned at level 1, and the player must now expand his or her repertoire to include how walls can be used to control mice indirectly. Additionally, the player may have picked up another method, the pattern in figure 3.26. This is a "staircase" pattern: sending the mice up in the lower right corner leads them to the

(a)

(b)

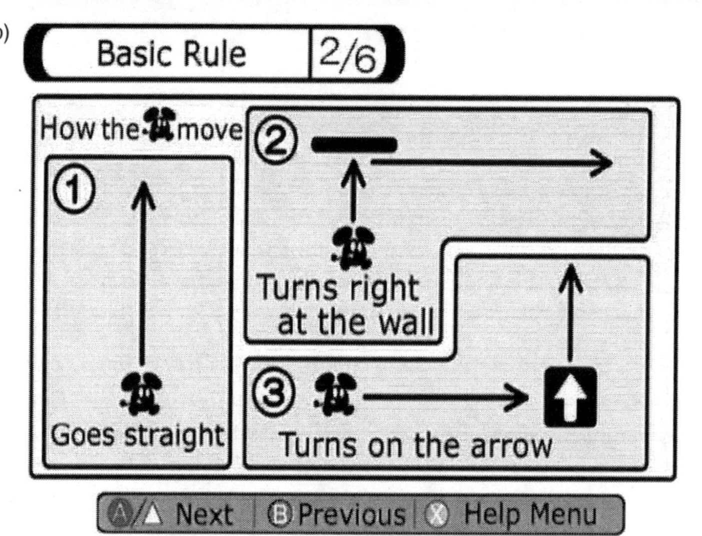

| **Figure 3.23** |

ChuChu Rocket (Sonic Team 2000). Basic rules for mouse movement.

(a)

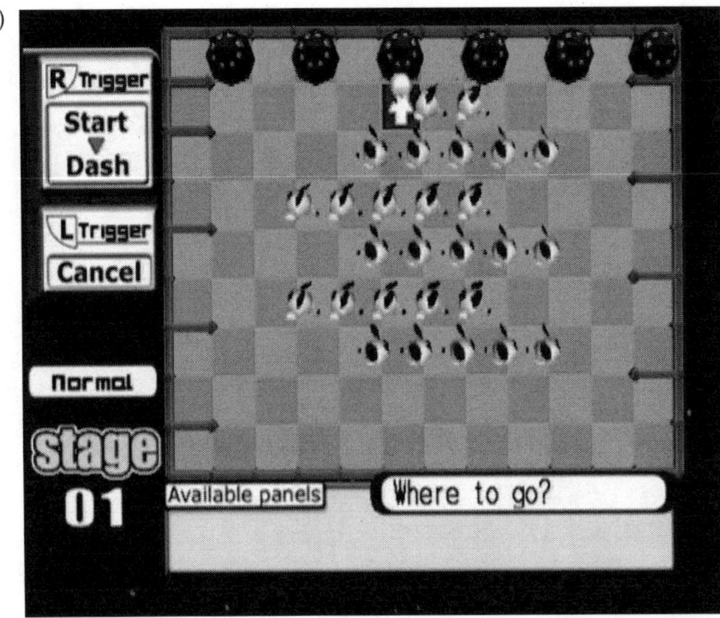

(b)

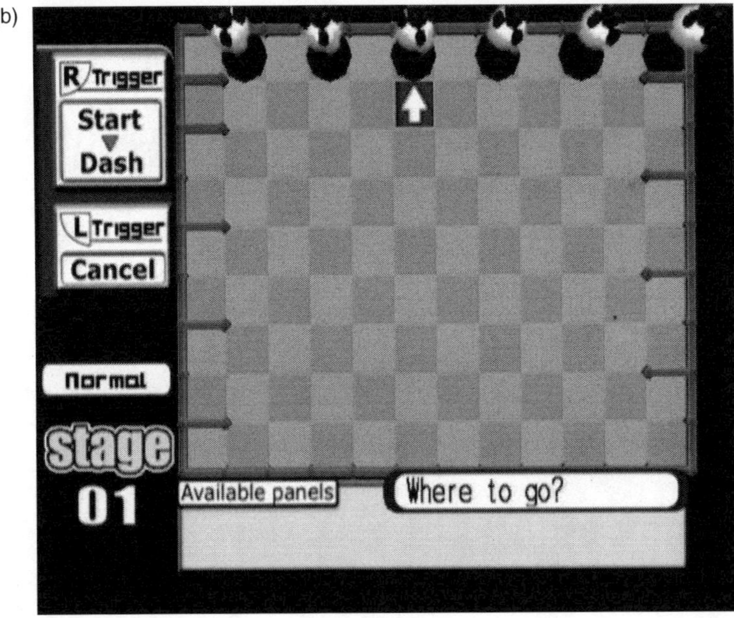

| **Figure 3.24** |

The mice follow the arrow to a spaceship. The spaceships take off.

(a)

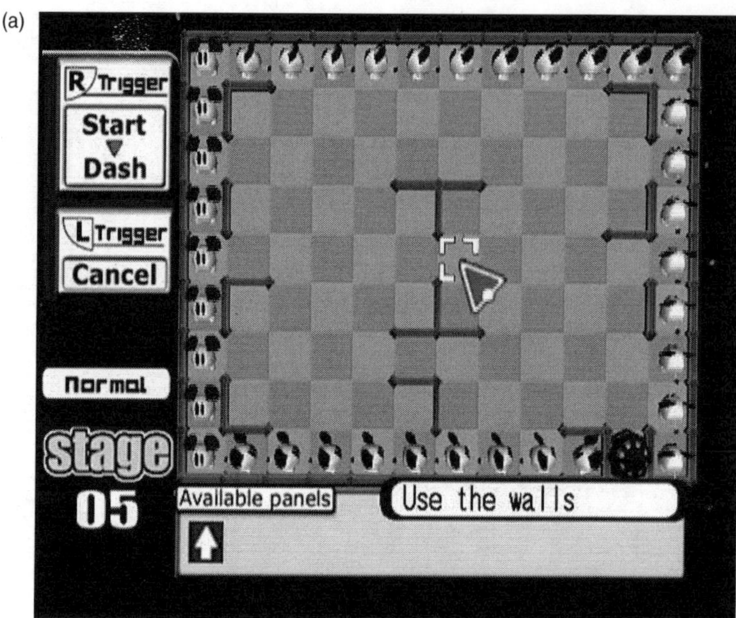

(b)

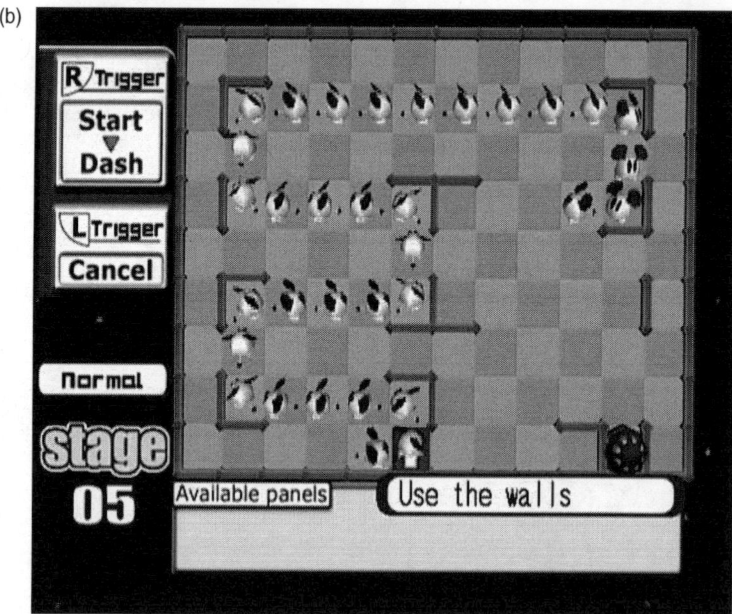

| **Figure 3.25** |

Only an up arrow is provided, but the mouse needs to go down. However, the up arrow can be used indirectly.

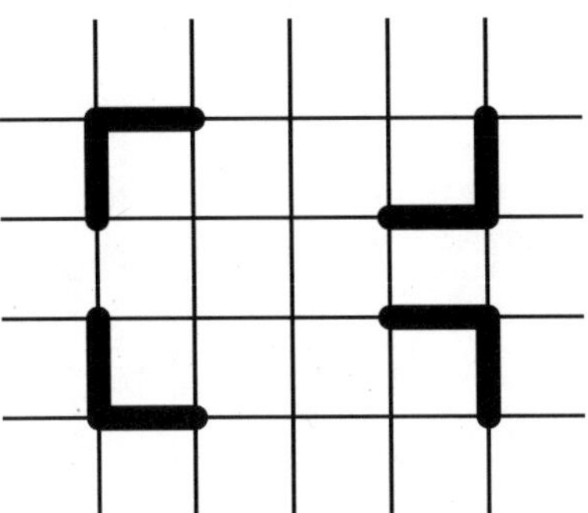

| **Figure 3.26** |
Staircase pattern in *ChuChu Rocket.*

lower left corner, upper left corner, and upper right corner. Any number of these can be stacked and mirrored; it is a good strategy to look for such patterns on the screen on the later stages. Stage 5 may therefore have expanded the player's repertoire with two additional methods. The staircase pattern is also a *chunk* as described by Newel and Rosenbloom previously.

The skilled puzzle designer can thus work with the player by foregrounding a specific kind of method that then turns out not to work. For example, in stage 10 of the "special" puzzles, the puzzle is set up to divert the player from the solution (figure 3.27). Stage 10 is divided into four squares. I solved the top right one first: Here I had to set an arrow to make the mouse go to the spaceship without colliding with the cat. I then worked for a while to solve the other three challenges with success except for the bottom left square. No matter how I placed the arrow, I could not make the mouse avoid the cat. The puzzle design foregrounded a specific method of solving the problem, that of controlling the mouse. The solution turned out to be to control the cat rather than the mouse (figures 3.28–3.29). According to Danesi, a puzzle tries to conceal its own answer, and the foregrounding of the wrong solution—only controlling the mouse—is an instance of that. It helps explain the attraction of *ChuChu Rocket:* The game also works well because it has cats *and* mice; this lets the game cue the players into foregrounding either mice or cats, thereby playing with their expectations and tricking them into focusing on the wrong parts of their repertoire.

| **Figure 3.27** |
Level ten: four arrows, one for each mouse?

(a)

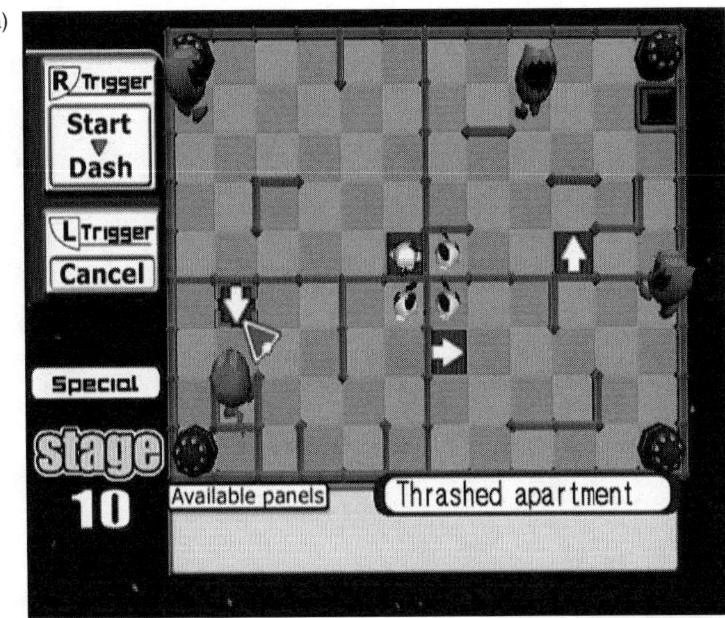

(b)

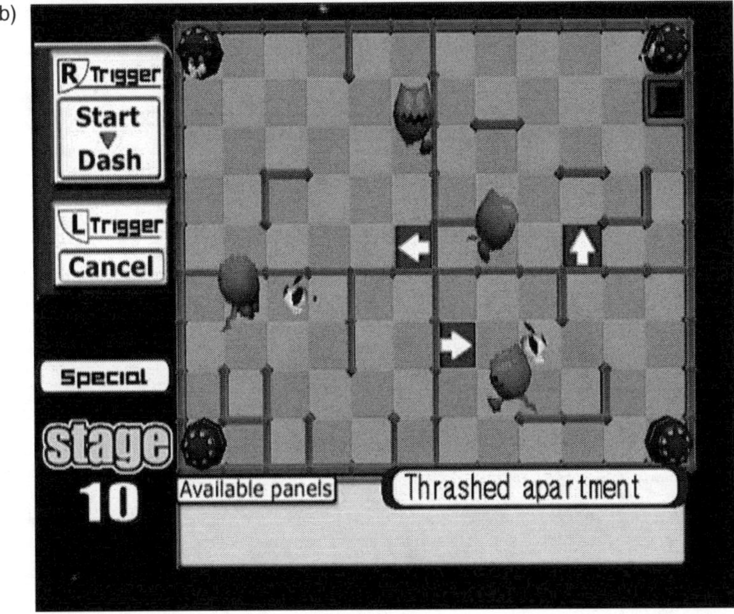

| **Figure 3.28** |

Solution to level ten. Bottom left cat hits the arrow, turns down.

(a)

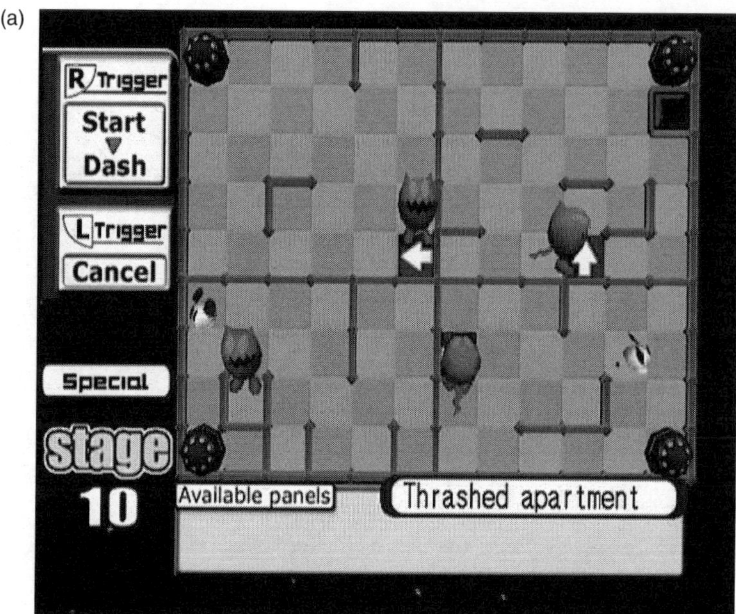

(b)

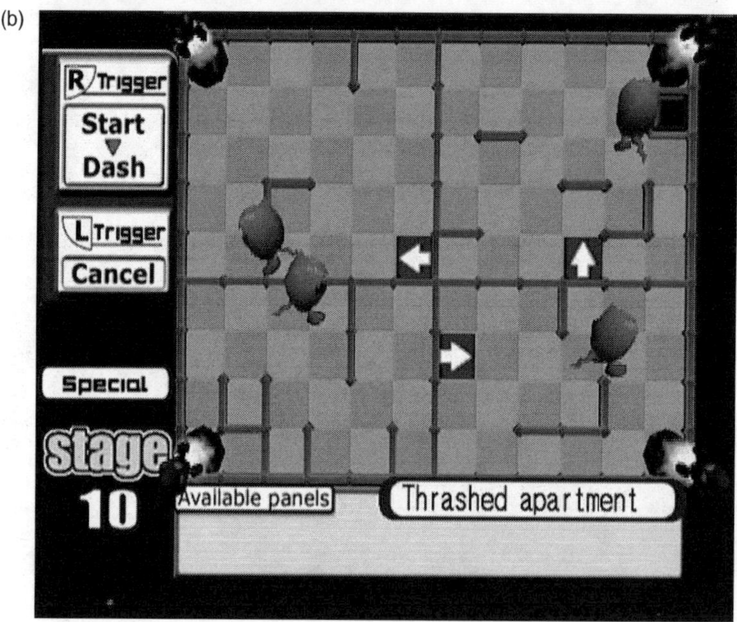

| **Figure 3.29** |
Just in time to let the mouse pass. Success.

Emergence: Naturally Occurring Challenges

Games of progression allow for challenges that are explicitly designed to trick the player into focusing on the wrong aspect of the game, but some puzzle-like situations occur "naturally" in games of emergence. Chess puzzles, such as the one in figure 3.30, are a prime example. For a mediocre chess player like me, the easiest way to produce a checkmate is by threatening the king with one piece while protecting this piece with another piece—this is one of the most basic methods in my chess repertoire. In this puzzle, I therefore immediately focused on moving the queen to G8, thus threatening the black king while being protected by the knight on H6. However, I realized that the black rook on F8 would capture the queen, and I therefore abandoned this scheme. The solution turns out to be:

| **Figure 3.30** |
White to move and checkmate in two (*The Tech* 2003).

1. QG8+ RxG8
2. NF7x

The queen does go to G8, is captured by the black rook from F8, but since that rook is now at G8, the white knight can move from H6 to F7, thereby checkmating the king who is locked in the corner of the board due to the rook at G8. In other words, the chess puzzle foregrounds using the queen to checkmate, then tricks me into rejecting this solution, which in fact turns out to be part of the correct solution after all. While this chess puzzle may be designed explicitly, it is also a naturally occurring position in chess—in a normal game of chess, the players may actually reach the position of this chess puzzle. Emergence games may automatically create puzzle-like situations that foreground wrong solutions, tricking the players to activate the wrong parts of their repertoire, and this is an effect of emergent systems' ability to surprise. In a multiplayer game, players may also try to trick their opponents into focusing on the wrong part of their repertoire by signaling that they intend to attack somewhere they are not going to attack, and so on.

This chess puzzle also demonstrates that the element of surprise in games of emergence is due to the way humans think about the world. A computer program that dumbly considers every possible position of chess will not be surprised or thrown off track. Humans are tricked because we play games not by going through every possible position in the game tree, but by finding patterns in the game by chunking or by ignoring information. These ways of playing the game are often imprecise simplifications, and so games surprise us.

Standard Types of Emergent Challenges

That emergent systems are unpredictable also means that they cannot *consistently* surprise the player, nor can they be consistently satisfying in relation to the player's repertoire. There are, however, a number of standard ways or patterns by which challenges can be automatically generated by the rules of a game. While it would be interesting to create a comprehensive and well organized collection of ways in which an emergent game can create challenges, this is certainly outside the scope of this book, and I will instead discuss a few recent attempts at this. Inspired by the work of Christopher Alexander, Bernd Kreimeier and others have initiated the *game design patterns* project.[19] This project aims to collect and describe a large number of game design patterns, each pattern being a description of a name, a problem, a solution, and its consequences (Kreimeier 2002). For example, Björk, Holopainen, and Lundgren (2003) describe a *mutual goal* pattern where several players share a common goal thus encouraging team play. This pattern is an alternative to the pattern of *symmetrical goals*, where players have mutually exclusive goals.

Let us examine three patterns that in different ways demonstrate how games of emergence are not necessarily unpredictable: triangularity, which relates to the question of interesting choices; individual bases, which is a very general pattern that creates tradeoffs between offensive and defensive play styles; and choke points, which show how the physical layout of a game affects gameplay.

Triangularity and Orthogonal Unit Design

Kreimeier notes that the first game design pattern to have been explicitly described is the rock-paper-scissors device previously mentioned, as this provides the most basic type of "semi-interesting choice," in that no single option is consistently preferable over any other. This kind of three-step relation between choices has been described in different ways. Chris Crawford (1982) has termed it *triangularity*. Rollings and Morris use the term *intransitivity* to describe the fact there is no fixed hierarchy between choices, units, strategies, or moves: the relation between them changes (2000, 40). *Intransitive* relations in games are first described by Neumann and Morgenstern (1953, 39, 52). The simplest form of intransitivity is found in games where three types of units are locked in a circular relationship (figure 3.31). In this case, the archer is stronger than the warrior, the warrior is stronger than the barbarian, and the barbarian is stronger than the archer. In actual gameplay, this will mean that each player has to second-guess the actions of the other players and, depending on terrain, economics, recognizance, and other factors, build an army with a suitable combination of units.

Harvey Smith has described this type of relation in a more general way as *orthogonal unit differentiation* (2003). This means designing the game so that every unit has strengths and weaknesses along several different axes: An archer may be weak in melee battle, strong at a distance, but slow to move. Another unit may be strong in melee, but weak at a

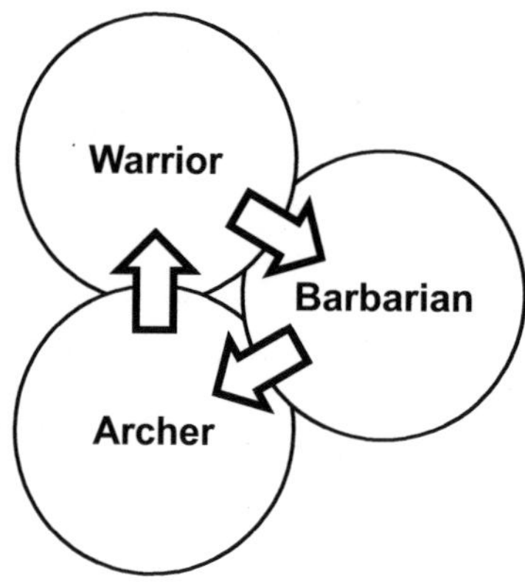

| **Figure 3.31** |
An intransitive relationship between three units in a game (Rollings and Morris 2000, 42).

distance. The key is to make sure that there are a number of different non-overlapping axes that the units can be placed along rather than just one axis such as "strength." If units simply have varying degrees of strength, the player's choices are simple and actual gameplay is predictable. With orthogonal unit design, many different kinds of unexpected gameplay may occur.

A More Basic Pattern: Individual Bases

The basic pattern of individual bases can be found in multiplayer action games, strategy games, soccer, baseball, tennis, chess, and many other games. Any game in which each player (or team) has a personal base or unit that needs protection (to prevent goals from being scored, the base from being captured, a flag from being captured, or just a player from being killed) inevitably generates a tradeoff and thereby interesting choices between offensive and defensive strategies: An offensive strategy focuses on attacking the opponent's base; a defensive strategy focuses on defending your own.

Choke Points

First-person shooters tend to contain a number of *choke points:* These are locations on a specific game level or map where opposing teams tend to

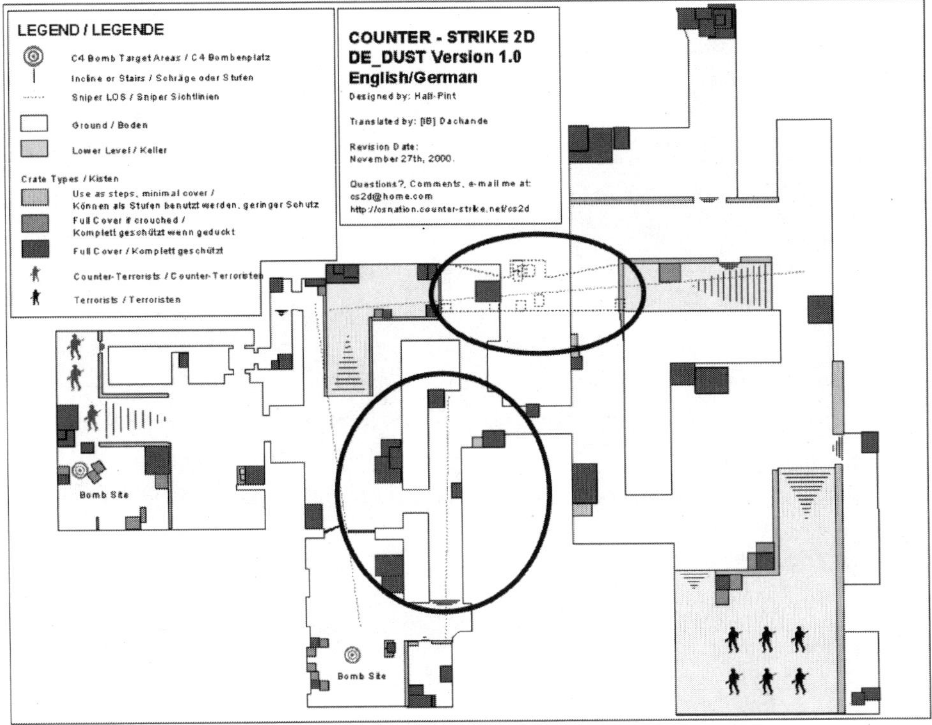

| **Figure 3.32** |

Counter-Strike, the DE_DUST map: Choke points are marked with black ellipses (Andersen, Güttler, and Folmann 2001).

meet in decisive confrontations. Andersen, Güttler, and Folmann (2001) analyzed a number of *Counter-Strike* maps using computer-controlled players to pinpoint the choke points of each map. The popular DE_DUST map features two locations where teams tend to meet (figure 3.32). The existence of choke points leads to a number of potential strategies. The two teams will tend to have a shared awareness of the choke points on a map, and can therefore mutually work with the expectations of the other team. Switching between the choke points that are the focus of their movements, they can fake an offensive against one choke point using only a few players, thus foregrounding that choke point, while secretly preparing to attack through another choke point.

Changing Game Design Patterns

There is probably a limit to how detailed and comprehensive a collection of game design patterns can be since actual patterns may be loosely defined, changing or overlapping. There are some additional issues regarding how patterns should be expressed: Since games are not strictly designed to solve problems, it makes little sense to describe game design patterns exclusively as being responses to "problems"—in many cases the "problem" is only meaningfully described as "the game is not interesting." Two parallel enterprises, covered in the articles "Better by Design: The 400 Project" (Falstein 2002) and "Formal Abstract Design Tools" (Church 1999) have slightly different philosophies: The 400 project consists of informally stated design principles that (using a card game metaphor) can trump each other, while the formal abstract design tools, despite its name, works on a more detailed level but in no fixed format.[20] While these three projects are useful and interesting they are also Herculean, volatile and subject to fads and fashions, as such projects would be for any other area such as film, literature, or music.

The Aesthetics of Challenges

Players come to a game with very different qualifications and repertoires. A few different solutions have been proposed for dealing with this, the most simple of which is allowing players to select their skill level. *Save games* are considered a more controversial technique, whereby the player can store a snapshot of the game session and resume it later. Save games are accused of decreasing the dramatic tension of the game since the player simply reloads if something goes wrong. Another argument against save games is that saving makes the game too easy. Counterbalancing these two arguments is the immense frustration to be had if you are forced to replay an entire game level simply because you made a mistake at the very end.[21] For example, the recent games *Hitman: Codename 47* (IO Interactive 2000) and *Giants: Citizen Kabuto* (Planet Moon Studios 2000) have been criticized for lacking an in-level save function (Osborne 2000a, 2000b). A third argument is that the possibility of saving destroys the player's sense of immersion because it shifts the focus to the game on a meta level. Chris Crawford's position is the more categorical—that save games are a symptom of design flaws:

> Experienced gamers have come to regard the save-die-reload cycle as a normal component of the total gaming experience. . . . Any game that requires reloading as a normal part of the player's progress through the system is fundamentally flawed. On the very first playing, even a below-average player should be able to successfully traverse the game sequence. As the player grows more skilled, he may become faster or experience other challenges, but he should never have to start over after dying. (qtd. in Rollings and Morris 2000, 80)

It seems that Crawford is mostly thinking about replayable games rather than exploratory and adventure games. There are scarcely any games that fit Crawford's description of being possible to complete in the first go and being replayable and interesting afterwards. Additionally, save games are part of what has allowed video games to develop beyond the classic game model. The only way most players can play a game that takes fifty or hundreds of hours is by using save games. Save games are probably not an evil to be avoided at all costs. They are by now a staple of video games on personal computers and consoles, and one of the ways in which players with different skills and repertoires can adjust the difficulty of the challenges in a game: the skillful player can overcome a challenge quickly, while the inept player can retry any number of times without having to replay all the previous challenges of the game.

Single or Multiple Solutions?

One of the assumptions behind Harvey Smith's (2001) call for emergence and systemic level design is that having multiple solutions to a problem is always better than having a single solution. Smith's argument is that players will prefer being able to solve challenges in their own ways, thus expressing their personalities rather than having to second-guess the designer's intention. But this is probably not all there is to it. Most of the puzzle examples mentioned earlier have a single solution, and Danesi's notion of an *aesthetic index* focuses on single-solution problems. Another writer on puzzles, Stewart T. Coffin, says of a puzzle that "it has only one solution, usually a mark of good design" (1974, chap. 1). The disagreement may to some extent be a question of genre and the cuing of player expectations. Harvey Smith's prime example, *Deus Ex*, promises an elaborate and fairly open world where the player will probably expect to be able to solve problems in any number of ways. In the puzzle genre, the player seems to *expect* that there will be one single, perfect solution.

The stronger argument for systemic level design is probably the question of *consistency*—that the players can perform the actions that they have been cued into believing they can do. It can be a problem when the representation of the game cues the player into attempting to perform an action that is not implemented in the rules. This is covered in more detail in chapter 5.

The Problem with Challenges

A compelling aspect of the focus on challenges is that it is a perfect match for Mihaly Csikszentmihalyi's flow framework (1990): Csikszentmihalyi claims that *flow* is a mental state of enjoyment shared by people in a variety of situations such as rock-climbing, chess-playing, and composing music. According to the flow framework, the player will enjoy playing if the challenges match the player's abilities and thereby lead to a state of flow. If the game is too hard, the player will experience anxiety or frustration. If the game is too easy, repetition or triviality of choice will make the player bored. In diagram form, any given challenge has a *flow channel* in which the player will be in an enjoyable state of flow. Outside this channel, the player will be either bored or anxious. As the player's skills improve—that is, as the player expands his or her repertoire—the game needs to provide harder challenges to keep the player interested (figure 3.33). Ideally, this would give us a complete description of the attraction of games, going from the formal system of the game rules, to how different game rules can provide different kinds of challenges, to the experience and enjoyment of the player. Unfortunately, even though flow is a compelling angle on games, it does not explain everything: David Myers (1992) has noted that the fascination with mechanically repeating trivial tasks in some games contradicts flow—repetition should lead to boredom but does not always.

In fact, there are enjoyable aspects of games that cannot simply be explained as challenges. *Galaga* (figure 3.34) (Namco 1981) provides the player with many choices such as how aggressively to seek out diving opponents and whether to risk a ship in order to get increased firepower. These are not the only things going on: In the second picture, the player faces a single remaining enemy exactly above the player's ship. There is

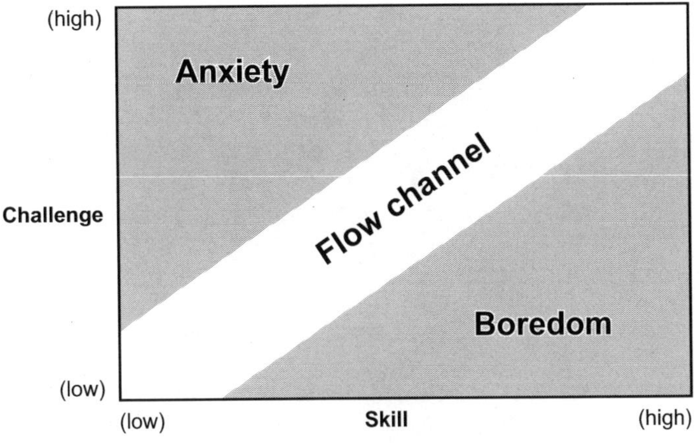

| **Figure 3.33** |
The flow channel (Csikszentmihalyi 1990, 74).

no conceivable argument against shooting this enemy. Thus parts of the gameplay in *Galaga* consist of unchallenging choices, but these parts may nevertheless be quite enjoyable. If we look at most other games, we may at first glance accept the theory that all of them are based on interesting choices and challenges, but a second look will reveal a lot of *unchallenging* moments as well. However, something not challenging can still be a positive experience—executing a plan; hitting the beat; performing the final kill; doing a routine to perfection. The variation between challenges and lack of challenge is one of the ways in which a game can modulate its intensity.

This does not weaken the claim that challenges are a core aspect of the enjoyability of a game; it simply points out that challenges can range widely, and that the way in which they are created, their difficulty, and the order in which they are presented to the player all contribute to the player's subjective experience and enjoyment of different games. Consider the quite special Playstation game of *Vib-Ribbon* (NaNaOn-Sha 1999) in figure 3.35. In *Vib-Ribbon*, the player controls a character moving along a white line. The object of the *Vib-Ribbon* is simply to hit the right buttons on the Playstation controller at the correct time (in time with the beat). Various shapes on the line correspond to specific buttons on the controller. Since the only thing the player can do is to press the right button at

(a)

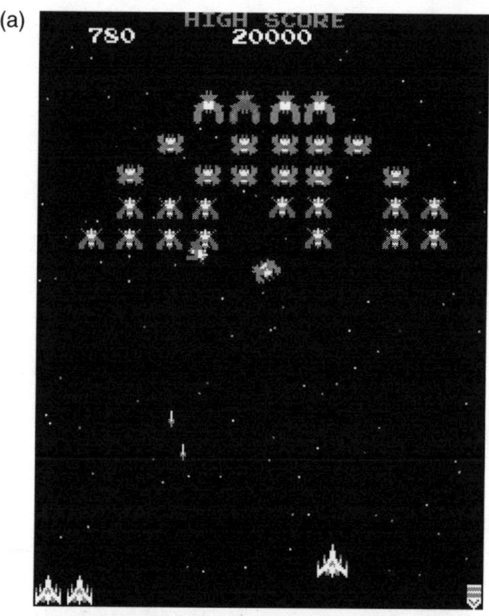

(b)

| **Figure 3.34** |
Galaga (Namco 1981): Most of the game is challenging, but some situations are not challenging at all.

| **Figure 3.35** |
Vib-Ribbon (NaNaOn-Sha 1999).

the right time or fail to do so, *Vib-Ribbon* does not contain any interesting choices whatsoever. *But it is still an enjoyable game*. Performing the non-interesting choices is augmented by another form of enjoyment, that of being in time with the music. *Vib-Ribbon* is, of course, a game of skill or motor challenges rather than strategy; the fun factor of *Vib-Ribbon* is connected to a larger, primarily Asian, genre of music and rhythm games where the primary object of the game is to be in time with the music. (The most famous of these games is *Dance Dance Revolution* [Konami 2001]). This shows that we cannot have one definitive description of what makes challenges enjoyable. Even though all challenges likely produce some enjoyment when they are overcome, different challenges can be enjoyable for other reasons as well.

The Conventions of Challenge Consistency

While nothing prevents a game from combining all imaginable kinds of challenges, there is a convention that the challenges presented throughout a game must have a similarity that allows the player to face them by refining the same basic repertoire. Even if the real-time strategy game *StarCraft* (Blizzard 1998) requires strategic planning as well as high-speed mouse skills; and even if a game session goes through many different phases (from buildup to expansion to large battles), there is a consistency in the game where many basic methods such as building structures and units, creating groups, and upgrading technology remain constant. A very small number of games make an exception to this convention of consistency.

Some older game types contain a disused way of combining challenges by having a number of completely independent screens that are part of the same fictional world. *Defender of the Crown* (Cinemaware 1986) is basically a strategy game with the overall goal of conquering England. This is achieved by way of a number of very different mini-games: jousting (first-person perspective), raiding (fencing in 2-D perspective), and attacking castles (controlling a catapult). It is only the fictional world that ties different mini-games together; each mini-game calls for a special repertoire with little connection to the repertoire needed for the other mini-games.

The ironic meta-game *WarioWare Inc.* (Nintendo 2003b) has a unique twist in that it presents itself as a number of "bad" games supposedly designed by various friends of Wario (Mario's evil cousin). *WarioWare* consists of a number of utterly unrelated mini-games. Each mini-game lasts less than ten seconds and is simply presented as a task that the player must quickly figure out how to perform (figures 3.36–3.38). *WarioWare* contains many of references to different games and game *genres* and the challenges and repertoires that they contain. Playing *WarioWare* involves identifying the challenge of a given game within a very short time frame, and the repertoire needed to play it is a meta-repertoire of being able to identify different game types and the methods needed for playing them. *WarioWare* is unique in that it is a parody of video games. I point to these two games because they—by their exception—highlight the convention that a game should challenge the player in a consistent way.

Enjoying Rules

This has presented a general view of the rules of games, as well as a description of different ways in which games can be structured by these rules. It may still seem paradoxical that the rules of a game have to be

(a)

(b)

| **Figure 3.36** |
WarioWare (Nintendo 2003b): Catch the toast!

(a)

(b)

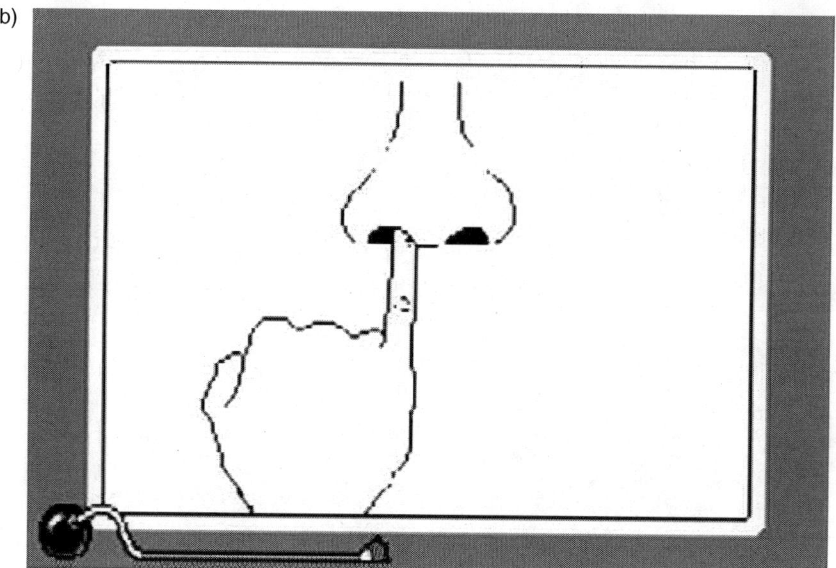

| **Figure 3.37** |

WarioWare: Pick the nose!

(a)

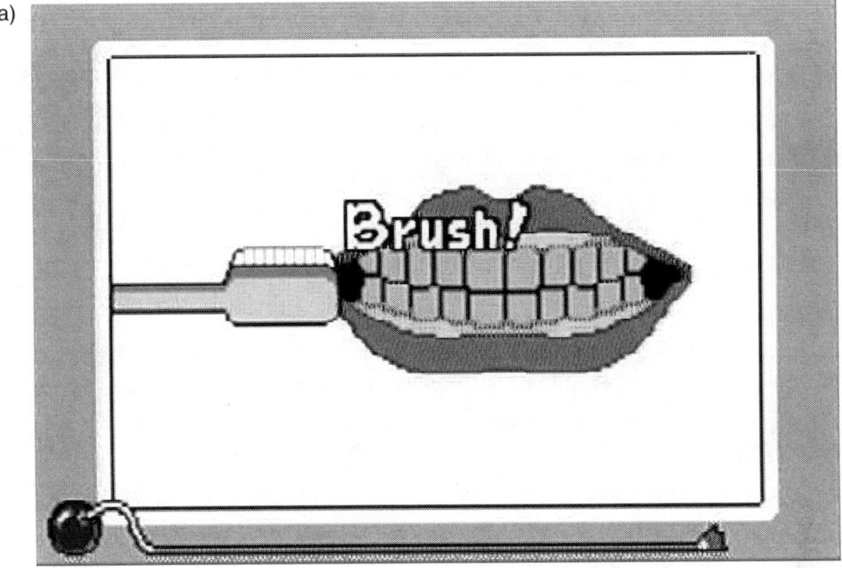

(b)

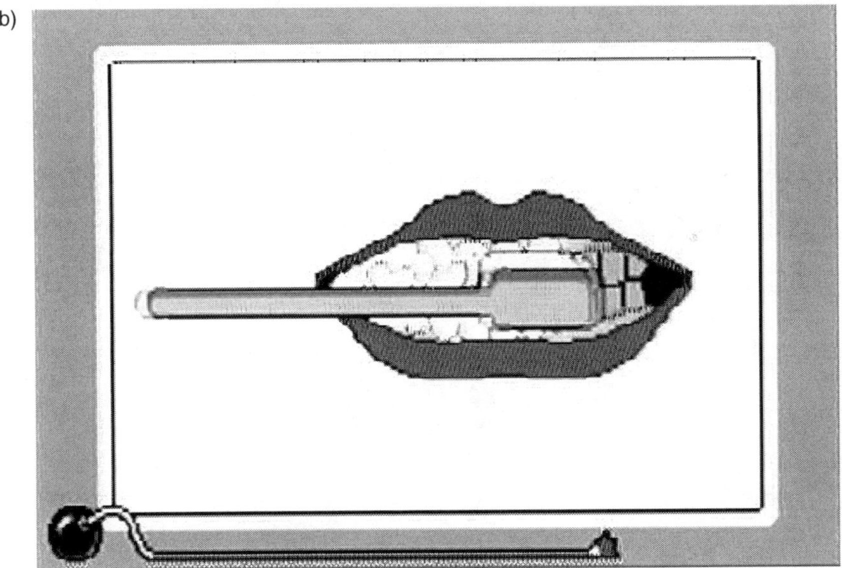

| **Figure 3.38** |
WarioWare: Brush the teeth!

algorithmic and implementable without any ingenuity, yet the game immediately becomes boring if the player has a complete strategy and can thus *play* it without using any ingenuity. This is an effect of the quality that the behavior of simple rules can be unpredictable and highly complex, and thus a game can be easy to learn but difficult to master.

In a game of emergence, the player is challenged because aspects of the game—the rules and the game entities—continually influence each other. This creates variation. Emergence in games makes interesting strategies possible, but a dominant strategy may render a game uninteresting. Likewise, micromanagement or too much low-level work may become uninteresting when the player is thinking about strategy on a higher level. Most of the interesting challenges of games require a continued refinement of the player's repertoire.

In this chapter, I have examined rules from a number of different perspectives. But this is what games are like: Games are an interaction between the algorithmic game rules and the human players who often enjoy themselves. Games are formal systems that provide informal experiences.

4
FICTION

While all games have rules, most video games also project a *fictional world:* The player controls a character; the game takes place in a city, in a jungle, or anywhere else. Such fictional game worlds, obviously, do not actually exist; they are worlds that the game presents and the player imagines. The focus of this chapter is *what kind of worlds* we find in games and *how games cue players into imagining worlds*.

Rules and fiction compete for the player's attention. They are complementary, but not symmetrical: Since all games have rules and since rules are a distinct aspect of games, it was possible in the previous chapter to discuss rules mostly without mentioning fiction. However, it is not possible to deal with fiction in games without discussing rules. The fictional world of a game is projected in a variety of ways—using graphics, sound, text, advertising, the game manual, *and* the game rules. The way in which the game objects behave also influences the fictional world that the game projects. Though rules can function independent of fiction, fiction depends on rules.

In chapter 3, we found that rules are designed to be objective, obligatory, unambiguous, and generally above discussion. With fiction in games, we find the opposite to be true: a strong part of the attraction of fiction in games is that it is highly subjective, optional, ambiguous, and generally evocative and subject to discussion. Rules and fiction are attractive for opposite reasons.

Games project fictional worlds through a variety of different means, but the fictional worlds are imagined by the player, and the player fills in any gaps in the fictional world. Many games also present fictional worlds that are optional for the player to imagine, and some present worlds that are contradictory and incoherent.

Fiction is commonly confused with *storytelling*. I am using *fiction* to mean any kind of imagined world, whereas, briefly stated, a story is a fixed sequence of events that is *presented* (enacted or narrated) to a user. Herman Melville's *Moby Dick* is a story and a fiction, whereas a painting such as Georges Seurat's *La Grande Jatte* is a fiction but not a story since it only presents one moment in time. I will examine the question of games and stories at the end of this chapter.

Fictional Worlds

What kinds of places are Norrath in *EverQuest* or the Black Mesa complex in *Half-Life* (Valve Software 1998)? They are not fixed stories, but fictional worlds. The theory of fictional worlds is derived from concept of *possible worlds* in analytical philosophy. In its most basic form, "possible worlds can be understood as abstract collections of states of affairs, distinct from the statements describing those states" (Pavel 1986, 50). In fictional worlds, there is an important distinction between the description of a fictional world and the fictional world as it is actually imagined. The text of *Hamlet* directly describes a rather small world, mostly a castle in Elsinore with some hints of foreign countries. At the same time, the fictional world of *Hamlet* is presumed to be as large and detailed as the actual world. The work not only cues the reader to imagine the states of affairs described by the play, but also to make inferences about the larger world of *Hamlet* on basis on the text. Thus, the reader performs much work in order to imagine a fictional world, and consequently different readers and game players will imagine a fictional world differently.[1]

This is because all fictional worlds are *incomplete*. No fiction exists that completely specifies all aspects of a fictional world: "For several writers, incompleteness constitutes a major distinctive feature of fictional worlds. About complete worlds, one can decide whether for any proposition *p*, either *p* or its negation non-*p* is true in that world" (Pavel 1986, 107). They are incomplete because is not possible to specify all the details about any world (Pavel 1986, 75). For example, it is not possible to determine the number of children that Lady Macbeth has—this is an undecidable question (Ryan 1992, 532–533). Any fictional world will be missing such pieces of information, some of which will be filled in by the user, some of which will remain subject to controversy: "The laws of nature that are not specifically contradicted by the text belong to its worlds:...every child

———

born in fiction having been engendered by a human father, there is no reason to doubt this regularity as long as the text signals no exception" (Pavel 1986, 105). In most cases, the incompleteness of a fictional world leaves the user with a number of choices in the imagining of the world. Marie-Laure Ryan has proposed the *principle of minimal departure*, which states that when a piece of information about the fictional world is not specified, we fill in the blanks using our understanding of the actual world (Ryan 1991, 48–60). In a specific genre, we fill in the missing pieces by using a combination of knowledge of the real world and knowledge of genre conventions. In an adventure tale, we fill in the blanks using a combination of knowledge of the adventure genre and our knowledge of the real world, so although we have no real-world experience with witches, we assume that a witch in an adventure has magical powers.

Why Does Mario Have Three Lives?

Half-Life takes places in a world where a scientific experiment goes wrong and an alien invasion ensues, but the fictional world of this a game is also incomplete: Not much can be inferred about the outside world of *Half-Life*. Likewise, we cannot deduct the technical details of the units in a game strategy game and we do not know the names of Mario and Luigi's parents. This does not prevent us from imagining such things, but the games do not give much information to go by.

In addition to incomplete worlds, some games, and many video games, present game worlds that are *incoherent worlds*,[2] where the game contradicts itself or prevents the player from imagining a complete fictional world.[3] Historically, the arcade game gave the player three lives before the game was over. This is the case in *Donkey Kong* (Nintendo 1981), where we face serious difficulties trying to imagine the world (figures 4.1–4.3).

The fictional world of *Donkey Kong* is only very superficially described, but it is possible to imagine a world in which Mario's girlfriend is kidnapped by an evil gorilla and has to be rescued. This is repeated on levels 1 and 2. On level 3, Donkey Kong kidnaps Mario's girlfriend again and apparently returns to the original hideout. It is harder to understand why Mario has three lives: Being hit by a barrel, by a fireball, or by an anvil should reasonably be fatal. Furthermore, the player is rewarded with an extra Mario at 10,000 points. This is not a question of *Donkey Kong* being

(a)

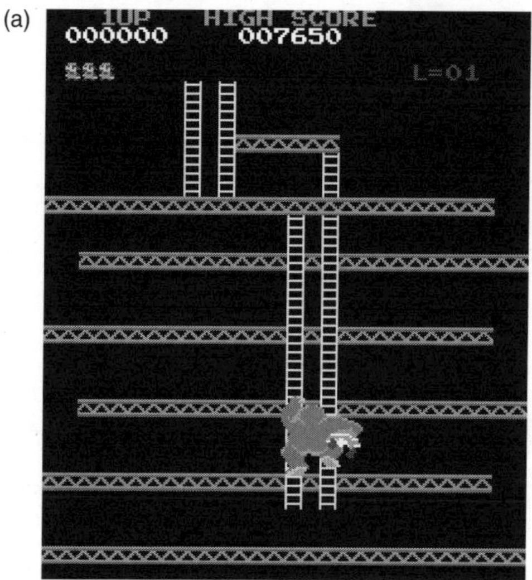

(b)

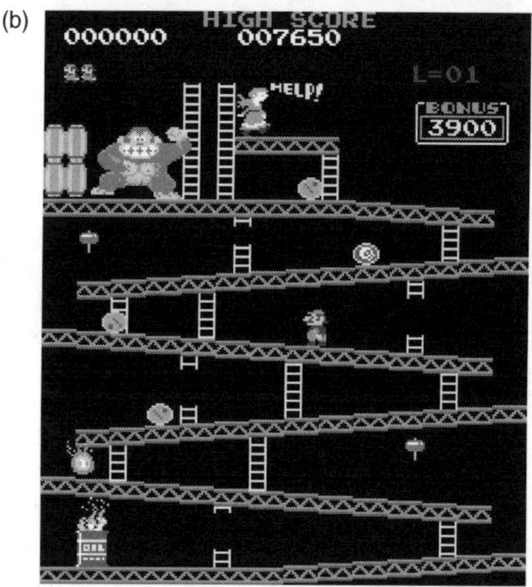

| **Figure 4.1** |

Donkey Kong (Nintendo 1981): Girl abducted. Playing. Hit by barrel. Hit by barrel again.

(c)

(d)

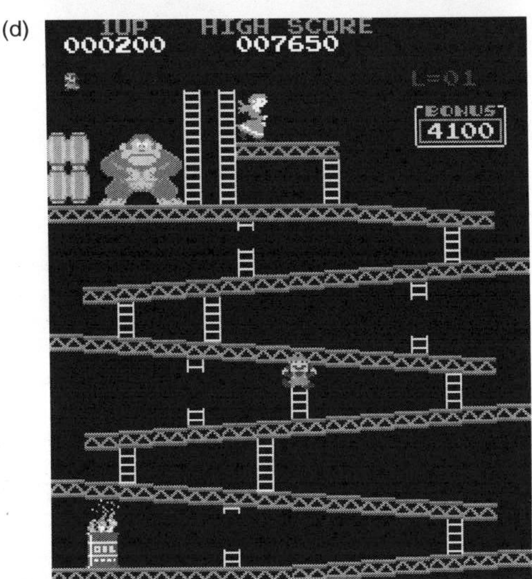

| **Figure 4.1** |
(continued)

(a)

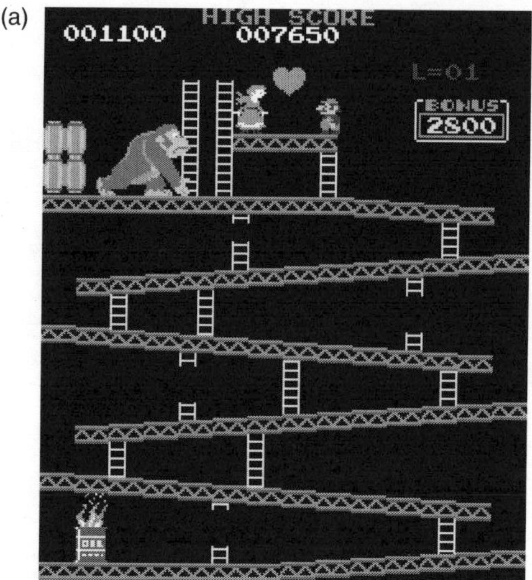

(b)

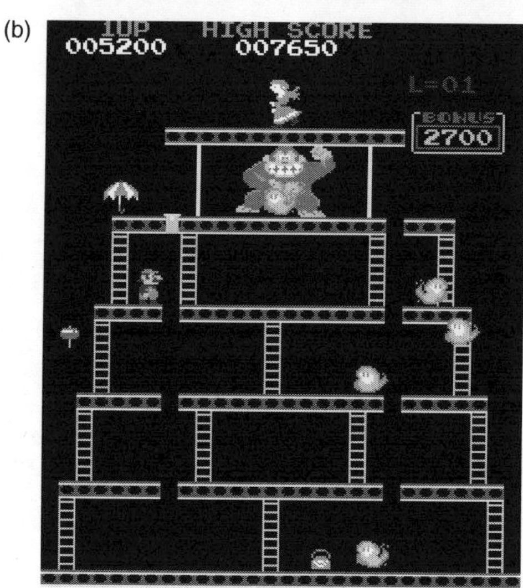

| **Figure 4.2** |
Success. Level 2: Abducted. Success. Abducted. Success.

(c)

(d)

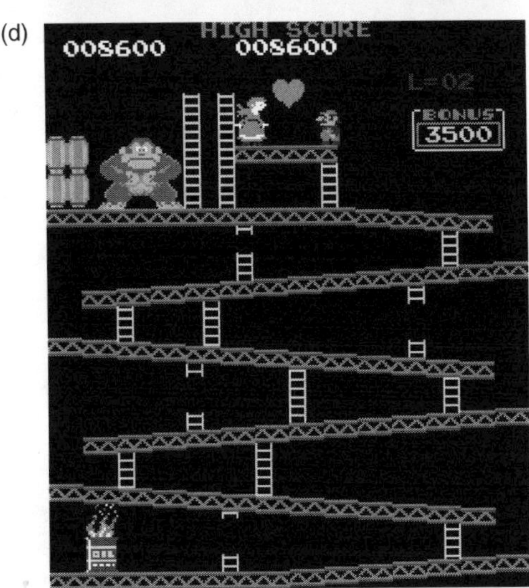

| **Figure 4.2** |
(continued)

(a)

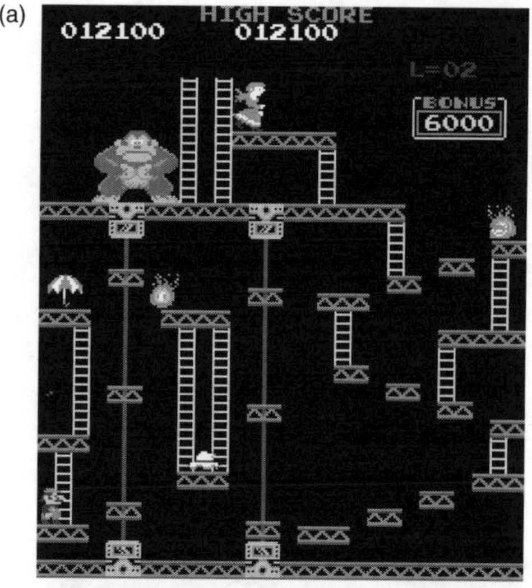

(b)

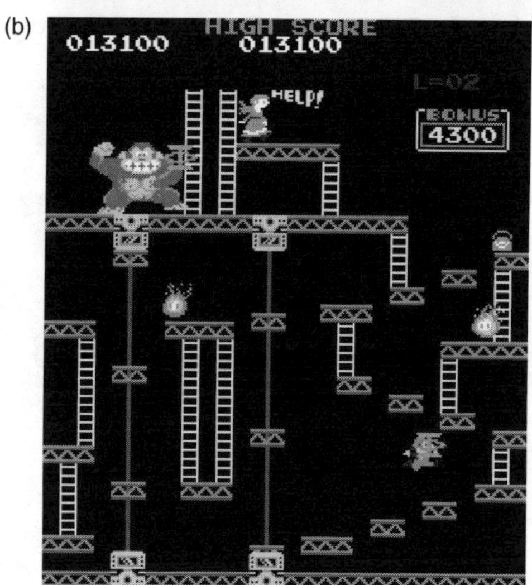

| **Figure 4.3** |

Level 4: Lifts. Hit by spring (?). Game over. Enter your name.

(c)

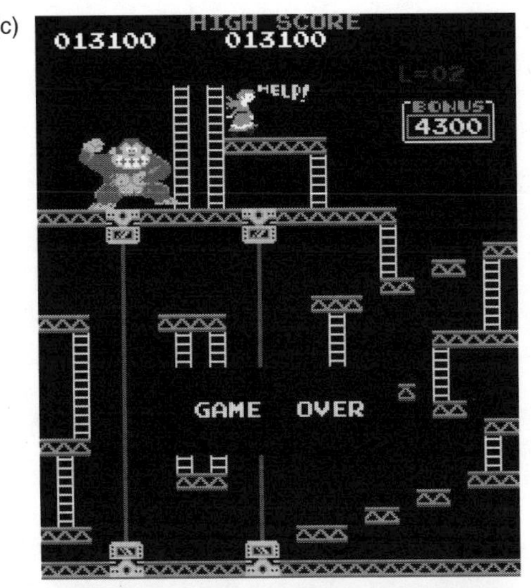

(d)

| **Figure 4.3** |
(continued)

incomplete, but a question of the fictional world being *incoherent* or unimaginable. While, technically, any world *can* be imagined, and we could explain Mario's reappearance by appealing to magic or reincarnation, the point here is that nothing in *Donkey Kong* suggests a world where people magically come back to life after dying. In an informal survey of *Donkey Kong* players, all players explained the three lives by appealing *to the rules of the game:* With only one life, the game would be too hard.

This means that when we find it too hard to imagine a video game fiction, we can resort to explaining the events in the game by appealing to the rules. Mario is not reincarnated (fiction); the player just has three Marios (rules). If the effort required to fill in a blank in the game world becomes too big, we have to resort to a rule-oriented explanation. I propose that we call this type of fictional world an *incoherent world,* meaning that there are many events in the fictional world that we cannot explain without discussing the game rules. Still, if we focus on the rules of the game, the *experience* of playing *Donkey Kong* is not incoherent. This relation between rule coherence and fictional world coherence is discussed in further detail in chapter 5.

From Abstract to Representational

There is a big difference between an abstract game and a modern video game with an elaborate fictional world. It is tempting to describe games as being either abstract or representational, but in *The Oxford History of Board Games,* game scholar David Parlett rejects this as a distinction that we cannot completely uphold. Different players will imagine different things and some players will forget the representation and think in terms of rules: "In short, no hard and fast distinction can be drawn between abstract and representational as a classification of games. How representational a game is depends on the level at which it is being played and the extent of its player's imagination" (Parlett 1999, 6).

I completely agree with Parlett's argument that we cannot draw a hard distinction between abstract and representational games, but it is nevertheless an interesting area to explore, particularly the muddled ground between abstract and representational games in terms of games as objects, in terms of the player's experience of the games, and in the player's use of a single game. So rather than dismissing the question, we can consider it in greater detail:

- There are many abstract games, such as *Tetris.*
- There are many games that project fictional worlds, such as *Counter-Strike.*
- A game like chess falls in a strange space in between: It is not abstract, but neither is it entirely representational in the sense that it projects a world. Chess represents a conflict between two societies, but most of the events in chess are not comprehensible as descriptions of events in a fictional world. How long time does it *really* take to move the pawn? Is chess about a world where the queen moves eight times faster than the king? Therefore, like *Donkey Kong,* chess is an *incoherent world game*—these are games that project some kind of world, but where it is impossible or very difficult to imagine a complete fictional world from the game, not because the world is incomplete (all fictional worlds are), but because there are events in the game that cannot be explained without referring to the game rules.
- A parallel type is the almost abstract game where the individual pieces have iconic meaning—an example would be the standard deck of cards with its kings and queens.
- Finally, some games are abstract, such as *Denki Blocks* (Denki Limited 2001) or *Bust-A-Move* (Taito 1998), which are based on a gameplay that is abstract; in both cases the game is about connecting elements with the same color, but they are also framed as being a contest against cute in-game characters (figure 4.4).

This leads us to a list of five main types of games:

1. *Abstract games.* An abstract game is a game that does not in its entirety or in its individual pieces represent something else: The game of checkers is a set of pieces that do not mean something else; the game is the rules. There are some conventions around the shape of the pieces and the board, but they do not stand for something else. *Tetris* is the best-known abstract video game.

2. *Iconic games.* An iconic game is one whose individual parts have iconic meaning: The king of hearts in the standard deck of cards suggests a king; it is not clear what relation this king has to other kings in the deck of cards or to other cards in the same suit. Presumably, the king and queen of hearts are married and the jack is somehow part of the court, but it is hard to take this any further.

| Figure 4.4 |

Bust-A-Move (Taito 1998): The abstract game is presented as being played between in-game characters.

3. *Incoherent world games.* An incoherent world game is a game with a fictional world but where the game contradicts itself or some game events cannot be explained as part of the fictional world. While in an incomplete fictional world there are blanks that the player must fill in, an incoherent world *prevents* the player from filling in the blanks. In the *Donkey Kong* example, we cannot easily explain why Mario has three lives except by referring to the rules of the game. Chess represents a conflict between two societies at war, but it is not possible to explain the movements of the pieces except by referring to the rules of the game.

4. *Coherent world games.* Some games contain coherent worlds, where nothing prevents us from imagining them in any detail. Most adventure games fall in this category.

5. *Staged games.* Staged games are a special case where an abstract or somewhat representational game is played in a more elaborate world.

These are games like *Denki Blocks* or *WarioWare Inc.* where the simple puzzles and games to be solved are presented as having been created by characters in a very cursorily sketched larger world. A more complex variation is in the ambitious role-playing/adventure *Shenmue* (Sega-AM2 2000) where the protagonist can play games on in-game arcade machines. This can obviously be done on any number of levels, but the major limitation seems to be that you can only stage a game in a game with a fictional world. You can play an abstract game against characters in a fictional world, but you cannot play *EverQuest* inside *Tetris*. It is not that it is *graphically* impossible to place *EverQuest* inside a game of *Tetris*; it is just that it does not make sense.

These categories can work on a purely textual level as well as in the mind of the player: The player may fail to understand the representation, strongly misinterpret the representation, fill out the inevitable holes in the representation in idiosyncratic ways, or add an element of make-believe to an abstract game. Arguably, many amateur sports are often played with some fictional world element. The amateur soccer player may imagine that he is David Beckham during the match, thus combining the abstract game with an imagined, fictional world.

Likewise, any game can potentially be read as an allegory of something else. Janet Murray has famously read *Tetris* like this: "a perfect enactment of the overtasked lives of Americans in the 1990s—of the constant bombardment of tasks that demand our attention and that we must somehow fit into our overcrowded schedules and clear off our desks in order to make room for the next onslaught" (1997, 144). When we consider that *Tetris* is a Russian game, Murray's reading does not say that *Tetris* was *intended* as a comment on American lives or that *Tetris is* a comment on American lives, but only that it is *possible* to make this allegorical reading. Any game can potentially be *read* as an allegory of something else, but some readings will be more convincing than others.

Ways of Creating Worlds

A game cues a player into imagining a fictional world. Games can do this in a number of different ways: using graphics, sound, text, cut-scenes, the game title, box, or manual, haptics,[4] and rules. Additionally, the actions that the player performs by moving a mouse, pressing a key on a

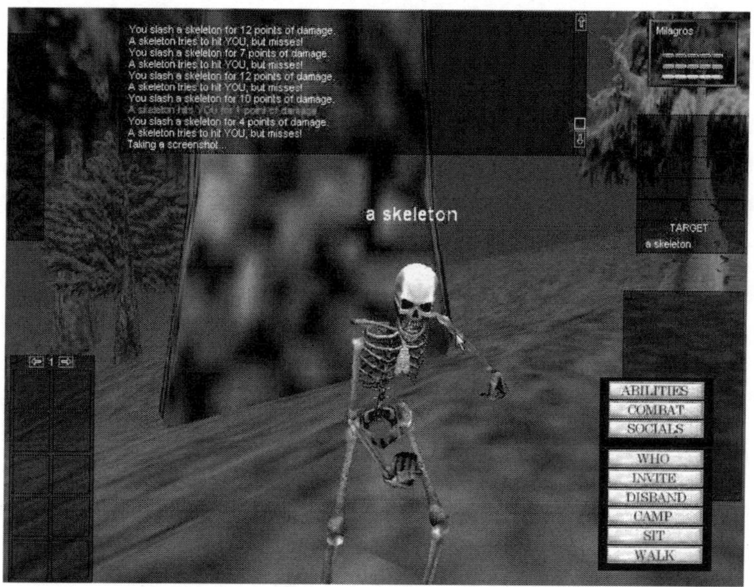

| **Figure 4.5** |
EverQuest (Verant Interactive 1999).

keyboard, or using a game controller signify actions in the game world: Pressing the mouse button may signify shooting a gun; pushing the stick on the game controller to the right may signify moving a character to the right in the game world. Finally, personal idiosyncrasies and even rumors may influence the way a player imagines the game world.

Graphics

The most obvious way of projecting a world is by using graphics. In figure 4.5, the player faces a skeleton in *EverQuest:* The graphics project a world with trees and skeleton monsters. Graphics are probably the most important way in which games project worlds.

Sound

In the same example, the *sound* is less expressive but, certainly, the simple noises played when the player is attacked also project a fictional game world. In game development, fewer resources are usually spent on sound than on graphics, and there is a tendency for sound in games to be mostly mood-enhancing and not quite as informative than graphics.

Text

EverQuest is something of a combination of the old and new, combining 3-D graphics with the text-based MUD (multi-user dungeon) game of the 1980s. Consequently, much of the action is also described using *text*, as in the previous *EverQuest* example: "*A skeleton tries to hit YOU, but misses!*" Even though dialogue has traditionally been exclusively represented by text, advancements in computer sound and storage have allowed it to be included as audio as well. Nevertheless, the vast majority of games for current handheld game systems rely on text for dialogue.

Cut-Scenes

A somewhat controversial way of creating game fiction,[5] a *cut-scene* is a non-interactive sequence of a game that typically provides backstory or informs the player of the task to be undertaken (figure 4.6). Cut-scenes are often considered problematic because they prevent the player from doing anything and are in a sense a non-game element in a game. Still, they play an important role in projecting fiction in modern video games.

Game Title, Box, and Manual

Several non-game elements can contribute to the projection of the game world: The *title* of the game sometimes creates expectations about the fictional world; for example, the title *Space Invaders* is by itself sufficient to describe a science fiction setting with battling spaceships. The game *box* usually features specially designed graphics rather than screenshots from a game, as in the case of *EverQuest* in figure 4.7. The images on the box—screenshots as well as specially designed graphics—cue the player into imagining the fictional world of the game. It is also common for games to provide some element of textual background story in the manual or on the box.

Haptics

The least developed way of projecting fictional worlds is using the haptic facilities of the controllers for modern consoles: The Playstation 2, Xbox, and GameCube consoles' standard controllers can be programmed by

| **Figure 4.6** |
Metal Gear Solid 2: Sons of Liberty (Konami 2001b).

games to vibrate at specific times. At the current state of the art, this is, in my opinion, not done very artfully, being mostly a default vibration that is triggered when, for example, your car crashes in a racing game.

Rules

The *rules* of a game also contribute to the fictional world. Even if the graphics were the same, the fictional world-skeleton of *EverQuest* would be perceived quite differently if it never attacked the player, if it always ran away, or if it was stronger or weaker. In this way, the rules work with the representational layer of the game to project the game world. This is explored in more detail in chapter 5.

Player Actions and Time

Since a player uses time and effort to play a game, that time and effort acquire a dual meaning in a game with a fictional world. The actions that the

| **Figure 4.7** |
The *EverQuest* box.

player performs also influence events in the fictional world, and the time taken to play is projected onto the fictional time of the game world.

Rumors

Like other fictional worlds, the fictional world of a video game is incompletely specified. But where the viewer of a film or the reader of a novel is certain to have seen all the material that presents the fictional world of the story, video games are special in that skill is required to access all parts of the game. Video games are therefore uniquely prone to rumors and imaginings about the world of a game. In the arcade game *Battlezone* (figure 4.8) (Atari 1980), the player controls a tank in a simple 3-D environment; a mountain range and a volcano can be seen on the horizon. Atari engineer Lyle Rain recalls: “One letter came from a *Battlezone* fan who said that if you drove far enough you finally got to the volcano, and if you drove over the top of the volcano, you could go down into the crater.

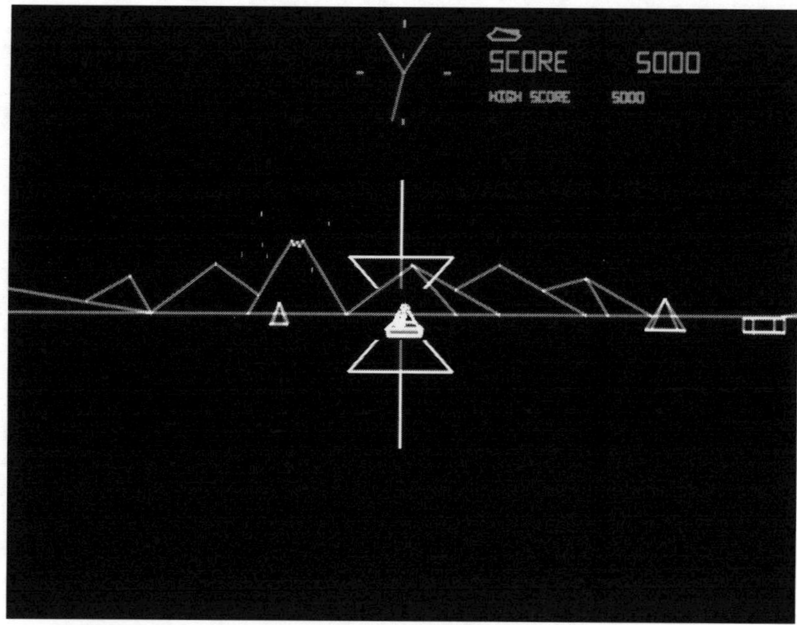

| **Figure 4.8** |
Battlezone (Atari 1980).

And he said that inside the crater there was a castle, and that you could go inside and explore the castle. Of course, none of this was true" (qtd. in Burnham 2001, 216). The game designer cannot control the player's interpretation of the game world, and the player may additionally believe that the game contains nonexistent elements and imagine the world accordingly. There is nothing in *Battlezone* that indicates the existence of a castle, but this player nevertheless believed that the game contained indications that he would find if only he got sufficiently far into the game.[6]

Optional Worlds and Incoherent Worlds

If we play a game of *Quake III Arena*, we are invited to imagine a fictional world where players can change directions in mid-air, and attack each other using a wide range of futuristic weapons. However, we can also refuse the invitation and still play the game. It is a common characteristic that with sustained playing of the same game, the player may become less interested in the representational/fictional level of the game and more focused on the rules of the game. In a survey of *Quake III Arena* players, Retaux and Rouchier (2002) discovered that *Quake III Arena* players were initially attracted to the graphics of the game, but that as they played more, they would modify the graphical settings on their machine to get higher frame rates (and thereby faster feedback) at the expense of graphical detail: The more experienced a player was, the less the graphics mattered. In figure 4.9a, graphical detail is high and the game as a fictional world is therefore emphasized, in figure 4.9b, graphical detail is low and the game as a set of rules is therefore emphasized. Experienced players shift their focus from the fictional world of the game to the game as a set of rules. This corresponds with Haider and Frensch's theory of information reduction (1996) discussed in chapter 3, about how improved performance includes learning to ignore information that is not relevant to the performance of the task. This is something that users generally do intuitively, and in this case they do it explicitly by tweaking the options of the game: Skilled players know that the textures on the wall are not relevant to the playing of the game.

Incoherent Worlds

An incoherent world is characterized by the fact that we cannot reasonably fill in the gaps in the world. It is not easy to generalize about where the

(a)

(b)

| **Figure 4.9** |

Quake III Arena (ID Software 1999) with high and low graphics detail (Retaux and Rouchier 2002).

border lies, but an informal test is the *retelling test:* For a given game, is it possible to describe *what really happened* in the game without resorting to describing the rules, props, or the real-world situation where the game was played? In *Donkey Kong,* we are likely to simply refer to the game convention that the player has three lives, rather than explain Mario's three lives as an aspect of the fictional game world. The same applies to chess. What we find is that small and local aspects of such games can be retold: Each level and individual life in *Donkey Kong* can be retold; the checkmating of a king can—with extraordinary leaps of imagination—be retold; but a full session of an incoherent world game cannot be retold in its entirety without describing the rules of the game or the real-world play situation.

I think the best explanation for incoherent world games is that by *game conventions,* the player is aware that it is optional to imagine the fictional world of the game. In non-electronic make-believe games, this makes perfect sense since a game of make-believe is not required to be rhetorically persuasive (nobody else needs to be convinced) nor does it need to be logically coherent. We can agree to believe in the fiction, and we can agree not to.

Time in Games

In Pavel's (1986) terms, make-believe is a *dual structure* where something in the real world (primary universe) is assigned a place in a fictional world (secondary universe). If we play a board game such as *Axis & Allies* (Nova Game Design 1984), all our actions have a double meaning. We move a piece around a board, but this *also* means we are invading Scandinavia with our troops. In *Tomb Raider* (Core Design Ltd. 1996), we click the keys on the keyboard, but we are also moving Lara Croft. In these examples, the *actions* that we perform have the duality of being real events and being assigned another meaning in a fictional world. Additionally, since our actions take place in time, that time shares the duality of being both real time *and* fictional world time. The fictional world of an incoherent game is provisional, and we can examine this from a temporal perspective to see how it works during the course of a game session: how a game can shift between prompting the player to imagine a fictional world and preventing the player from imagining the game world.

Here, I have chosen to examine time rather than space, as the time the player uses to play a video game has an additional meaning in the

| **Figure 4.10** |
Time in abstract games.

fictional world, whereas space in video games primarily exists *inside* the game world. Chapter 5 contains a general discussion on space in games.[7]

Time in Abstract Games

To play a game takes time. A game begins and it ends. I would like to call this time *play time*. Play time denotes the time span taken to play a game. As a first example, we may look at checkers. In abstract games like checkers or *Tetris* it would seem that this is all there is to it: Everything in the game happens *now*, while we play. In soccer—which is really just a physical abstract game—the same thing would be true. To draw a diagram of time in such a game is trivial (figure 4.10).

Games such as checkers, tennis, or *Tetris* do not cue the player into imagining a fictional world, but all games contain a change of game state, the movement from the initial state (the outcome has not been decided) to another state (the outcome has been decided). As discussed in chapter 3, a game is a *state machine*. When you play a game, you are interacting with the game state. The difference between a real-time abstract game and a turn-based abstract game is that in the latter case the game state only changes when the player takes a turn. In a real-time game, not doing anything also has consequences. Additionally, turn-based games usually do not specify the amount of play time that the player can use on a specific move (unless this is specified by tournament rules or social pressure).

Real-time Games with Worlds

In a real-time game like *Quake III Arena* or *Unreal Tournament* (Epic MegaGames 1999), we experience the duality described above: As a player, you are "yourself" and a character in the game world. I propose the term *fictional time*[8] to denominate the time of the events in the game world. In most action games and in the traditional arcade game, the play time–fictional time relation is presented as being 1:1. In such real-time

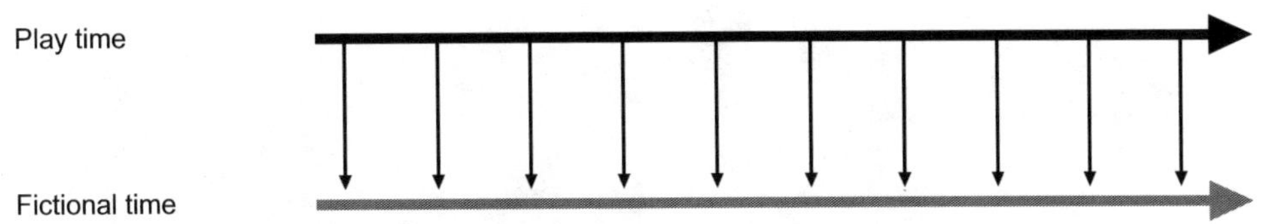

| **Figure 4.11** |
Real-time games: The play time has a 1:1 projection to the game world's fictional time.

games, pressing the fire key or moving the mouse immediately affects the game world. Therefore, the game presents a parallel world, happening in real time (figure 4.11).

Other Games with Worlds

In the original *SimCity* and in *SimCity 4* (Maxis 2003) in figure 4.12, we also find play time and fictional time, but the events in the *fictional time* (investing in infrastructure, building houses) happen faster than we would expect them to. Fictional time depends on explicit marks, such as dates, and on cultural assumptions about the duration of the game events. *SimCity* has both: We know that building a power plant takes more than a few seconds, and the interface displays the current date of the fictional time. Playing for two minutes can make a year pass in the fictional time/game world (figure 4.13).

Projection

The link between play time and fictional time can be described as *projection*. Projection means that the player's time and actions are projected onto the game world where they take on a fictional meaning. The arrows of the figures correspond to a basic sense of *now* when playing a game. Games require at least one situation where the player interacts with the game state, and games that are not abstract also require at least one instance of projection—one instance where the player performs some act such as moving a piece on a board or pressing a key on a keyboard, and where this act is projected as having a specific meaning in the fictional world.

As described, action games tend to have a 1:1 projection of the play time to the fictional time. In some games such as *Shogun: Total War* (Creative Assembly 2000), or *The Sims*, the player can select the game speed,

(a)

(b)

| **Figure 4.12** |

SimCity 4 (Maxis 2003): Building a power plant in a few seconds.

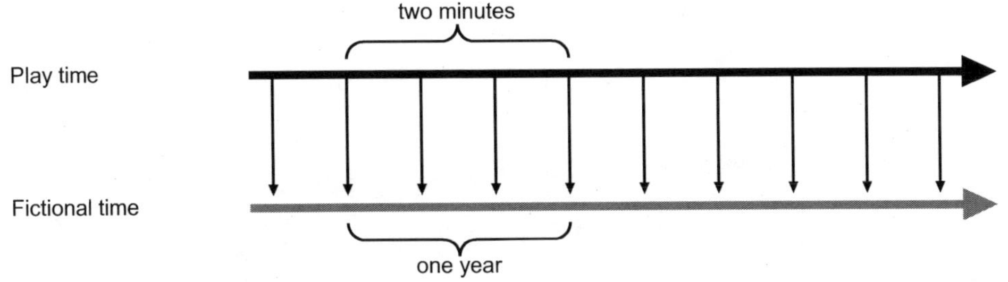

| **Figure 4.13** |
A fictional time of a year takes a few minutes of play time.

thus specifying the relation between play time and fictional time.[9] The play time is projected in to the fictional time with a specific *speed*, determining how a period in play time will translate to fictional time.

There is one extra aspect of the projection itself, since many games claim to depict historical events. *Axis & Allies*, about World War II, may be a good example, as well as *Age of Empires II* (Ensemble Studios 1999). In these games, the fictional time is placed in a specific historical period. It is perfectly possible to play a real-time game that takes place in fifteenth-century France or in space in the thirty-second century. This can be something determined as simply as using text on the box, "The year is 3133," or it can be something the player deduces from the game setting. The year specification in *SimCity* serves the same purpose. The play time can be projected onto fictional time with a specific *speed* and it can be *placed* historically.

Modern Game with Cut-Scenes

Not all fictional time is projected from play time: It is quite common for contemporary video games to contain intro-sequences and cut-scenes. As an example, consider the sequence from *American McGee's Alice* (Rogue Entertainment 2000) in figures 4.14–4.16. This single-player game is a mission-based real-time game where each mission is framed by *cut-scenes*. Cut-scenes depict events in fictional time (in the game world). Cut-scenes are not a parallel time or an extra level, but a different way of projecting the fictional time. They do not by themselves modify the game state—this is why they can usually be skipped and why the user cannot do anything

| **Figure 4.14** |
American McGee's Alice (Rogue Entertainment 2000). Navigating the game world.

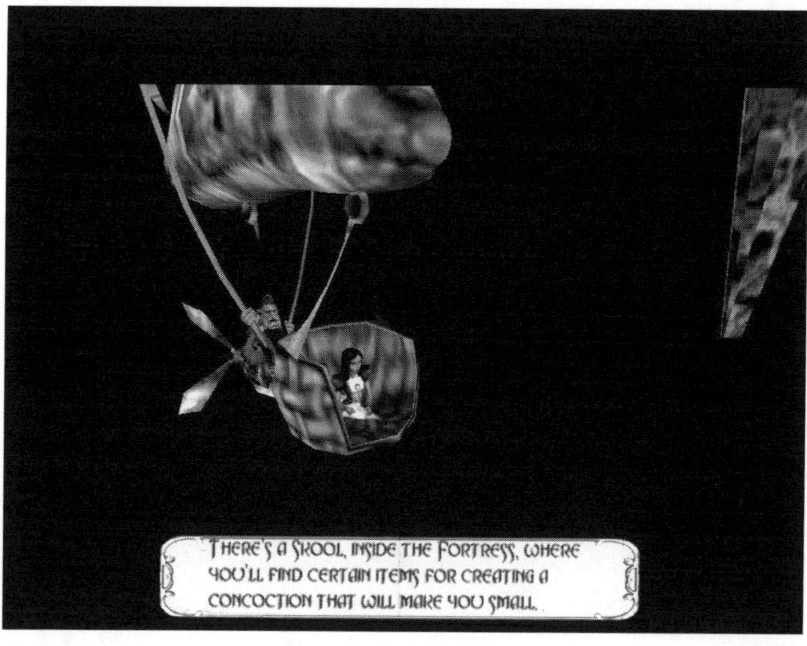

| **Figure 4.15** |
Having traversed a part of the game world, the player is rewarded with a cut-scene, which gives information about the next task.

| **Figure 4.16** |
Navigating the game world in search of the promised concoction.

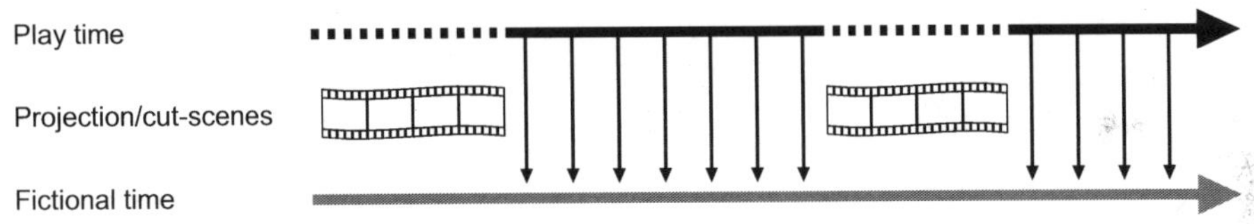

| **Figure 4.17** |
Alternation between play time being a prop for fictional time and fictional time being narrated by cut-scenes.

during a cut-scene. While play time is projected to fictional time in interactive sequences, cut-scenes disconnect play time from fictional time (figure 4.17).

The Chronology of Time in Games

Notwithstanding inspirations from cinema, time in games is almost always chronological, and there are several reasons for this. Flash-forwards are highly problematic, since to describe events-to-come would mean that

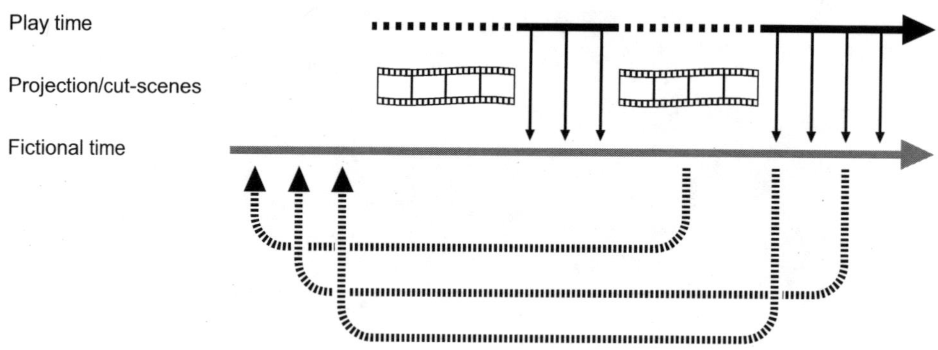

| **Figure 4.18** |
Game objects may bring information about earlier events.

the player's actions did not really matter.[10] Using cut-scenes or in-game artifacts, it is possible to describe events that led to the current fictional time, but an *interactive* flashback leads to the time machine problem: The player's actions in the past may suddenly render the present impossible.[11] This is the reason why time in games is almost always chronological.[12]

One of the more interesting developments in recent years is that game designers have become better at creating games where objects *in* the game world point to past events. Modern adventure games tend to contain not only cut-scenes, but also artifacts in the game world (fictional time) that tell the player what happened at a previous point in fictional time. This is the basic detective game model. In *Myst* (Cyan 1993), books in the game world inform the player of events that happened prior to the time of the playing, or at least outside the time that you can interact with (figure 4.18).

Adventure *and* Pong*: Coherent Time versus Level Time*

Many, especially newer, games are careful to craft fictional time as continuous, creating a believable world. *Half-Life* is a coherent world game (figure 4.19). When the game needs to load new data, this is indicated by the word "loading." This creates a continuous fictional time, but disconnects play time (figure 4.20). This is logically the case in all coherent-world games, where the game only presents one coherent world and one coherent time, but many games are imprecise with fictional time. In the

| **Figure 4.19** |
Half-Life (Valve Software 1998). Paused while loading.

Play time

Fictional time

| **Figure 4.20** |
Moving through the game, play time is paused while loading.

classic arcade game, the changing of levels has no logic in the game world: Arcade games tend to present several ontologically separate worlds that simply replace one another without indicating any connection. One way to soothe the passage between two levels is, of course, to use cut-scenes. One of the earliest examples of this can be found in *Pengo* (figure 4.21) (Sega 1982). This cut-scene does not actually make sense: It does not mean that something happens in the game world, so *Pengo* is therefore an

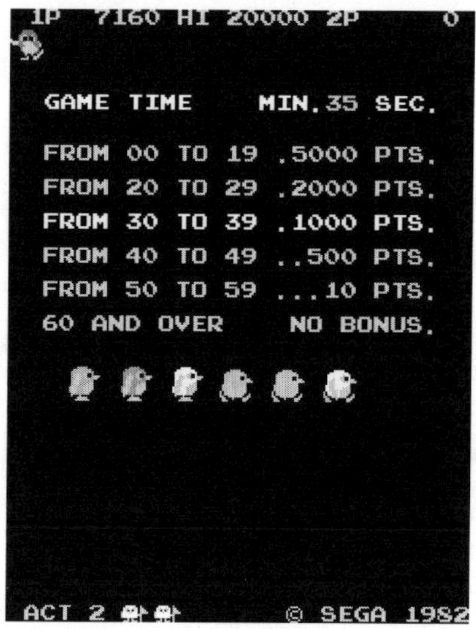

| **Figure 4.21** |
Pengo (Sega 1982): After level two, penguins dance to Beethoven's *An Die Freude*.

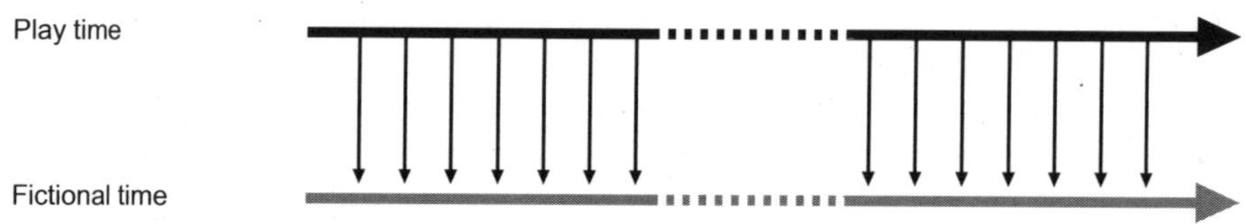

| **Figure 4.22** |
Changing level, both play time and fictional time are undefined.

incoherent world game. The cut-scene rather presents a break between two separate worlds in the game, thus breaking the timeline of both play time and fictional time. Here, play time is not projected onto fictional time, and there is no connection between the fictional time of the previous level and the upcoming level (figure 4.22). *Pengo* is an incoherent world game, but the individual levels are coherent. Similarly, in newer games like *Battlefield 1942* or *Counter-Strike*, the jump between different rounds is not explained.

This kind of abrupt jump can seem unwarranted, but can incoherent worlds in games be understood by way of their time? When we consider this historically, *Space Invaders* also features several levels: Having destroyed all the advancing aliens, the player is presented with an unexplained new wave of aliens.

The popularity of this kind of incoherent time may be due to the early history of video games. *Pong* presents itself as table tennis, and each session is played with several balls. It is structured like a meta-game consisting of separate rounds, but it makes sense here—this is, in fact, just like table tennis. *Space Invaders* borrows the concept of rounds *and* projects a fictional world. Incoherent round-based worlds seem connected to the rounds found in sports and other pre-electronic games. The rounds make sense on the rule-level, as an activity in play time, but not in the fictional world and time.

Broken Time: Standard Violations of Game Time

In addition to the lack of connection between levels in some games, there are a few standard violations of the play time/fictional time relationship. Since play time is projected onto fictional time, pausing the play time should logically also pause the fictional time and hence the fictional world. A common violation of this principle regards sound: In *Black & White* (Lionhead Studios 2001), the environmental sounds continue playing when the game is paused. In *The Sims*, the CD player purchased for the game's inhabitants continues to play when the game is paused. This breaks the logic of game time, and it signals that the sound is in some way not part of the game world at all. The film theorist David Bordwell makes a distinction between *diegetic* space—the fictional world—and *nondiegetic* space—that which is not part of the fictional world (in the same way that the musical score is external to the fictional world of a movie) (Bordwell 1985, 118–120). The sounds that continue even when the game world is paused keep the player "in the mood" of the world, even though the world is technically paused.

Another type of subtle breach of game time logic is when it is unclear whether the actions of the game are real-time events—in play time—or if they refer to the fictional time of the game. In the soccer game *FIFA 2002* the on-screen clock counts forty-five minutes for each half, signifying a full-length soccer match. In real time each half lasts four minutes, a speed-up of 11.25 times. Since the clock shows the duration of a normal soccer match, it follows that the action on the playing field is also 11.25

times faster than real life. Subjectively, the game action appears quite fast, but if our point of reference is the game clock, the action in the game is painfully slow. In figure 4.23, the normally agile David Beckham takes an amazingly slow twelve seconds *according to the clock* to run the few meters from the edge of the goal zone to the point from where he shoots. In play time, this takes a more reasonable one second. But how long did it take in the time of the game world, in fictional time? We cannot determine this in any definite way: The fictional time of the game flickers between being a real-time game of 2 × 4 minutes and an imagined full-length soccer match of 2 × 45 minutes.

A more explicit version of incoherent time can be found in *Grand Theft Auto III*. According to the in-game clock, the fictional time in the game runs sixty times faster than the play time. (An hour of fictional time lasts one minute in play time.) Like in the example of *FIFA 2002*, most of the events within the game appear nevertheless to proceed at real-time speeds. The cars drive fairly fast, but they are excruciatingly slow in fictional time. Many of the tasks and missions that the player has to perform have to be completed within a time limit *in play time*. In the taxi mission in figures 4.24–4.25, the player has forty-nine seconds in real time to deliver the passenger to his destination. According to the clock stating the time of day (at the top of the screen), the journey took twenty minutes, but according to the clock stating the time taken to deliver the passenger, the journey took twenty seconds. While the overall picture is clear, namely that the top clock refers to the fictional time, and the bottom clock refers to play time, this makes it impossible to decide how long time passed in the game world—like in *FIFA*, the fictional time of the game world is incoherent. While this may be surprising, it is even more surprising that this broken time goes unmentioned—the Gamespot.com review (Gerstman 2001) does not discuss it, which suggests how common it is for games to have incoherent fictional worlds.

A World Standing Still: Subjective Time?

There are situations in which the time of a game acquires a subjective quality. In *Space Invaders*, the whole game is paused slightly whenever the player hits an alien (figure 4.26). The moment of success for the player is extended by a slight pause. We find the same occurrence in a number of other games, mostly platform games like *Super Mario 64* (Nintendo 1996)

(a)

(b)

| **Figure 4.23** |

FIFA 2002 (Electronic Arts 2002): David Beckham sprints to the goal area. 12 seconds later, he is ready to shoot.

| **Figure 4.24** |

Grand Theft Auto III (Rockstar Games 2001): The passenger is waiting.

| **Figure 4.25** |

Grand Theft Auto III: Two clocks at the same time.

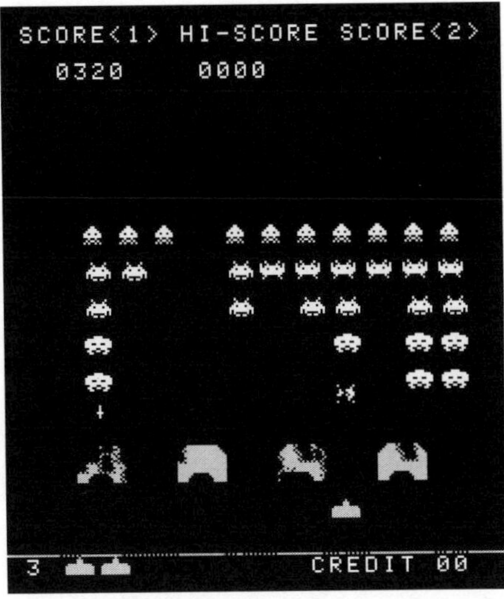

| **Figure 4.26** |
Space Invaders (Taito 1977): Time is paused briefly when an alien is hit.

or *Super Mario Sunshine* (Nintendo 2002). If this is not experienced as a jarring incoherence, it is likely due to the fact that the player is occupied with the enjoyment of his or her accomplishment, *and* because challenges influence the subjective experience of time (Csikszentmihalyi 1990, 66–67). In film, slow motion is a well known device for signaling that a moment in time has strong emotional significance.

The Experience of Time

How does the player experience the duration of the game? The objective, linear time described in the game time model feeds subjective time experiences. The experience is a product of both the play time–fictional time relation, and of the challenges that the rules present to the player. Games are supposed to be enjoyable experiences, but this is obviously not always the case. There are moments that have been described as *dead time:* Dead time is when you have to perform unchallenging activities for the sake of a higher goal. For example, to progress in *EverQuest* or *Ultima Online* (Origin Systems 1997), you must spend hours or days doing mundane tasks such as walking, waiting for monsters to respawn, or even fishing or chopping wood. It makes perfect sense within the context of the game world but it is a dull experience because the player's repertoire is not expanded or challenged—this is the dead time. A specific task has to be performed to advance in the game, but the task in itself holds no interest.

Games and Narratives

I have so far mostly refrained from discussing games and narratives, but the focus on fictional time in games makes it necessary to describe this in more detail. The primary predicament with such a discussion is that the term *narrative* has such a wide range of contradictory meanings and associations for different people and in different theories that it is practically meaningless unless specified in great detail. I have previously expressed my frustration with indiscriminate use of the term *narrative:*

> The narrative turn of the last 20 years has seen the concept of narrative emerge as a privileged master concept in the description of all aspects of human society and sign-production. Expanding a concept can in many cases be useful, but the expansion process is also one that blurs boundaries and muddles concepts, be this desirable or not. With any sufficiently broad definition of *x*, everything will be *x*. This rapidly expands the possible uses of a theory but also brings the danger of exhaustion, the kind of exhaustion that eventually closes departments and feeds indifference: Having established that everything is *x*, there is nothing else to do than to repeat the statement. (Juul 2001a)

This is not to say that we cannot discuss narrative, but to emphasize that our interest is in concepts rather than words. Let me point to six different meanings of *narrative:*

1. Narrative as the presentation of a number of events. This is the original and literal meaning of the word: story*telling* (Bordwell 1985; Chatman 1978).
2. Narrative as a fixed and predetermined sequence of events (Brooks [1984] 1992).
3. Narrative as a specific type of sequence of events[13] (Prince 1987).
4. Narrative as a specific type of theme—humans or anthropomorphic entities[14] (Grodal 1997).
5. Narrative as any kind of setting or fictional world (Jenkins 2003).

---

6. Narrative as the way we make sense of the world (Schank and Abelson 1977).

This list allows us to escape the simple question of whether games are narrative or not. Using the tools created so far for describing how games are structured and what kinds of fictional worlds they create, we can make a straightforward comparison of video games and narrative (table 4.1).

In a 2001 article, I argued that while a novel based on *Star Wars* will tell a story that is recognizable from the movie, the *Star Wars* video game (Atari 1983) does not (Juul 2001a). Henry Jenkins disagrees on this point:

> Arguing against games as stories, Jesper Juul suggests, "you clearly can't deduct the story of *Star Wars* from *Star Wars* the game," whereas a film version of a novel will give you at least the broad outlines of the plot. This is a pretty old fashioned model of the process of adaptation. Increasingly, we inhabit a world of transmedia story-telling, one which depends less on each individual work being self-sufficient than on each work contributing to a larger narrative economy. The *Star Wars* game may not simply retell the story of *Star Wars*, but it doesn't have to in order to enrich or expand our experience of the *Star Wars* saga. (Jenkins 2004, 124)

My argument used definitions one and two of narrative as the presentation of a fixed sequence of events. Jenkins focuses on the fifth definition of narrative as well as taking the perspective of the broader media landscape. My article discusses the differences between video game and movies. Henry Jenkins emphasizes that both play a role in a broader media ecology. This does not seem to be an actual disagreement.

Most of the writers critical of applying narrative theory to games have focused on the first, second, and third definitions of narrative, whereas writers emphasizing similarities between games and narratives have focused on the fifth and sixth. Are games narrative? The answer depends exclusively on which meaning of "narrative" we are using and what aspects of games we are focusing on.

Emergent Narrative and Player Story?

The term *emergent narrative* or player story calls for a special discussion. Emergent narrative tends to be described very loosely[15] as the player's

Table 4.1
Video games and six definitions of narrative

	Novels/movies/ general storytelling	Video games
1. Narrative as the presentation of events (story *telling*/narration)	Yes	No: Games as activities and rules—games are not just *representations* of events, they *are* events. Yes: Games as fictional worlds.
2. Narrative as a fixed and predetermined sequence of events (*story*)	Yes	Generally: No. Yes: In progression games as the predetermined sequence that the player has to perform to complete the game, but not as all the failed attempts of the player.
3. Narrative as a specific type of sequence of events (story)	Yes	Generally: No. Yes: Progression games can contain this.
4. Narrative as a specific type of theme (human or anthropomorphic actors)	Yes	Depends on the fictional world of a game.
5. Narrative as any kind of general setting or fictional world	Yes	No: Games as activities and rules. Yes: Games as fictional worlds, with the caveat that games uniquely tend to present incoherent worlds.
6. Narrative as the way we make sense of the world	Yes, like everything else in the world.	Yes, like everything else in the world.

experience of the game (Pearce 2004), or the stories that the players can tell about the game, or, perhaps, the stories that players can create using the game. As Jenkins has explained: "Emergent narratives are not pre-structured or pre-programmed, taking shape through the game play, yet they are not as unstructured, chaotic, and frustrating as life itself.... Most players come away from spending time with *The Sims* with some degree of narrative satisfaction. Wright has created a world ripe with narrative possibilities, where each design decision has been made with an eye towards increasing the prospects of interpersonal romance or conflict" (2004, 128). Since any emergent game as defined in the previous chapter is neither pre-structured nor as chaotic as life itself, this is not much of a criterion. Emergent narrative tends to be associated with games like *The Sims* or *EverQuest*. This seems to be an association with narrative as described in definition four, as a type of fictional world where the events contain much human interaction: in *The Sims* because the focus is on the interaction between a small group of people; in *EverQuest* because the gameplay often involves playing in groups or guilds. As long as it is not specified, emergent narrative is a nearly meaningless term, but it does point out the fact that the content of some games are thematically closer to traditional narratives than others.

Time in Games versus Time in Narratives

My two-level description of time in games as *play time* and *fictional time* is in some ways parallel to the traditional narratological distinction between story and discourse. A narrative consists of two distinct levels:

- *Story*, denoting the events told, in the order in which they were described as having occurred.
- *Discourse*, denoting the telling of events, in the order in which they are told. This is the narrative as a sequence of signs, be it words or shots in a movie.

To read a novel or to watch a movie largely consists of reconstructing a story on the basis of the discourse presented (Chatman 1978). In Orson Welles's movie *Citizen Kane* (1941), the first scene shows the protagonist on his deathbed. Then the movie cuts back in time to the beginning of the story. This means that when watching *Citizen Kane*, we reconstruct the

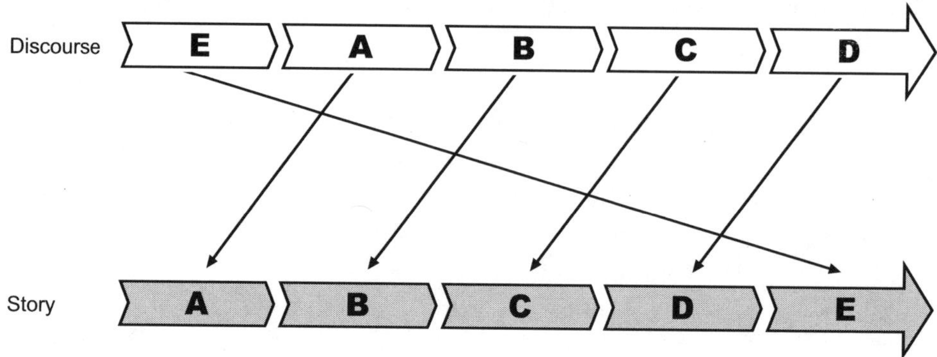

| **Figure 4.27** |
Narratives: The discourse presents the story, but often achronologically.

timeline of the story even though the events are presented to us in achronological order (figure 4.27).

In my description of time in games, play time is comparable to discourse time, and fictional time is comparable to story time. In both cases, the user uses some real time to comprehend a fictional time. There are five crucial differences: (1) The fictional time is not predetermined when the player plays the game. (2) Games tend to be chronological. (A flash-forward generally means that the outcome of the game *is* determined, and hence is not a game, whereas an *interactive* flashback can render the present impossible if the player fails to complete a task.) A story is a predetermined sequence, and users are aware of this in their reception of the game/story. (3) The actions of the player have a dual quality of occurring in play time and also being assigned meaning in the fictional world, thus the connection between the play time and the fictional time in a game is more direct than the connection between story and discourse. (4) Abstract games do not have a fictional time, and therefore have only one level. (5) Games often project incoherent worlds that cannot be described using a coherent timeline.

The Player and the Fictional World

In the world of storytelling, film and novels are largely about humans (or anthropomorphic things) that the viewer/reader identifies with. Stories without anthropomorphic actors are generally considered uninteresting (Grodal 1997), but abstract games have no human or anthropomorphic actors. If games were simply storytelling media, this would be radically uninteresting. The interest of the rules themselves is the reason why games can be abstract and without points of identification and yet be interesting. In a game, the real-world player works to overcome challenges, and overcoming them is considered a positive experience. The goal in the fictional world must mimic the player's real-world situation by being emotionally positive as well. For example, it is hard to imagine an *Anna Karenina* game based on Tolstoy's novel where the goal of the player is to commit suicide by throwing his or her character under a train (Ryan 2001a). The goal has to be one that the player would conceivably want to attain. Likewise, consider this hypothetical advertisement for a game based on *Hamlet:* "Your father has been murdered! With much effort, fail to avenge him and die a meaningless death!" This relates to the player association described in the game definition. Superficially, it would seem that the player is only attached to the outcome on the level of the rules, and as such, it would be irrelevant whether the goal of the game is to commit suicide or to save the universe. Yet, players undoubtedly also want to be able to identify with the fictional protagonist and the goal of the game in the fictional world, and hence the fictional world is very important to the player's motivation. The relation between the player and the protagonist is often discussed as *identification* (Walker 2001).

This does not rule out ironies, but most examples work by putting the player in an active position where he or she must do things normally considered negative: destroying houses and killing people in *Rampage* (Bally Midway 1986), and killing pedestrians in *Death Race* (Exidy 1976) and *Carmageddon* (Sales Curve Interactive 1997).[16] It is hard to create a tragic video game—tragedies are about events beyond our control that are then transformed into something more meaningful through the tragedy, but games are mostly about having power and overcoming challenges. A bad game is one in which the player dies without being able to prevent it. This is not to say that it cannot be done, but just that there are some inherent problems in the game format that makes creating tragic games difficult. *Burnout 2: Point of Impact* (Criterion Studios 2002), discussed in chapter 5, is one of the only video games where the player has to seek out personal destruction—but this is presented in a depersonalized way, as a game of disconnected rounds.

Fiction in Games

Games have their roots in rules and play time, and this allows them to define their worlds much more loosely and less coherently than we would accept in most other cultural forms. At the same time, the continued developments in processing power and data storage make it possible to craft fictional worlds with increasing detail and precision. While video games are also games, they have several unique strengths that support the projection of fictional worlds:

- Since the rules of a video game are automated, video games allow for rules that are more complex and hence for more detailed fictional worlds.
- Since the rules are hidden from the player, video games allow the player's initial focus to be on the appearance of the game as a fictional world, rather than on the game as a set of rules.
- Because video games are immaterial, they can depict fictional worlds more easily than non-electronic games.

Recent video games provide more elaborate worlds than previous games and, often, more coherent worlds. In combination with the improvements in computer graphics and storage, this results in an increased emphasis on game *fiction*. Conversely, contemporary games give the player more freedom in his or her use of the game: The player no longer has three lives, but can continue or even save the game; developers publish semi-official cheat codes for their games; players can set up the games the way they want. These are two movements in opposite directions: One is aimed at creating more coherent worlds on their own terms; the other is aimed at paying more heed to the real-world player by providing difficulty settings, retries, and/or cheat codes.

Video games project incomplete and sometimes incoherent worlds. Game fiction is ambiguous, optional, and imagined by the player in uncontrollable and unpredictable ways, but the emphasis on fictional worlds may be the strongest innovation of the video game.

5
RULES AND FICTION

Rules and fiction interact, compete, and complement each other. A video game may project a world and the game may be played in only a part of this fictional world. Examining a number of game examples in detail, it turns out that fiction in video games plays an important role in making the player understand the rules of the game. A statement about a fictional character in a game is *half-real*, since it may describe both a fictional entity and the actual rules of a game.

In the game design process, the game designer must select which aspects of the fictional world to actually implement in the game rules. The player then experiences the game as a two-way process where the fiction of the game cues him or her into understanding the rules of the game, and, again, the rules can cue the player to imagine the fictional world of the game.

Rules and fictions can rarely match completely; there are many examples of jarring mismatches between them. It is therefore tempting to describe their relation as inherently problematic, but when rules and fictions do not match perfectly it can still generate a *positive* effect, working as a way of playing with the player's expectations, as a way of creating parody, and finally as a way of foregrounding the game as a real-world activity.

However, space in games is a special case. The level design of a game world can present a fictional world *and* determine what players can and cannot do at the same time. In this way, space in games can work as a combination of rules and fiction.

With the ideas developed throughout the book, I will finally consider what a game *means*.

World Space and Game Space

In the introduction, I mentioned Roger Caillois's empirically incorrect claim that games are *either* ruled *or* make-believe. Let us revisit his argument:

> Despite the assertion's paradoxical character, I will state that in this instance the fiction, the sentiment of *as if* replaces and performs the same function as do rules. Rules themselves create fictions. The one who plays chess, prisoner's base, polo, or baccara, by the very fact of complying with their respective rules, is separated from real life where there is no activity that literally corresponds to any of these games. That is why chess, prisoner's base, polo, and baccara are played *for real. As if* is not necessary. (Caillois 1961, 8)

While his conclusion is incorrect, Caillois does point to an interesting similarity between rules and fiction in that both contain an element of separation from the rest of the world. Rules separate the game from the rest of the world by carving out an area where the rules apply; fiction projects a world different from the real world. The space of a game is *part of* the world in which it is played, but the space of a fiction is *outside* the world from which it is created.

Building on Johan Huizinga, Katie Salen and Eric Zimmerman have used the term *magic circle* to describe the border between the context in which a game is played and what is outside that context: "The term is used here as shorthand for the idea of a special place in time and space created by a game.... As a closed circle, the space it circumscribes is enclosed and separate from the real world.... In a very basic sense, the magic circle is where the game takes place" (2004, 95). Soccer is played within a designated playing field; a board game only takes place on the board. This can be expanded to provide a more general description of the relation between the space in which a game is played and the space of the world around it. In sports or board games, *the game space* is a subset of the space of the world: The space in which the game takes place is a subset of the larger world, and a magic circle delineates the bounds of the game (figure 5.1). When a ball game has a rule prescribing that the game stops if the ball leaves the playing field, this relates to the border between game space and world space. But in video games, the magic circle is quite

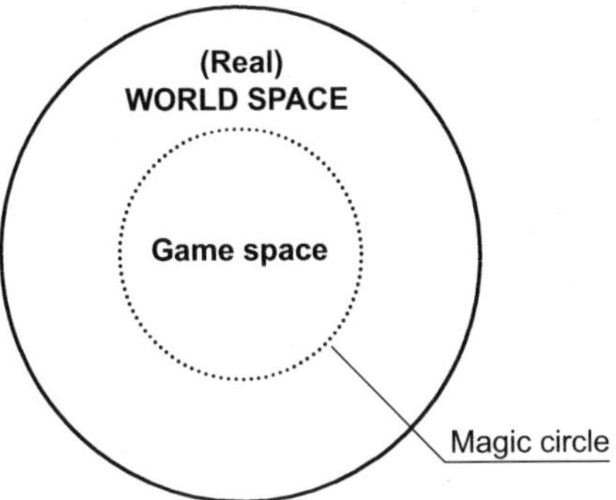

| Figure 5.1 |
A physical game (such as soccer): The game space is a subset of the space of the real world.

well defined since a video game only takes place on the screen and using the input devices (mouse, keyboard, controllers), rather than in the rest of the world; hence there is no "ball" that can be out of bounds.[1]

In a computerized soccer game such as *FIFA 2002*, the game is delineated by the screen and input devices, but the game itself projects a fictional world quite similar to the real world of FIFA world cups, inside which a game space is delineated by a magic circle and a soccer game is played (figure 5.2). This is typical of sports adapted to video games (and many other video games): A fictional world is projected and a game is played in a part of that fictional world. Since it adds meaning to a game to place it inside a larger fictional world, this is a common way of constructing a game. The simplest setup is to claim that the series of rounds that make up the individual game are part of a tournament. This is the case in *Unreal Tournament* and *Tekken 4* (Namco 2002). The relationship between game space and world space becomes more interesting in games with more elaborate fictional worlds, where the end of the game space has to be marked in more subtle ways than by using a white line or a wall. In *Battlefield 1942*, the player approaching the edge of the game space is informed by a textual message, "*Warning! You are leaving combat area. Deserters will be shot.*" This is known as *invisible walls:* The fiction gives no clue that the world ends, but for no apparent reason, the game space ends. When the game magazine *Edge* reviewed Shigeru Miyamoto's game *Super*

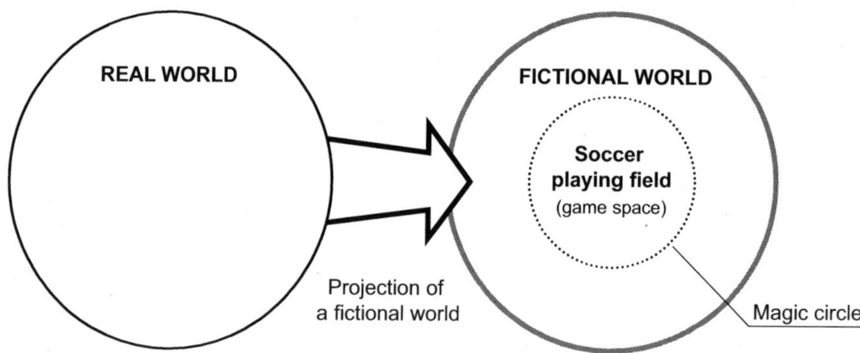

| **Figure 5.2** |
FIFA 2002 projects a fictional world, with a playing field on which soccer is played.

Mario Sunshine, disappointment was high since the game in this area fell short of its predecessor, *Super Mario 64:*

> [In Super Mario 64] There was always somewhere to go, always something to do; levels thrilled and baffled in equal measure; there were tiny polished touches that you might not discover for days, months, years. So lucid and solid, too. No obvious invisible walls.
>
> *Sunshine* begins on an island, and the island is surrounded by invisible walls. There are more around the island's central hub, the town and in each of the seven worlds that lead off it. That is disconcerting, unnerving in the follow-up to a game that used coherence as one of its central tenets. (Edge 2002, 80)

It is a hallmark of a coherent world game that the bounds of the game space are reasonably motivated by the fictional world: *Grand Theft Auto III* has a very elegant solution, where the player is initially stuck on an island whose bridge to the mainland was destroyed when the player was freed from a prison transport in the beginning of the game. It is only when the player has solved a number of tasks that the bridge is reopened and the second and third islands become accessible.

One type of incoherent world game is the game with several rounds which have no clear connection. This covers *Pengo* (chapter 4) and the newer game of *Counter-Strike* where two teams compete in a number of ontologically unconnected fictional worlds. In these games, the magic circle is inverted, and the space in which the game is played becomes larger than the space of the world in which it is played. The entire game becomes a superset of world space, and a series of fictional world spaces with magic circles inside are created and deleted during the course of the game.

Half-Real Games

In addition to containing a fictional space, the fictional world also influences the players' understanding of the game rules. Let us examine the following statement: "Hamlet is Prince of Denmark." It is a philosophical problem whether this statement is true or not (Pavel 1985, 13–17). On the one hand, there is no real person called Hamlet who is Prince of Denmark. On the other hand, it is more correct to say that Hamlet is Prince of Denmark than to say that he works as a banker. That is, Shakespeare's play describes a fictional world that does not actually exist, but in which there is a character by the name of Hamlet who is Prince of Denmark. "Hamlet is Prince of Denmark" is true in the fictional world that the play creates, and we normally accept the statement "Hamlet is Prince of Denmark" because we take it to refer to the possible world of the play. Now consider this statement: "Tennis is a game where two people hit a ball using a racket." This statement is true in the normal sense: It is about the real world, and it describes how the game of tennis is actually played. Let us then look at a computer game, *Tetris,* in figure 5.3. We can make the following statement about *Tetris:* "In *Tetris,* when you have covered an entire row, it disappears." This is a statement about the real world much like the previous statement about tennis. The rules of *Tetris* are not physical but programmed; but this does not change the fact that it is a verifiable statement about the real world. Looking at *Tekken 3* (figure 5.4), a game that is not abstract, consider the statement: "Eddy Gordo is Brazilian and fights using the martial art of capoeira." Is this true? In this case, we have to combine the question about Hamlet with the question about the rules of tennis:

1. There is no real-world person called *Eddy Gordo,* but in the *fictional world* of *Tekken 3,* there is a person by the name of Eddy Gordo who fights using the martial art of capoeira.

| **Figure 5.3** |
Tetris (Atari 1986).

2. *And:* In the real world, it is factually true that you can choose Eddy in *Tekken 3*, and that you can control the character of Eddy so that he attacks his opponent using capoeira moves.

The first point looks at *Tekken 3 as fiction;* the second point looks at *Tekken 3 as real activity*. The description of the fictional character of Eddy *also* describes the real-world fact that having selected that character in *Tekken 3* gives the player the option of performing a number of special moves. *That Eddy Gordo fights using capoeira moves describes the fictional world of the game, and it describes the real rules of the game.*

The fictional world of a game strongly depends on the real world in order to exist, and the fictional world cues the player into making assumptions about the real world in which the player plays a game.

(a)

(b)

| **Figure 5.4** |

Tekken 3 (Namco 2000): Eddy Gordo fights using capoeira.

Implementing a Fictional World: Stylized Simulations

On a basic level, a game with a fictional world can be seen as a simulation, as the implementation of a fictional world in the rules of a game. A racing game is a simulation of racing; *FIFA 2002* is a simulation of soccer. Simulation can have varying degrees of fidelity to what is being simulated.[2] *Tekken 3* simulates fighting in general and capoeira with the character of Eddy. A practitioner of capoeira, however, would undoubtedly feel that the game was an extreme simplification. Countless moves have been omitted, and the available moves have been simplified and are only available as either/or options: perform a handstand or do not perform a handstand. Here, capoeira has lost much of its expressive potential. *Tekken 3* is a very imprecise and low-fidelity simulation of capoeira.

If we assumed that the quality of a game hinged on its degree of realism and the detail of its simulation of the real world, this would be a serious detriment to the experience of playing *Tekken 3*. Another example of a low-fidelity simulation is when the player enters a car in *Grand Theft Auto III*. Simply being near the car and pressing △ on the Playstation 2 controller makes the protagonist run to the nearest car door, open the door, remove any person in the car, get in, and close the door. This is also a very low-fidelity simulation: In real life, we can enter a car in any number of different ways. But unlike in the capoeira example, we are unlikely to feel any significant loss here, since entering a car is generally not considered a very interesting activity. Simplification and stylization can be found in most games with fictional worlds. The player cannot lie down, do handstands, or simply leave the playing field in *FIFA 2002* or *Virtua Tennis*. Game fictions and rules are not perfect and complete simulations of the real world; they are flickering and provisional by nature. But stylization is an expressive device that games can use.

In his seminal book, *Understanding Comics* (1993), Scott McCloud demonstrates the expressiveness of simplification in comics (figure 5.5). The drawing of the cup in McCloud's example represents not as much a cup as the *idea* of a cup. By removing detail, the comic appears closer to the world of concepts than to the minute details of the real world. This provides a more positive account of what simplification provides: By removing detail from the source domain, the game focuses on a specific *idea* of what the game is about such as capoeira, soccer, tennis, driving

(a)

(b)

(c)

| **Figure 5.5** |

"By de-emphasizing the appearance of the physical world in favor of the idea of form, the cartoon places itself in the world of concepts" (McCloud 1993, 41).

cars. A game does not as much attempt to implement the real world activity as it attempts to implement a specific stylized *concept* of a real-world activity. The tennis and soccer games implement only what are considered interesting core parts of the real-world game; since entering a car is ultimately an uninteresting detail in the larger world of *Grand Theft Auto III*, the simulation of that activity is reduced to the pressing of one button.

Even though the actual design and development of a game are also subject to financial and time constraints, this goes to show how games are often *stylized simulations;* developed not just for fidelity to their source domain, but for aesthetic purposes. These are *adaptations* of elements of the real world. The simulation is oriented toward the perceived interesting aspects of soccer, tennis, or being a criminal in a contemporary city. In the case of sports games, the fact that sports are typically experienced on television also shapes the game: Most sports games contain slow-motion replays of the most dramatic moments in the game. The stylization of a simulation is, of course, a subjective art that must take into account common perceptions of whatever domain is being simulated.[3] *Virtua Tennis* simulates lobs, smashes, and other dramatic aspects of tennis, whereas tennis elbow and broken rackets are omitted. In many strategy games, humans pop into existence within a few seconds; in *Age of Empires II*, a villager can be created at the click of a button (figure 5.6).

To Win the Sword Fight, Solve the Puzzle: Difficulty Metaphors

Many aspects of computer-based games are not just simplifications of real-world activity, but something quite different. In the tennis game *Top Spin* (Power and Magic 2004), a perfect serve must be performed by pressing the front right controller button and releasing it at the precise time when the bouncing yellow mark is in the middle of the serve indicator (figure 5.7). What is the connection between serving in real tennis, throwing the ball into the air, twisting your body to achieve maximum power while retaining enough control to direct the ball to the right position on the other side of the net, and pressing and releasing the front right button on the Xbox controller at the right moment? The basic answer seems to be that both tasks are *difficult:* instead of performing a serve by mimicking the actual tennis activity, the serve has been replaced by another difficult

| Figure 5.6 |

Age of Empires 2 (Ensemble Studios 1999): Create a villager by clicking a button.

task. The video game activity is a metaphor for the tennis activity. *Puzzle Pirates* (Three Rings Design 2003) works explicitly with this type of metaphorical substitution. Challenging another player to a sword duel leads to a two-player duel in a puzzle game. This is a duel of sorts, but the activity bears no relation to what the fictional setting of the game would lead us to expect. Likewise, when being on board a ship, the task of bilge pumping turns out to be the playing of another action puzzle (figure 5.8).

Puzzle Pirates stands out because it foregrounds how video games often substitute one difficult task for another. Again, this does not mean that the in-game fictional task is always replaced by arbitrary real-world tasks that the player has to perform. It simply means that in games that emphasize a fictional world, there has to be a metaphorical substitution between the player's real-world activity and the in-game activity performed.

(a)

(b)

| **Figure 5.7** |

Top Spin (Power and Magic 2004): Release the button when the yellow bar is in the middle to perform a perfect serve.

(a)

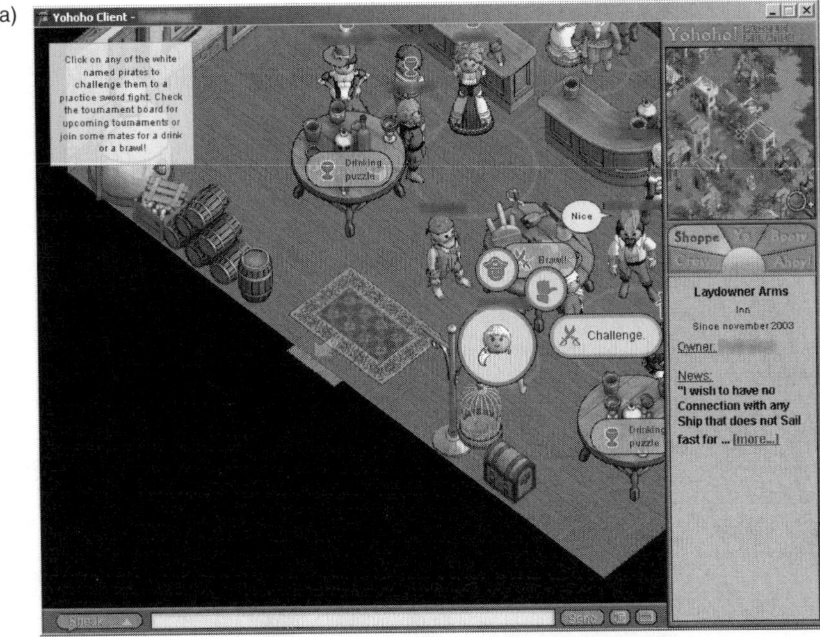

(b)

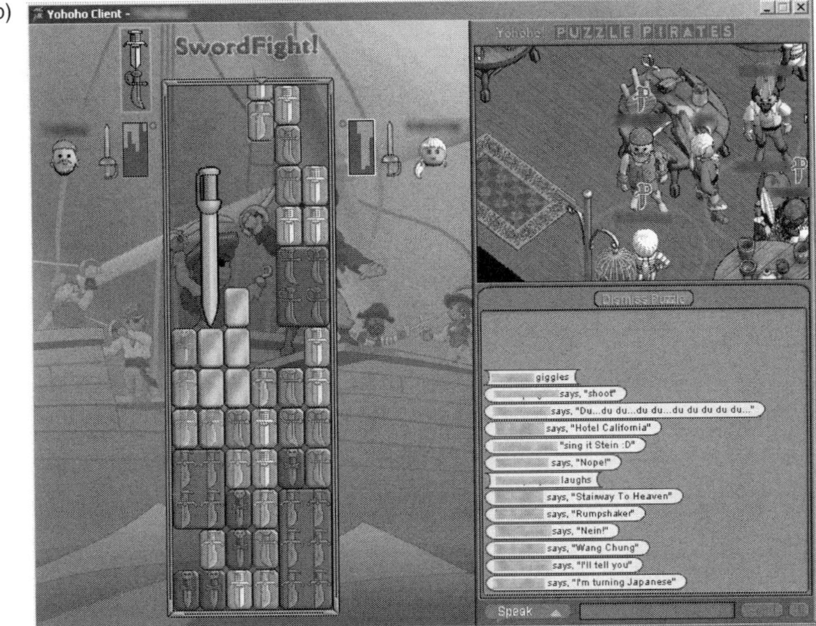

| **Figure 5.8** |

Puzzle Pirates (Three Rings Design 2003): A sword fight using a puzzle.

Fiction Cuing Rules and Rules Cuing Fiction

While the *design* of a game can work by choosing a domain or fictional setting and then subjectively designing rules to implement that domain, the player of a video game experiences this in an inverted way, where the representation and fictional world presented by the game cue the player into making assumptions about the rules of the game. In a computerized soccer game, the fictional world of the game will cue the player to assume that the game implements whatever concept the player has of soccer, including the normal soccer rules. An object that looks like a car is likely to be drivable. The even marginally experienced player is additionally likely to be aware that some aspects of the fictional world may not be implemented in the rules, and that generally the rules of a game are selective stylizations of the domain they are supposed to simulate. As such, the player is unlikely to expect to be able to leave the playing field in *FIFA 2002* or to disassemble a car for spare parts in *Grand Theft Auto III*. Only selected aspects of our assumptions about the fictional world are actually implemented in the game: The player does not have to eat; the car never runs out of gas.[4]

The vast majority of video games present fictional worlds in one way or another, whereas the vast majority of traditional non-electronic games are abstract. This is not, however, a sufficient description of this split—the majority of commercial board games are also representational (this may be because it is easier to market a representational game)—among other reasons because the potential buyer cannot possibly predict the gameplay of a game simply by reading the rules. In video games, the rules are initially hidden from the player—this means that the player is more likely to use the game world to make inferences about the rules. In fact, the player may need a fictional game world to understand the rules. In an article discussing their rhythm game *Amplitude* (Harmonix 2003) and its predecessor *Frequency* (Harmonix 2001), Greg Lopiccolo and Alex Rigopulos explain how the introduction of recognizable elements can help the player understand the rules of the game (figure 5.9):

To make sure new players could get the feel of the game right away, we redesigned the interface in a number of ways, introducing a spaceship that the players steer to shoot lasers at targets. This way, when a prospective player

———

sees a screenshot of Amplitude, or watches someone else play the game, he or she immediately reacts. "Oh, I get it. I'm, supposed to shoot things."

Interestingly, this interface change really only affects players for the first few moments they play. Thereafter, the player's attention ends up focused on the same three little target spots that were the center of the interface in Frequency. But the key point here is that those first few moments are absolutely crucial for luring in the new player. (Lopiccolo and Rigopulos 2003, 43)

Even though fiction and rules are formally separable, the player's experience of the game is shaped by both. The fictional world of a game can cue the player into making assumptions about the game rules: In a game with a first-person perspective, the player facing evil-looking monsters is likely to assume that the monsters are to be avoided or possibly destroyed. If the images of the monsters were replaced by something benign, perhaps large flowers, the player will likely make different assumptions about the rules of the game. It is not just the graphical representation, but also the rules of the game that project the fictional world. The way a given object or character behaves will characterize it *as a fictional object;* the rules that the player deducts from the fiction and from the experience of the playing of the game will also cue him or her into imagining a fictional world.[5]

Conflicts between Rules and Fictions: The Good and the Bad

In previous writings, I have assumed that the incongruence between rules and fiction was an insurmountable obstacle for games (or game scholars) wanting to emphasize games as fictional worlds (Juul 1998, 1999). A game may exhibit the problem that the rules and the representation do not match; the representation may give the players reason to make assumptions about the rules that turn out to be false; and the representation may fail to give the player important information. There are certainly many examples of such problematic relationships between rules and fiction. *Myst,* for example, is extremely inconsistent in implementing the fictional world in the rules. Here, the player can manipulate the switch, but the ship model cannot be touched (figure 5.10). This is a problem many games exhibit, but it especially happens in the adventure game genre since the progression structure means that all possible interactions in the game

(a)

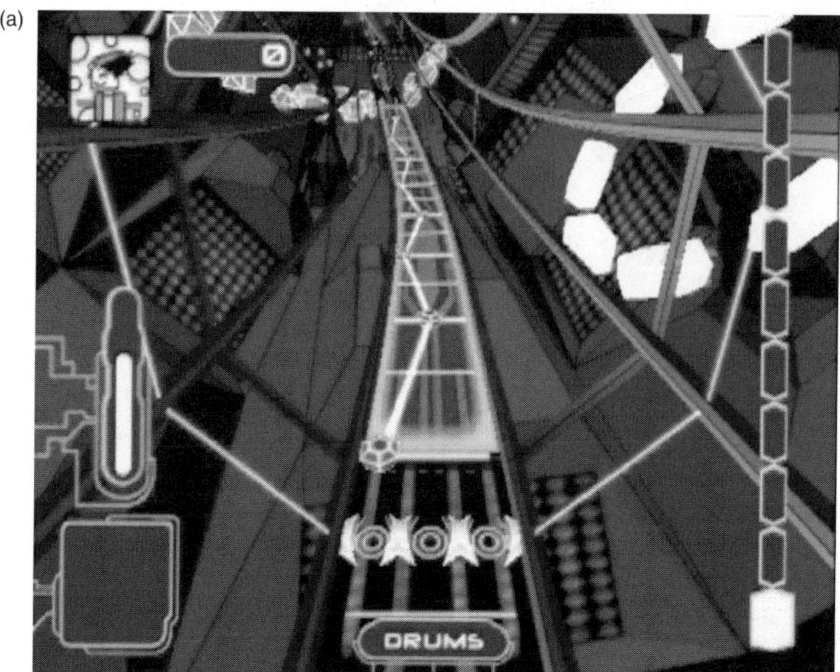

(b)

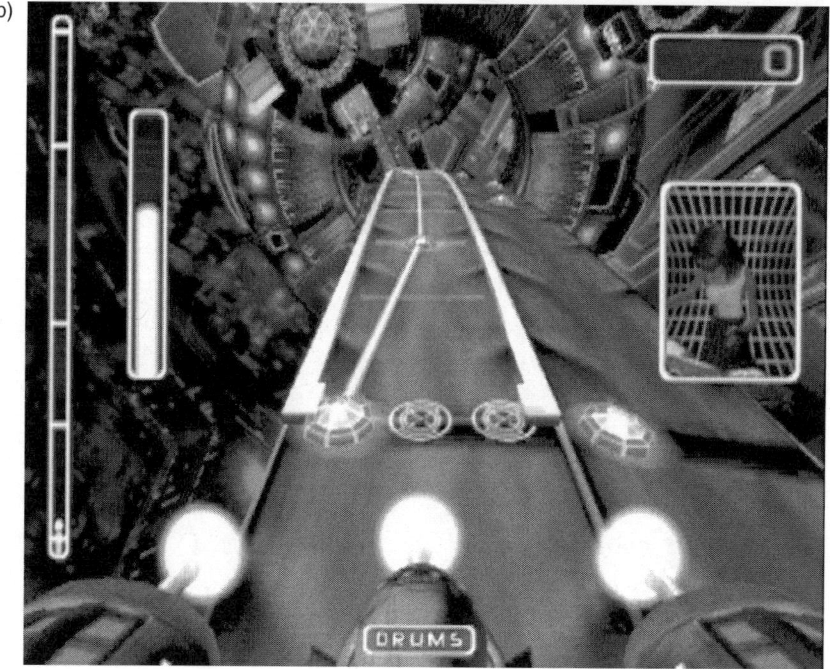

| **Figure 5.9** |

Frequency (Harmonix 2001) and Amplitude (Harmonix 2003): Identical rules, but easier to grasp with a spaceship metaphor.

have to be explicitly programmed, and implementing even the most obvious interactions requires more resources than are available for the development of the game. In text-based adventure games, the mismatches can be even more jarring, such as in this example from *Witness* (Infocom 1983):

>wait
The rain is falling heavily now.

>drink rain
(Sorry, but the program doesn't recognize the word "rain.")

In *Myst* and *Witness*, the fictional world gives the impression that many things are possible that are not implemented in the rules. The reverse case is when the rules allow for actions that the fictional word does not cue the player into expecting. Many first-person shooters of the late 1990s featured wooden crates that turned out to contain medical kits and other items that the player could pick up. For an inexperienced player, this is nonsensical and not cued by the representation: Only the trained player knowing the conventions of the game genre would understand it.

In the game of *Hitman: Codename 47*, the player has to perform a number of assassinations using any combination of stealth and violence. One of the stealth tricks is to render harmless another character and steal his clothes. Since the protagonist, 47, is a very tall bald man, the stolen clothes often do not look very credible, but the in-game characters generally take no notice of this. The representation gives the impression that the disguise is unconvincing, but the rules dictate that the other characters are convinced.[6] This appears incongruous, but such incongruities can also be used as expressive devices. In the fighting game *Tekken 4*, players can choose between a number of different characters. In this case, we have chosen the small girl, Xiaoyu versus the big muscular Marduk (figure 5.11). The representation of the game leads us to believe that Marduk is a stronger character than Xiaoyu but, in actuality, her strength is on par with all the larger characters in the game (figure 5.12). In my experience, the discrepancy between the outward appearance of the characters and the rules governing their behavior tends to be considered humorous. Here,

(a)

(b)

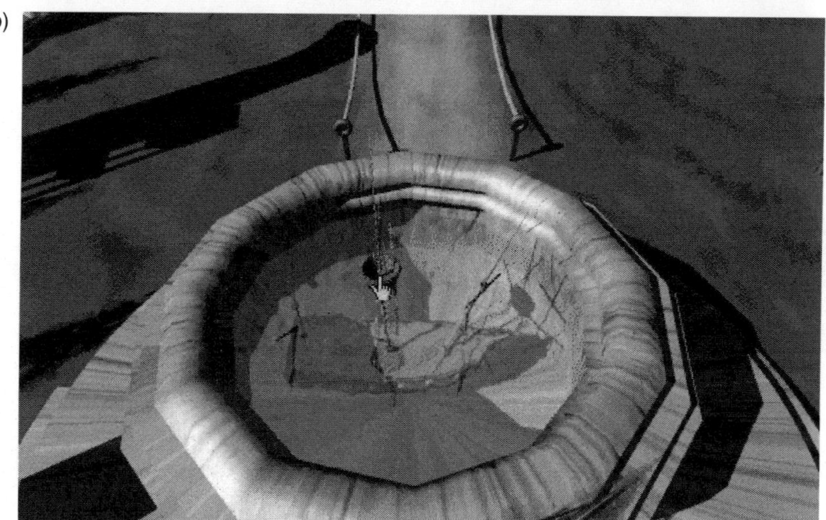

| **Figure 5.10** |
Myst (Cyan 1993): The player can manipulate the switch, but not the ship model.

(a)

(b)

| **Figure 5.11** |

Tekken 4 (Namco 2002): Xiaoyu versus Marduk.

(a)

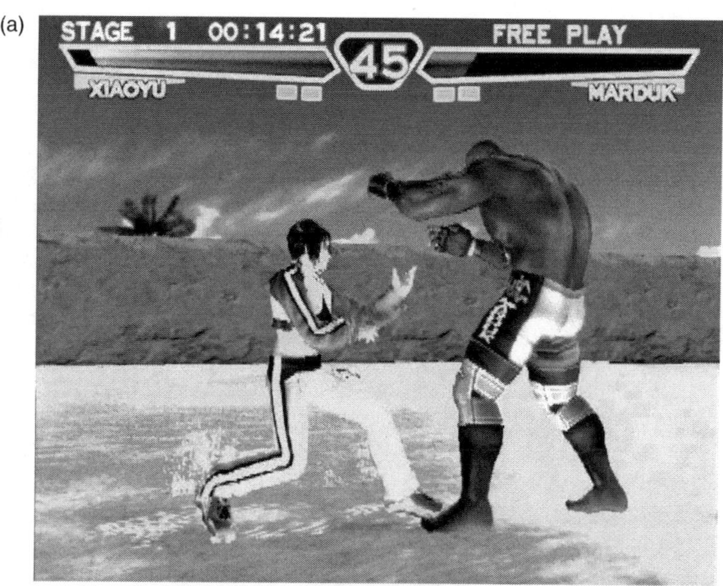

(b)

| **Figure 5.12** |
Xiaoyu defeats Marduk.

the surprising difference between what the representation suggests and what the game rules determine adds depth to the characters in the game. It also ties into the story of David versus Goliath, and the supposedly amazing powers of martial arts. In this case, the representation cues something that is contradicted by the rules, but this incongruence is an interesting effect.

Through the Glass Barrier: Characters Who Know You

If we assume that the fictional world of the game is a *world*, it would make sense to assume that the characters in that world are therefore generally unaware of their being fictional characters or being part of a game at all. In *Super Mario Sunshine*, many contextual clues are provided to the player. In the following figure, the circled B signals that the player should press the B button on the GameCube controller in order to engage in conversation (figure 5.13). The B is a contextual clue from the game interface, even if it is also a pseudo-three-dimensional object *in* the game world. In a surprising twist, an in-game object called the *FLUDD* talks about the layout of the GameCube controller (figures 5.14–5.15). It is a mixing of fictional levels when an object in the fictional world knows about things in the real world and knows that it is part of a GameCube game.

In another GameCube game, *Pikmin* (Nintendo 2001), the protagonist is a scientist stranded on an unknown planet. As the game progresses, the scientist takes notes in a diary that is displayed on the screen, including notes about the game controller (figure 5.16). In *Pikmin*, the mixing of levels has an extra twist in that it is the protagonist, and by extension the player, that is taking notes in a diary. From that perspective, taking notes on the game controller makes sense, since this is exactly the kind of thing we would write down if we were to take notes about our playing of the game.

We could easily frame this as being an interesting self-reflexive avant-garde praxis in the tradition of French nouvelle vague cinema, but it has a more immediate effect when we experience it. When an in-game character talks about how to use the controller, it rhetorically befriends us, not just as in-game characters, but also as real-world players. The breakdown of fictional levels is a positive emotional experience.

| **Figure** 5.13 |
Super Mario Sunshine (Nintendo 2002): Press B for conversation.

Satire

Any incongruity between rules and fiction can also be productive. As in any aesthetic field, there is a chance that what is considered a problem can also be used as a positive *effect*. Helene Madsen and Troels Degn Johansson examined how incongruities can be used as satirical devices (2002). Following their analysis, I discussed two similar games in chapter 1 that do not display an arbitrary relation between rules and fiction: They are satires where the love/hate relation that viewers have with TV presenters and the activity of creating video game theory are both staged metaphorically as space battles. Countless satirical games follow this pattern of framing a complex issue within a well-known video game genre.

(a)

(b)

| **Figure 5.14** |

Meeting the FLUDD device. FLUDD introduces itself.

| **Figure 5.15** |
FLUDD provides instructions. FLUDD knows the buttons on the GameCube controller.

(a)

(b)

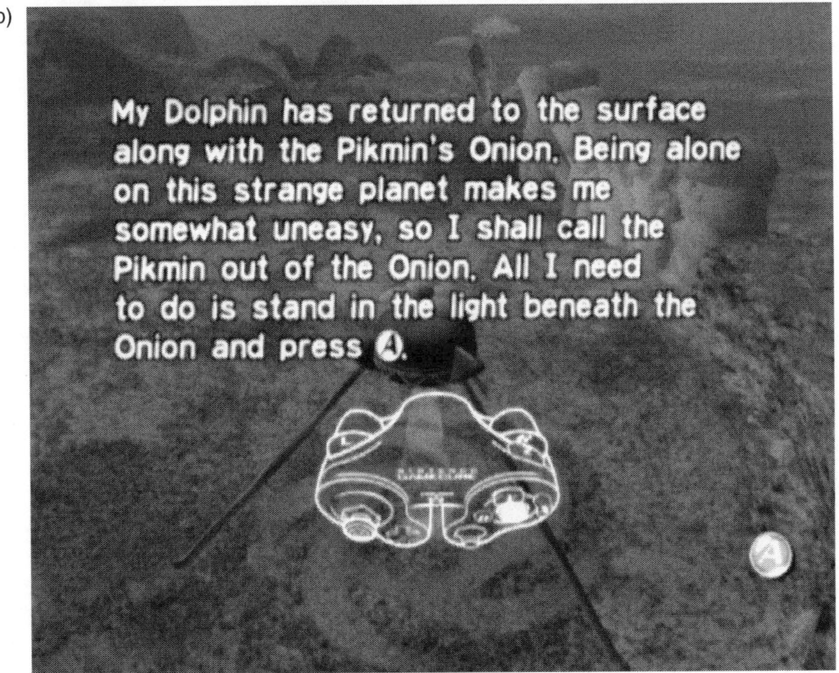

| **Figure 5.16** |

Pikmin (Nintendo 2001): The protagonist's diary discusses the controller.

Can Rules and Fiction Match? Space in Video Games

Focusing on the differences between rules and fiction and the ways they can work against or with each other, it is easy to overlook how they can, in some situations, completely overlap: *Space* is a special issue between rules and fiction. The level design in a game may create an emotionally evocative landscape and at the same time determine the shape of the game tree and hence the gameplay of the game. On the "Wake Island" map in *Battlefield 1942*, the U.S. side holds a U-shaped island, and the Japanese side must invade the island.

In figure 5.17, the topography of the island not only cues the player into imagining an island, it also provides cover and hides information. The player can only see the attacking airplane when it is too late. The shape of the island determines choke points, which points are easily defendable or very vulnerable, and more generally what strategies will

| **Figure 5.17** |
Battlefield 1942 (Digital Illusions 2002): The "Wake Island" map.

work for either side on this map. At the same time, the physical layout of the level prompts the player into imagining an island in the Pacific. As such, level design, space, and the shape of game objects refer simultaneously to rules and fiction. This is a case in which rules and fiction *do* overlap.

Implementing a World

Viewing games as rules, there is a sense in which all games are created equal, the difference between different games being merely their rules and the challenges they present. This suggests that any set of rules can in principle be made to be about anything, but as we have seen, rules and fiction are quite intertwined. From a rules perspective, the most crucial role of fiction is to cue the player into understanding the rules, and this easily leads us to the assumption that games are *themable* (Juul 2001b), that the representation and fiction of any game can simply be replaced with something else. Since an attractive feature of games is the way they challenge their players, games do not *need* an interesting fictional world or *any* fictional world to be considered interesting, but this does not mean that fiction is irrelevant for player experience or game quality.

A serious game design challenge is that at least some aspects of the fictional world have to be implemented in rules, but that some things are easier to implement than others. Games resist many of the more complex themes we can imagine, such as love, ambition, and social conflict, because they are not easily implemented in rules. When games actually are about these things, the actions that the player can perform are often simple, but the "complex" events in the game are only presented in the fictional world, or happen as a result of the player's simple actions. *Myst* contains a love story as well as a conflict between two brothers, but neither of these are implemented in the rules of the game, they are simply presented to the player once the player has performed some very simple mechanical tasks such as turning stone wheels or moving objects about.[7] *The Sims* deals with this issue by letting characters speak to each other using only simple sounds rather than actual language, and the player can then imagine a dialogue from these sounds. This shows that the technical issue of what is readily implemented in rules and/or programming influences the content of the fictional worlds of video games.

The Blue Arrow of the Video Game

The importance of coherence in the fictional world of a game is an ongoing discussion in game development circles. Noah Falstein has initiated the *400 project*, a project of collecting rules for creating good games. This is rule #7:

7. *Maintain Suspension of Disbelief*[8]

- With narrative, keep player in story
- Don't remind them "it's only a game"
- Domain is games with any narrative.

(Barwood and Falstein 2002)

As previously discussed, it is not entirely clear what definition of narrative is being used here, but surely *Grand Theft Auto III*, with its numerous cut-scenes and linear overall structure, qualifies in Falstein's view. However, the game also has numerous incoherencies in its fictional time (chapter 4), and like the *Legend of Zelda* game of the introduction, this game also has large arrows that point to the rules of the game. Though Jeff Gerstman's review (2001) describes the game as a living, breathing place, he does not mention that the game also features large blue arrows that point to the game rules.

Janet Murray's book *Hamlet on the Holodeck* (1997) helped popularize the idea of *immersion*. Inspired by the *holodeck* of *Star Trek,* Murray claims that the ideal immersive system would be a perfected virtual reality system that was indistinguishable from the real world. This undoubtedly tapped into the then popular idea of *virtual reality*. Following Murray, immersion has commonly been described as the feeling of being transported to a fictional world, but as we have seen in the description of fiction in games, this is a misleading account of what is going on in a video game. The player may be completely absorbed by the game *as a real-world activity*, and the player may for the duration of the game or in isolated parts of the game also strongly *imagine* the fictional game world. In *Rules of Play*, Katie Salen and Eric Zimmerman name the exaggerated focus on immersion *the immersive fallacy* (2004, 466–471). Focusing exclusively on coherent worlds and well formed storytelling is a misunderstanding of what games are about.

What a Game Means

Even if games are not exclusively fictional worlds, they are nonetheless subject to constant interpretation. But what does a game mean? It is very hard to create convincing interpretations of *the rules in a game themselves.*[9] One of the most discussed games is *SimCity*, where as the mayor of a city, the player has to control land development, tax levels, and so on (see figure 4.12). *SimCity* is not the actual world, but a model, and this model is obviously based on a set of assumptions. Ted Friedman has claimed that "most fundamentally, it rests on the empiricist, technophilic fantasy that the complex dynamics of city development can be abstracted, quantified, simulated, and micromanaged" (1999). It shines through that Friedman is against this fantasy. But if we actually play *SimCity*, the experience is one of *not* being able to control a city. *SimCity* is an excellent example of a game of emergence where the complexity of the game is far higher than the complexity of the rules. In this way, *SimCity* is a prime example of how a city is unpredictable and uncontrollable. The most important issue here is that Friedman not only ignores what it is actually like to play the game, but also sidesteps the possibility of things like irony, parody, and poetic license. We need to take a step back to consider how we interpret other art forms.

Where Is the Moral?

As a first example, consider Cecil B. DeMille's film *The Ten Commandments* (1956). With Charlton Heston playing the part of Moses, we follow the biblical tale of the birth of Moses, his adoption, the exodus from Egypt, his parting the Red Sea, and his finally receiving the Ten Commandments from God. In this film, it is clear that the protagonist is *good*, and that his actions are *good*. We see the protagonist as the film's moral center, but are protagonists always good? We can compare the Ten Commandments to Mozart's opera *Don Giovanni:* The personal goal of Don Giovanni is to seduce as many women as possible, at which he is sublimely skilled. Toward the end of the opera, Don Giovanni is offered the option of repenting his sins, but he refuses and is finally swallowed by the flames of hell. It should be clear that the moral of the opera is that God punishes sinners, and that the protagonist demonstrates what we *should not* do. We do not automatically assume that the actions of a protagonist are "good" or "right."

Bret Easton Ellis's novel *American Psycho* (1991) is a more complex case. Here, the protagonist commits a number of gruesome murders, all of which are described in great detail. *American Psycho* is critical of modern society (that is, it is a warning against the values and actions of the protagonist), but it can also be criticized for aestheticizing violence. The same kind of criticism is easily directed toward Oliver Stone's movie *Natural Born Killers* (1994), which presents itself as a critique of media fascination with violence while being quite susceptible to the same kind of criticism. Such cases tend to be framed in discussion of whether the violence is gratuitous or motivated within the context of the work. Is the violence a part of the message or just a cheap trick for increasing sales? This is not easily determined, and it is hard to reach any kind of clear interpretation of a movie or novel concerning a dangerous or unpleasant aspect of the world: They can always be interpreted as enjoying or glorifying a tragic aspect of reality or as warning against the same.

What Does Monopoly *Mean?*

Let us return to games. It has been a common assumption that the board game *Monopoly* promotes the values of capitalism. *Monopoly* is of course a game with the goal of acquiring as much money and property as possible, and this was straightforwardly interpreted as a statement that we should acquire as much money and property as possible *in real life*. As a response to this, Ralph Anspach created a countergame called *Anti-Monopoly* (Anspach 1973), in which the explicit goal is to break rather than create monopolies. As a game, however, *Anti-Monopoly* is quite similar to *Monopoly* except for the names of the pieces used: Players also move pieces around the board and collect other pieces, but rather than collecting property, they collect assets to use for breaking monopolies. Following the publication of *Anti-Monopoly*, Parker Brothers sued Ralph Anspach for violating the copyright of *Monopoly*, but during the legal proceedings, it turned out that *Monopoly* was itself a copy of Elizabeth J. Magie's 1903 game *The Landlord's Game*.[10] *The Landlord's Game* had been developed to educate the public about the *evils* of monopolies on land and, more specifically, to promote the single tax system proposed by the economist Henry George where only land is taxed. The instructions of *The Landlord's Game* state: "The object of this game is not only to afford amusement to players, but to illustrate to them how, under the present or prevailing system to land tenure, the landlord has an advantage over other enterprisers, and also how the single tax would discourage speculation" (Salen and Zimmerman 2004, 520). This demonstrates that two games with identical rules *and* fiction can be interpreted as promoting *and* rejecting the creation of monopolies. The entire story of *Monopoly* and its precursors can be found in Ralph Anspach's book *The Billion Dollar Monopoly (R) Swindle* (1998).

A Meaningful Car Crash

It would be a misunderstanding to see a game as an expression of the players wanting to perform the in-game actions in reality. Games—like stories—are things we use to relate to death and disaster. Not because we want them to happen, but because we know they exist. Consider the game *Burnout 2*. *Burnout 2* can be played in a special *crash mode*, where the object is to drive into a busy intersection at full speed in order to create the largest pile-ups possible (figure 5.18). It should be obvious that we do not play this game because we *want* traffic accidents, but because we know they exist and because we want to consider the possibility of death and destruction. The audience of a movie does not automatically assume that the protagonist *does good*, and neither does the player of a video game believe that the protagonist of the game *does good*. A game is a play with identities, where the player at one moment performs an action considered morally sound, and the next moment tries something he or she considers indefensible. The player chooses one mission or another, tries to complete the mission in one way or another, tries to do "good" or "evil." Games are playgrounds where players can experiment with doing things they would or would not normally do.

Literary theorist Stanley Fish has argued that the meaning of any given text is something that is not strictly in the text, but is negotiated in a specific *interpretive community* (Fish 1980). There is no long tradition for interpreting video games, and hence no conventions or community for upholding a specific interpretation. I do not think this should be followed to a conclusion of blanket subjectivity; I think that having the tools for discussing games, and remembering how we interpret other cultural forms, can prevent us from making naïve, literal interpretations of games.

(a)

(b)

| **Figure 5.18** |

Burnout 2: Point of Impact (Criterion Studios 2002), crash mode: Create the largest traffic accident possible.

The Interplay between Rules and Fiction

Different games contain different types of fictional worlds. The rules of a game relate to the kind of fictional world it can project. There is a general correlation between the progression game structure and coherent worlds, perhaps because the fictional aspect of a game is more important when the player only sees it once, and because it is easier to create a variety of different actions when the implementation only has to work in a few selected cases.

Incoherent fictional worlds are often emergence games, perhaps because emergence games have a stronger focus on their rules, and the incoherence of the fictional world is less likely to be experienced as a problem in an emergence game than in a progression (adventure) game. Breaking the coherence of the fictional world does not so much foreground the way the game projects a fictional world as it foregrounds the rules, the game as an activity. In a multiplayer game, breaking the coherence of the fictional world can work as a foregrounding of the game as a real-life social activity. The lack of coherence in some game worlds appears to originate in games being rule-based, and the resulting issues such as creating interesting gameplay, modifying difficulty, and giving the player multiple attempts at the same task.

Can rules and fiction ever match? Level design and the spatial layout of a game are the prime examples of things that are part of rules as well as fiction. *Should* rules and fiction match? Generally speaking, the mismatches may be a larger problem for novice players because they are more likely to use cues from the fictional world in order to understand the game rules. Seasoned players have more knowledge of game conventions and are therefore more skilled at explaining fictional incoherence as the product of game rules. Fictional incoherence and rules/fiction incongruities may in some circumstances make games inaccessible to new players.

Finally, we can point to a set of conventions regarding rules and fiction in games:

- A game can use *functional stylization* to implement selected interesting aspects of the fictional world.
- Space and level design in games are special areas where rules and fiction can overlap: The shape of a fictional island, for example, also works like a rule in that it determines what the player can or cannot do.

- Rules can cue the player into imagining a world.
- Fiction can cue the player into understanding the rules of the game.
- The player's real-world actions have a metaphorical relation to the fictional in-game action: Pressing of a controller button at the right time means making a perfect serve.
- The interplay between rules and fiction of video games is what makes them *half-real:* real rules and fictional worlds.

6
CONCLUSIONS

The intention of this book has been to create a basic theory of video games: Video games are a combination of rules and fiction. Rules are definite descriptions of what can and cannot be done in a game, and they provide challenges that the player must gradually learn to overcome. Fiction is ambiguous—the game can project more or less coherent fictional worlds that the player then may imagine. The classic game model describes games on three levels: the game itself, the player's relation to the game, and the relation between playing and the rest of the world. The entire theory can therefore be described as the intersection between games as rules and games as fiction, and the relation between the game, the player, and the world (table 6.1). The player may pick up a game, invent a game, or negotiate game rules with other players. A game may exist before the player plays it, but the player generally plays it because he or she *wants to*. Fiction cues the player into understanding the rules, and rules can cue the player into imagining a fictional world. This table does not imply causality—the theory has no first principle or starting point, but many simultaneous parts that interact.

The Classic Game Model

The classic game model is a way of capturing what a game is by describing it in terms of the game itself, the player's psychological relation to the game, and the relationship between the playing of the game and the rest of the world. I have called this model *classic* because it describes almost all games from 3000 BC to the end of the twentieth century. The classic game model points out shared traits between most of the things we call "games," and, because it is very open, can be used to differentiate games from each other. The letters of the novel, the sound waves of music, and

Table 6.1
Rules and fiction meet the game, the player, the world

	The game (The game as an artifact)	**The player** (The player and the game)	**The world** (The playing of the game and the rest of the world)
Rules	· The rules of the game · The state machine · The game tree	· Gameplay · Learning · The player repertoire	· Rule negotiations · Repertoire of skills the player brings · Social interaction · Winning and losing · Consequence negotiations
Fiction	· Signs that project a fictional world	· The way the player actually imagines the fictional world	· Film conventions · Game conventions · World knowledge · Interpretation conventions

the images of film are technical cores that are used for creating a diverse set of works that produce a diverse set of experiences. Similarly, the model describes a core that games share of rules, variable outcomes, values assigned to potential outcomes, player effort, emotional attachment to the outcomes, and negotiable consequences. The classic game model also helps us to see that games are created and played using different tools: Games are *transmedial*, and computers are a *game medium*. Sometimes it is easier to see a pattern when it is broken, and the classic game model has perhaps become easier to identify now that video games have evolved beyond it. In this way, the model describes historical change and shows how games develop.

Previously, I discussed to the dual origins of video games—the arcade game and the adventure game. The economical conditions surrounding arcade games demanded that play sessions be kept short. The promotional flyer for the original *Pong* game stresses this by announcing, "Ball Serves Automatically" (Gielens 2000, 6). The action game was initially tied to the arcade model of short sessions in games that could never be completed;

moving away from arcade game conventions became a significant part of the early commercial history of video games. This paved the way for persistent games and save games that modify how the game outcome is defined, and the proliferation of semi-official cheat codes has made it possible for players to bend the rules of video games to accommodate their own wishes. Still, arguably the most interesting departure is the appearance of games without a clear valorized outcome. Even if games conforming to the classic game model are hugely successful, they have a weakness: While a clear valorization (goal) and emotional attachment to the outcome afford the player an opportunity to succeed, they also mean that the player can fail miserably. Additionally, when there is a clear goal, players are more or less forced to focus on optimizing their strategies, but this may run counter to what players *want* to do. *SimCity*, *The Sims*, and many role-playing games do not have official goals, so the players are encouraged to set their own personal short- or long-term goals. Conversely, *Super Mario 64* and *Grand Theft Auto III* do have official goals, but the player is mostly not critically threatened, and can therefore choose to simply play around instead of trying to reach the goal. If the classical game model forces players to optimize their strategies and, to some extent, ignore the aesthetic value of the game pieces, removing or weakening the game goal accommodates a wider range of player types and game experiences. In such games, the player can choose to buy a *nice* couch rather than an *optimal* couch.

Half-Real

I have called video games *half-real*, but an alternative term would be *half-fictional*. On a formal level, games are *themable*, meaning that a set of rules can be assigned a new fictional world without modifying the rules. A game can be changed from one setting to another; the gun can become a green rectangle; the players can control wooden figures rather than humanoid characters. Nevertheless, fiction *matters* in games and it is important to remember the duality of the formal and the experiential perspectives on fiction in games.

As it turns out, the formal rules of a game matter greatly to the experience the player will have, but through a complicated process: Gameplay is the interaction between the rules, the game tree, the players pursuing a goal, and the players' personal repertoires and preferences. When playing a game, events may occur that the designer did not predict, but even if many emergent and *non-intentional* events can happen in a game, they still would not happen *without* the game—it is the game that allows them to happen. If we assume that the game designer will generally *try* to make the game enjoyable, this means that when the instructions of a game inform the player of a game goal, it is also implied that the game has been designed to be entertaining *when one pursues the goal*, and that there is no guarantee that pursuing a different goal will provide quality gameplay.

The fictional worlds that video games project cover a scale from the elaborate and coherent adventure game to incoherent worlds to abstract games. Chapters 4 and 5 gave examples of jarring contradictions and inexplicable events in the fictional worlds of games—events that can only be understood in the context of the rules of a game. The worlds that video games project are often ontologically unstable, but the rules of video games are very stable. While we may not be able to explain, in the game fiction, why Mario reappears in *Donkey Kong*, we always know how many lives we have left. That many fictional game worlds are incoherent does not mean that video games are dysfunctional providers of fiction, but that they project fictional worlds in their own flickering, provisional, and optional way. Of all cultural forms that project fictional worlds, the video game is a special form in which players can meaningfully engage with the game even while refusing to imagine the world that the game projects—the rules of a game are often sufficient to keep the player's interest. Perhaps this places games on par with songs, opera, and ballet—cultural forms that can project fiction but can also be enjoyed even when one does not imagine the worlds that they project.

The importance of the fictional level of a game can change over historical time. I am unaware of any examples of this in the relative short history of video games, but there are numerous cases in non-electronic games: Peter A. Piccione (1980) has described how the game of senet originally was an abstract game, but gradually became associated with the religious motif of the soul's travels in the afterlife. However, this game appears to be a precursor of Parcheesi and backgammon, in which this fictional association has been lost.

In the Game

The affinity between computers and games is one of the ironies of human history. The non-electronic games played and developed over thousands of years have turned out to fit the modern digital computer extremely well. Game players generally dislike having to argue about the rules of a game, and hence they learn to specify rules that are unambiguous and algorithmic. It is surprising that the rules of an old Egyptian game would fit something as modern (and perhaps Western) as the digital computer, but it is only surprising if we forget that the history of mathematics is long and, to a large extent, a shared European-Middle Eastern-Asian history. The word *algorithm* is derived from the name of the ninth-century Muslim mathematician al-Khwarizmi, specifically from the Latin translation of his treatise *Al-Khwarizmi Concerning the Hindu Art of Reckoning* (Encyclopædia Britannica 2003). The history of the algorithm is a shared European-Middle Eastern-Asian history, like the history of games.

We interpret an everyday word differently in the context of a poem, and an ordinary object takes on new meaning when displayed in a gallery. We prefer not to be involved in traffic accidents, but we may play video games about creating traffic accidents. We may prefer not to have to clean the house or take out the garbage, but we play video games about this anyway. A game is a frame in which we see things differently. Literature can make us focus on the words themselves. In the game, we can seek the beauty of the activity itself.

Brian Eno has suggested that pop music is interesting due to the wide range of people and expressions it can contain, covering a spectrum from conceptually oriented musicians to people who are merely in it for style (Kelly 1995). Perhaps what we are seeing is a widening of the video game market: Hardcore game players often dislike the big game hits. That game aficionados can scoff at the tastes of the general public is merely an indication that games are becoming like pop music. The rift between the hardcore and the casual gamer—and between different player types—is a sign of the maturity of the medium. Although there is a core that most video games share of challenges and fictional worlds, innovative games are often those that create interest in what has hitherto been considered boring or unimportant. Innovative games are also discussions about what a game is. From a historical perspective, *The Sims* mirrors the appearance of the realistic novel of the late nineteenth century, when, broadly speaking, novels began to describe everyday life rather than heroes and dramatic events. Art forms develop in part by shifting emphasis: The details of everyday life can be interesting; painting does not have to represent anything; rhythm can be as important as melody. Video games develop the same way.

That the rules of a game are real and formally defined does not mean that the player's experience is also formally defined. However, the rules help create the player's informal experience. Though the fictional worlds of games are optional, subjective, and not real, they play a key role in video games. The player navigates these two levels, playing video games in the half-real zone between the fiction and the rules.

Notes

1 Introduction

1. The shift from abstract to representational games is not just a shift from the non-electronic to the computer, but also from non-commercial games to commercial games.

2. Wittgenstein writes about "Spiele," which is a broader category than "games."

3. I have previously reviewed *The Study of Games* (Juul 2001c).

4. Foursquare is played on four squares painted on the ground. Hughes lists three basic rules of the game:

   - Hit a ball that lands in your square to another square.
   - Let the ball bounce once, but only once, in your square.
   - Don't hit a ball that lands in another square. (Hughes 1999, 99)

5. Hitting the ball very hard at an opponent.

6. Mateas and Stern's *Façade* project (2004) is arguably the most advanced attempt at building such a system to date.

7. See Fluegelman 1976 for a collection of mostly non-competitive, yet charming, games.

2 Video Games and the Classic Game Model

1. The idea of a describing a *classic* model of a historically changing field comes from Bordwell, Staiger, and Thompson 1985.

2. According to E. M. Avedon and Brian Sutton-Smith, cultures without games do exist (1971, 4–5).

3. Ring-a-ring o' roses is a children's game (game in a broad sense) where the participants hold hands and sing:

   Ring a-round the roses,
   A pocket full of posies,
   Ashes! Ashes!
   We all fall down!

   (Everybody falls over.)

4. In *Homo Ludens*, Huizinga devotes an entire chapter to an examination of the concept of *play* in different languages (1950, 28–45).

5. In the works quoted here, Wittgenstein's use of *Spiel* is translated as game; Roger Caillois's use of *jeux* is translated as play *and* games.

6. This table was inspired by Salen and Zimmerman's work on game definitions, where they provide a more fine-grained but less generalized table of eight different game definitions (2004, 95).

7. See Schneider and Butcher 1997 for a critique of the concept of prelusory goals.

8. The possibility of betting hinges on the quantitative outcome of a game—it is only possible to bet if the outcome is beyond discussion.

9. In the MIT Assassins' Guild game played on February 23, 2003, the rules stated the following:

   Non-Players: Not everyone in the world is playing in this game. Some non-players (**NPs**) like to sleep or study undisturbed; others just don't like having toy guns waved in their faces. . . . NPs may not knowingly affect the game. They may not be used to hold items or information. They may not help you kill someone. Do not use the presence of NPs to hide from rampaging mobs that want your blood.
   (MIT Assassin's Guild 2003, 1)

10. Some judged sports such as figure skating rely on the extra layer of judges to transform the qualitative movement of the skater into a quantitative outcome. See Suits 1995 for a discussion.

11. Some of the enjoyment of pen and paper role-playing games is due to the flexibility of the rules.

---

12. Conversely, Wolf (2001) has described the video game as a medium in itself in *The Medium of the Video Game*.

13. That the body of the computer game player is not part of the state machine gives flexibility since the player likely does not have the physical shape or skill needed to perform the sport on a professional level in real life.

14. Mapping between space and mathematics is in fact how a computer handles 3-D graphics—since the computer does not have a real space inside, the space in a computer game is handled as numerical values in the computer. (Technically, the computer does not *really* handle numbers—it only handles electrical signals which can be used to represent numbers.)

15. The equivalence between tic-tac-toe and the mathematical game was described by Newell and Simon (1972, 59–63).

3 Rules

1. Game theory generally uses strategy as an overall term that also encompasses the short-term planning often known as tactics.

2. If the players of a game become aware of a dominant strategy, this always makes the game uninteresting.

3. Video games of perfect information are mostly non-scrolling 2-D games.

4. See, for example, Selic, Gullekson, and Ward 1994.

5. Here are two concrete examples of state machines:

   In chess, the *initial state* is the setup of the board. The set of *input events* corresponds to the permissible moves. It has a *state transition function* (rules) that determines what happens in reaction to specific moves—such as moving pieces, capturing pieces, and more complex events such as castling. In the state machine perspective, it is the *output function* of the game that determines what output is produced at a given time. Since chess is a game of perfect information (the entire game state is visible to all players at all times), the *output function* of chess simply outputs the entire game state at every move.

   In a game like *Quake III Arena*, the *initial state* is the starting position of the players on a level. The set of *input events* is the different actions that each player can perform: move, jump, shoot, change weapon. The *state transition function* determines what happens as a consequence of the player actions and the current game state—players jumping, missiles moving through the air. The *output function* sends a specific view of the game state to each player, only showing them what is visible from their character's perspective in the game world.

6. Unless the machine is broken.

7. When *informally* playing soccer on an open field, rule #1 may be used.

8. According to Suber, "Nomic is a game in which changing the rules is a move. In that respect it differs from almost every other game. The primary activity of Nomic is proposing changes in the rules, debating the wisdom of changing them in that way, voting on the changes, deciding what can and cannot be done afterwards, and doing it. Even this core of the game, of course, can be changed" (1990, Appendix 3B, 362).

9. In the U.S. Open men's singles tennis final on September 8, 2003, Andy Roddick played against Juan Carlos Ferrero. In the third set Ferrero returned a ball that hit the top of the net, stopped almost completely, yet barely fell on Roddick's side of the net, with no chance for Roddick to reach it. Ferrero raised his hand, apologizing. What happened was entirely within the rules of tennis—the raised hand simply implied that it was a chance occurrence beyond his control.

10. Note the difference between the rules of *Pong* and the rules of the game of table tennis: In the real world, the ball will naturally bounce off the table and the player bats, in a video game this has to be explicitly specified in programming.

11. The progression/emergence distinction focuses on the overall structure of a game, whereas Crawford's distinction focuses on the way the game is programmed. These two distinctions will mostly overlap.

12. See also Crawford 1987.

13. See my article "The Open and the Closed" for a more detailed discussion of *EverQuest* and emergence (Juul 2002).

14. A more detailed history of adventure games can be found in Montfort 2003.

15. Gameplay is sometimes used in a broader sense to describe the total game experience, but I am focusing on gameplay as the dynamic aspect of games.

16. Tuning the relation between different weapons, units, or sides of a game is known as *balancing* (see also Rollings and Morris 2000, chap. 5).

17. In other words, it is wrong to assume that *Counter-Strike* is popular *either* because of the game itself or because of the community around the game: *Counter-Strike* is popular because the gameplay makes community-building a good meta-strategy for winning the game *and* because these communities were actually built.

18. Since the number of apples in the basket is doubled every minute, the basket was half full one minute before noon—at 11:59.

19. The home page of the project is www.gamedesignpatterns.org.

20. Kreimeier 2003 provides an overview of these three projects.

21. Then again, the joy of winning correlates positively to the amount of frustration experienced on the way, but the general trend from the 1980s on has been to make games easier, or at least to give the player more small victories and fewer long stretches of frustration.

4 Fiction

1. *Fictional* primarily means *imagined* here. It is not an evaluation of truth value.

2. This is also found in some avant-garde novels, such Alain Robbe-Grillet's *La Jalousie* (1957), which contain contradictory statements.

3. We might wrongly assume that since any game has multiple outcomes, any game is a contradictory world. This means that we might place games in the category of avant-garde fiction, but this is not entirely true. A better explanation is that while a given game can have many different outcomes, it still sets up a dynamic fictional world that can be coherent within a single game session.

4. Haptics (relating to the sense of touch) is the physical feedback from game controllers and other devices that typically vibrate in response to game events.

5. See Klevjer 2002 for a discussion of cut-scenes.

6. While any game can be imagined in any number of ways, this does not mean that all players imagine a specific world in completely different ways. An interpretation of a game world can be more or less convincing. (This interpretation of *Battlezone* has little credibility since we

can demonstrate that it is based on unsubstantiated rumors.) General conventions for how to interpret and imagine fictional worlds will influence the way the player imagines a game world.

7. Wolf (2001) categorizes different kinds of video game spaces in *The Medium of the Video Game.*

8. In *Introduction to Game Time* (Juul 2004a), I called this "event time." I believe that "fictional time" is a more descriptive term.

9. The play time–fictional time relation depends somewhat on the player's familiarity with the game events. The real-time strategy game *StarCraft* (Blizzard Entertainment 1998) is set in space, and the player does not have a strong expectation of the speed of the units of the Zergs or the Protoss. The speed selection is consequently not described in relation to the play time (such as "twice as fast"), but simply called "normal" or "faster."

10. Flash-forwards *can* be included to indicate either something outside the player's influence or something that the player has to fight to reach. (But this will not make sense as a flash-forward if the player does not reach it.)

11. This kind of paradox can be found in *Max Payne* (Remedy 2001), where the game simply restarts the flashback level if the player fails.

12. The prevalence of unchronological time in narratives is afforded by their fixed nature. Since the story is already determined, the events can easily be presented in non-chronological order for aesthetic effect.

13. There are several specific variations of this: narrative as a set of chronologically ordered events, narrative as a sequence of causally related events, and Greimas's canonical narrative, where a subject tries to attain an object from a giver for the benefit of receiver (cf. Prince 1987, 58–59, 91–92).

14. This is strictly speaking not a definition of narrative, but a characterization—most narratives are about human or anthropomorphic agents.

15. See Aarseth 2004a for another critique of the term.

16. These examples share a transgression of common morals, and that is probably a source of enjoyment.

5 Rules and Fiction

1. On the other hand, when a video game is played on a computer, the word processor is also inside the computer, yet outside the game. On the keyboard of a Windows machine, the Windows key is outside the game since pressing it stops the game and brings the user to the desktop; some keys on the keyboard are part of the game, and some keys are outside.

2. On simulation, see Frasca 2001b and Aarseth 2004a.

3. The stylization of a simulation corresponds quite closely to the editing of a film or a novel: It determines emphasis and works with player/viewer expectations.

4. Some games *do* include the possibility that the car can run out of gas; the point is that every game only implements selected aspects of the fictional world.

5. Even the movement of purely abstract shapes is easily interpreted as signifying something. In Valentino Braitenberg's book *Vehicles* (1984), a number of experiments are described in which extremely simple machines are attracted to or repelled by each other. Even such simple rules cue us into imagining emotions for these abstract shapes.

6. There are some precedents for this in folk tales and myths, and in premodern stories in general, where characters successfully pose as other characters using semi-magical disguises. For example, in Beethoven's opera *Fidelio*, Leonore disguises herself as a boy (named "Fidelio") and takes a job at the prison where her husband is wrongfully imprisoned in order to save him. Disguises also play major parts in several of Shakespeare's plays.

7. Freeman (2004) discusses various techniques for adding emotional depth to games.

8. The suspension of disbelief means that readers or viewers must willingly suspend their disbelief in order to accept that the person on stage is not an actor, but the person he or she represents. The idea is usually attributed to Coleridge.

9. See Petschar 1993 for a very unconvincing interpretation of the rules of chess.

10. *The Landlord's Game* is U.S. patent 748,626.

References

Literature

Aarseth, Espen. "Genre Trouble: Narrativism and the Art of Simulation." In *First Person: New Media as Story, Performance, and Game*, edited by Noah Wardrip-Fruin and Pat Harrigan, 45–69. Cambridge, Mass.: MIT Press, 2004a.

Aarseth, Espen. "Quest Games as Post-Narrative Discourse." In *Narrative Across Media*, edited by Marie-Laure Ryan 361–376. Lincoln, Neb.: University of Nebraska Press, 2004b.

Ajami, Amer, and Craig Campanaro. "Half-Life: Counter-Strike Game Guide." Gamespot.com, 2001. Available at http://www.gamespot.com/gamespot/guides/pc/counterstrike/ (accessed November 7, 2004).

Andersen, Klaus Silberbauer, Christian Güttler, and Troels Brun Folmann. "CS_CITYMALL: Design af et 3D Spilmiljø." Student report, IT University of Copenhagen, 2001. Available at http://www.half-real.net/resources/andersen_guttler_folmann-cs_citymall.pdf (accessed November 7, 2004).

Anspach, Ralph. *The Billion Dollar Monopoly (R) Swindle*. 1998. Available at http://www.antimonopoly.com (accessed November 7, 2004).

Atkins, Barry. *More than a Game: The Computer Game as Fictional Form*. Manchester: Manchester University Press, 2003.

Avedon, E. M., and Brian Sutton-Smith. *The Study of Games*. New York: John Wiley & Sons, 1971.

Barwood, Hal, and Noah Falstein. "More of the 400: Discovering Design Rules." Paper presented at the Game Developers' Conference, San José, Calif., March 20–24, 2002. Available at http://www.gdconf.com/archives/2002/hal_barwood.ppt (accessed November 7, 2004).

Björk, Staffan, Jussi Holopainen, and Sus Lundgren. "Game Design Patterns." In *Level Up: Digital Games Research Conference Proceedings*, edited by Marinka Copier and Joost Raessens, 180–193. Utrecht: Utrecht University, 2003. Available at http://civ.idc.cs.chalmers.se/publications/2003/gamedesignpatterns.pdf (accessed November 7, 2004).

Bordwell, David. *Narration in the Fiction Film*. London: Routledge, 1985.

Bordwell, David, Janet Staiger, and Kristin Thompson. *The Classical Hollywood Cinema*. New York: Columbia University Press, 1985.

Braitenberg, Valentino. *Vehicles: Experiments in Synthetic Psychology*. Cambridge, Mass.: MIT Press, 1984.

Brooks, Peter. *Reading for the Plot*. Cambridge, Mass.: Harvard University, [1984] 1992.

Burnham, Van. *Supercade: A Visual History of the Videogame Age, 1971–1984*. Cambridge, Mass.: MIT Press, 2001.

Caillois, Roger. *Man, Play, and Games*. New York: Schocken Books, 1961.

Chatman, Seymour. *Story and Discourse: Narrative Structure in Fiction and Film*. Ithaca, NY: Cornell University Press, 1978.

Chesire, Sophie. "The Hobbit FAQ/Walkthru." Gamefaqs.com, 2001. Available at http://db.gamefaqs.com/computer/c64/file/hobbit.txt (accessed November 7, 2004).

Church, Doug. "Formal Abstract Design Tools." *Game Developer Magazine* (August 1999). Available at http://www.gamasutra.com/features/19990716/design_tools_01.htm.

Coffin, Stewart T. *The Puzzling World of Polyhedral Dissections*. London: Oxford University Press, 1974. Available at http://www.puzzleworld.org/PuzzlingWorld/default.htm (accessed November 7, 2004).

Costikyan, Greg. "I Have No Words and I Must Design." 1994. Available at http://www.costik.com/nowords.html (accessed November 7, 2004).

Crawford, Chris. *The Art of Computer Game Design*. 1982. Available at http://www.vancouver.wsu.edu/fac/peabody/game-book/Coverpage.html (accessed November 7, 2004).

Crawford, Chris. "Process Intensity." *Journal of Computer Game Design* 1, no. 5 (1987). Available at http://www.erasmatazz.com/library/JCGD_Volume_1/Process_Intensity.html (accessed November 7, 2004).

Csikszentmihalyi, Mihaly. "Does Being Human Matter—On Some Interpretive Problems of Comparative Ludology." *Behavioral and Brain Sciences* 5, no. 1 (1982).

Csikszentmihalyi, Mihaly. *Flow: The Psychology of Optimal Experience.* New York: Harper Perennial, 1990.

Culin, Stewart. "Mancala, the National Game of Africa." In *The Study of Games*, edited by E. M. Avedon and Brian Sutton-Smith, 94–102. New York: John Wiley & Sons, [1894] 1971.

Culin, Stewart. *Games of the North American Indians.* Lincoln, Neb.: University of Nebraska Press, 1992.

Danesi, Marcel. *The Puzzle Instinct.* Bloomington, Ind.: Indiana University Press, 2002.

De Groot, Adriaan D. *Thought and Choice in Chess.* Hague: Mouton Publishers, 1965.

Edge Magazine. "Super Mario Sunshine Review." *Edge*, no. 114 (2002): 80–83.

Ellis, Bret Easton. *American Psycho.* New York: Vintage, 1991.

Encyclopædia Britannica. "Algorithm." Encyclopædia Britannica Premium Service, September 28, 2003. Available at http://www.britannica.com/eb/article?eu=5785 (accessed November 7, 2004).

Eskelinen, Markku. "Towards Computer Game Studies, Part 1: Narratology and Ludology." Paper presented at SIGGRAPH, Los Angeles, Calif., August 12–17 (2001b). Available at http://www.siggraph.org/artdesign/gallery/S01/essays/0416.pdf (accessed November 7, 2004).

Falstein, Noah. "Better By Design: The 400 Project." *Game Developer Magazine* (March 2002): 26.

Fish, Stanley. *Is There a Text in This Class?* Cambridge, Mass.: Harvard University Press, 1980.

Fluegelman, Andrew, ed. *The New Games Book.* Garden City, New York: Doubleday/Dolphin, 1976.

Frasca, Gonzalo. "Ludology Meets Narratology: Similitude and Differences Between (Video) Games and Narrative." 1999. Available at http://www.ludology.org/articles/ludology.htm (accessed November 7, 2004).

Frasca, Gonzalo. *SIMULATION 101: Simulation versus Representation.* 2001b. Available at http://www.ludology.org/articles/sim1/simulation101.html (accessed November 7, 2004).

Freeman, David. *Creating Emotion in Games: The Craft and Art of Emotioneering.* Indianapolis, Ind.: New Riders, 2004.

Friedman, Ted. "Semiotics of SimCity." *Firstmonday.dk* 4, no. 4 (1999). Available at http://www.firstmonday.dk/issues/issue4_4/friedman/ (accessed November 7, 2004).

Gerstman, Jeff. "Grand Theft Auto III review." Gamespot.com, 2001. Available at http://www.gamespot.com/ps2/adventure/grandtheftauto3/review.html (accessed November 7, 2004).

Gielens, Jaro. *Electronic Plastic.* Berlin: Die Gestalten Verlag, 2000.

Goffman, Erving. *Encounters: Two Studies in the Sociology of Interaction.* New York: Penguin, 1972 (1961).

Grodal, Torben Kragh. *Moving Pictures. A New Theory of Film Genres, Feelings, and Cognition.* Oxford: Clarendon Press, 1997.

Haider, Hilde, and Peter A. Frensch. "The Role of Information Reduction in Skill Acquisition." *Cognitive Psychology*, no. 30 (1996): 340–337.

Herron, R. E., and Brian Sutton-Smith. *Child's Play.* New York: John Wiley & Sons, 1971.

Hofstadter, Douglas. *Metamagical Themas: Questing for the Essence of Mind and Pattern.* New York: Penguin, 1985.

Holland, John D. *Emergence: From Chaos to Order.* Oxford: Oxford University Press, 1998.

Hughes, Linda A. "Children's Games and Gaming." In *Children's Folklore*, edited by Brian Sutton-Smith, Jay Mechling, Thomas W. Johnson, and Felicia R. McMahon, 93–119. Logan, Utah: Utah University Press, 1999.

Huizinga, Johan. *Homo Ludens.* Boston: Beacon Press, 1950.

IGN.com. "Grand Theft Auto III Refused Classification in Australia." IGN.com, December 13, 2001. Available at http://ps2.ign.com/articles/100/100454p1.html (accessed November 7, 2004).

Jenkins, Henry. "Congressional Testimony on Media Violence." May 4, 1999. Available at http://web.mit.edu/comm-forum/papers/jenkins_ct.html (accessed November 7, 2004).

Jenkins, Henry. "Transmedia Storytelling." *MIT Technology Review*, January 15, 2003. Available at http://www.technologyreview.com/articles/03/01/wo_jenkins011503.asp (accessed November 7, 2004).

Jenkins, Henry. "Game Design as Narrative Architecture." In *First Person: New Media as Story, Performance, and Game*, edited by Noah Wardrip-Fruin and Pat Harrigan, 118–130. Cambridge, Mass.: MIT Press, 2004.

Johnson, Steven. *Emergence: The Connected Lives of Ants, Brains, Cities and Software*. London: Penguin, 2001.

Juul, Jesper. "A Clash between Game and Narrative." Paper presented at the DAC conference, Bergen, Norway, November 1998. Available at http://www.jesperjuul.net/text/clash_between_game_and_narrative.html (accessed November 7, 2004).

Juul, Jesper. "A Clash between Game and Narrative." Master's thesis, University of Copenhagen, 1999. Available at http://www.jesperjuul.net/thesis/ (accessed November 7, 2004).

Juul, Jesper. "What Computer Games Can and Can't Do." Paper presented at the DAC conference, Bergen, August 2000. Available at http://www.jesperjuul.net/text/wcgcacd.html (accessed November 7, 2004).

Juul, Jesper. "Games Telling Stories? A Brief Note on Games and Narratives." *Game Studies* 1, no. 1 (2001a). Available at http://www.gamestudies.org/0101/juul-gts/.

Juul, Jesper. "Play time, Event Time, Themability." Paper presented at the Computer Games and Digital Textualities conference, Copenhagen, March 1–2, 2001b.

Juul, Jesper. "The Repeatedly Lost Art of Studying Games. Review of Elliott M. Avedon and Brian Sutton-Smith (eds.), *The Study of Games*." *Game Studies* 1, no. 1 (2001c). Available at http://www.gamestudies.org/0101/juul-review/.

Juul, Jesper. "The Open and the Closed: Games of Emergence and Games of Progression." In *Computer Game and Digital Cultures Conference Proceedings*, edited by Frans Mäyrä, 323–329. Tampere: Tampere University Press, 2002.

Juul, Jesper. "Just What Is It That Makes Computer Games So Different, So Appealing?" *Ivory Tower* column for IGDA, April 2003a. Available at http://www.igda.org/columns/ivorytower/ivory_Apr03.php.

Juul, Jesper. "The Game, the Player, the World: Looking for a Heart of Gameness." In *Level Up: Digital Games Research Conference Proceedings*, edited by Marinka Copier and Joost Raessens, 30–45. Utrecht: Utrecht University, 2003b.

Juul, Jesper. "Introduction to Game Time." In *First Person: New Media as Story, Performance, and Game*, edited by Noah Wardrip-Fruin and Pat Harrigan, 131–142. Cambridge, Mass.: MIT Press, 2004a.

Juul, Jesper. "Hvad Spillet Betyder: Om Grand Theft Auto III" [What the Game Means: On Grand Theft Auto III]. In *Digitale Verdener*, edited by Ida Engholm and Lisbeth Klastrup, 181–195. Copenhagen: Gyldendal, 2004b.

Kelley, David. *The Art of Reasoning*. New York: W. W. Norton, 1988.

Kelly, Kevin. "Gossip is Philosophy." *Wired* 3.05 (1995).

Kent, Steven L. *The First Quarter: A 25-Year History of Video Games*. Bothell, Wash.: BWD Press, 2000.

King, Geoff, and Tanya Krzywinska. "Computer Games/Cinema/Interfaces." In *Computer Game and Digital Cultures Conference Proceedings*, edited by Frans Mäyrä, 323–329. Tampere: Tampere University Press, 2002a.

King, Geoff, and Tanya Krzywinska, eds. *ScreenPlay: Cinema/Videogames/Interfaces*. London: Wallflower Press, 2002b.

Klevjer, Rune. "In Defense of Cutscenes." In *Computer Game and Digital Cultures Conference Proceedings*, edited by Frans Mäyrä, 191–202. Tampere: Tampere University Press, 2002.

Knuth, Donald. *The Art of Computer Programming. Vol. 1: Fundamental Algorithms*. Menlo Park: Addison-Wesley, 1968.

Kreimeier, Bernd. "The Case For Game Design Patterns." *Gamasutra*, March 13, 2002. Available at http://www.gamasutra.com/features/20020313/kreimeier_01.htm (accessed November 7, 2004).

Kreimeier, Bernd. "Game Design Methods: A 2003 Survey." *Gamasutra*, March 3, 2003. Available at http://www.gamasutra.com/features/20030303/kreimeier_01.shtml (accessed November 7, 2004).

Lantz, Frank. "Ironclad. A Game for 2 Players." In *Rules of Play: Game Design Fundamentals*, edited by Katie Salen and Eric Zimmerman, 286–297. Cambridge, Mass.: MIT Press, 2004.

Laurel, Brenda Kay. "Toward the Design of a Computer-Based Interactive Fantasy System." Ph.D. diss., Ohio State University, 1986.

Lever, Janet. "Sex Differences in the Games Children Play." *Social Problems* 23, no. 4 (1976): 478–487.

Lopiccolo, Greg, and Alex Rigopulos. "Harmonix's Amplitude. The Sound and the Fury." *Game Developer Magazine* (August 2003): 40–45.

Madsen, Helene, and Troels Degn Johansson. "Gameplay Rhetoric: A Study of the Construction of Satirical and Associational Meaning in Short Computer Games for the WWW." In *Computer Game and Digital Cultures Conference Proceedings*, edited by Frans Mäyrä, 73–87. Tampere: Tampere University Press, 2002.

McCloud, Scott. *Understanding Comics*. New York: Harper Perennial, 1993.

MIT Assassins' Guild. *Vive la Révolution*. Handout, February 23, 2003.

Montfort, Nick. *Twisty Little Passages*. Cambridge, Mass.: MIT Press, 2003.

Murray, Janet. *Hamlet on the Holodeck*. New York: The Free Press, 1997.

Myers, David. "Time, Symbol Transformations, and Computer Games." *Play & Culture*, no. 5 (1992): 441–457.

Neumann, John von, and Oskar Morgenstern. *Theory of Games and Economic Behavior*. Princeton, N.J.: Princeton University Press, 1953.

Newell, Allen, and Paul S. Rosenbloom. "Mechanisms of Skill Acquisition and the Law of Practice." In *Cognitive Skills and Their Acquisition*, edited by John R. Anderson, 1–55. Hillsdale, N.J.: Lawrence Erlbaum, 1981.

Newell, Allen, and Herbert A. Simon. *Human Problem Solving*. Englewood Cliffs, N.J.: Prentice-Hall, 1972.

Osborne, Scott. "Giants: Citizen Kabuto Review." Gamespot.com, 2000a. Available at http://www.gamespot.com/pc/action/giantscitizenkabuto/review .html (accessed November 7, 2004).

Osborne, Scott. "Hitman: Codename 47 Review." Gamespot.com, 2000b. Available at http://www.gamespot.com/pc/action/hitmancodename47/review .html (accessed November 7, 2004).

Parlett, David. *The Oxford History of Board Games*. Oxford: Oxford University Press, 1999.

Parlett, David. *The Penguin Encyclopedia of Card Games*. London: Penguin, 2000.

Pavel, Thomas. *Fictional Worlds*. Cambridge, Mass.: Harvard University Press, 1986.

Pearce, Celia. "Towards a Game Theory of Game." In *First Person: New Media as Story, Performance, and Game*, edited by Noah Wardrip-Fruin and Pat Harrigan, 143–153. Cambridge, Mass.: MIT Press, 2004.

Petschar, Hans. "Das Schachspiel als Spiegel der Kultur." In *Vom Ernst des Spiels: Über Spiel und Spieltheorie*, edited by Ursula Baatz and Wolfgang Müller-Funk, 122–135. Berlin: Dietrich Reimer Verlag, 1993.

Piaget, Jean. "The Rules of the Game of Marbles." In *Play—Its Role in Development and Evolution*, edited by Jolly and Sylva Bruner, 413–441. New York: Penguin, 1976.

Piccione, Peter A. "In Search of the Meaning of Senet." *Archaeology* 33 (July–August 1980): 55–58.

Prince, Gerald. *Dictionary of Narratology*. Lincoln, Neb.: University of Nebraska Press, 1987.

Propp, Vladímir. *Morphology of the Folktale*. Austin, Tex.: University of Texas Press, 1968.

Retaux, Xavier, and Juliette Rouchier. "Realism vs. Surprise and Coherence: Different Aspect of Playability in Computer Games." Paper presented at the Playing with the Future conference, Manchester, U.K., April 5–7, 2002. Abstract available at http://les1.man.ac.uk/cric/gamerz/abstracts/retaux.htm (accessed November 7, 2004).

Robbe-Grillet, Alain. *La Jalousie*. Paris: Les Editions de Minuit, 1957.

Rollings, Andrew, and Dave Morris. *Game Architecture and Design*. Scottsdale, Ariz.: Coriolis, 2000.

Rouse, Richard. *Game Design: Theory and Practice*. Plano, Tex.: Wordware, 2001.

Ryan, Marie-Laure. *Possible Worlds, Artificial Intelligence, and Narrative Theory*. Bloomington, Ind.: Indiana University Press, 1991.

Ryan, Marie-Laure. "Possible Worlds in Recent Literary Theory." *Style* 26, no. 4 (1992): 528–553.

Ryan, Marie-Laure. "Beyond Myth and Metaphor: The Case of Narrative in Digital Media." *Game Studies* 1, no. 1 (2001a). Available at http://www.gamestudies.org/0101/ryan/ (accessed November 7, 2004).

Salen, Katie, and Eric Zimmerman. *Rules of Play: Game Design Fundamentals*. Cambridge, Mass.: MIT Press, 2004.

Saltzman, Marc, ed. *Game Design. Secrets of the Sages*. Indianapolis, Ind.: Macmillan, 1999.

Saussure, Ferdinand de. *Course in General Linguistics*. London: Duckworth, [1916] 2000.

Schank, Roger C., and Robert P. Abelson. *Scripts, Plans, Goals and Understanding*. Hillsdale, N.J.: Lawrence Erlbaum, 1977.

Schneider, Angela J. and Robert B. Butcher. "Pre-lusory Goals for Games: A Gambit Declined." *Journal of the Philosophy of Sport* 24 (1997): 38–46.

Selic, Bran, Garth Gullekson, and Paul T. Ward. *Real-Time Object-Oriented Modeling*. New York: John Wiley & Sons, 1994.

Shannon, Claude. "Programming a Computer for Playing Chess." *Philosophical Magazine* 41, no. 314 (1950).

Shelley, Bruce. "Guidelines for Developing Successful Games." *Gamasutra*, August 15, 2001. Available at http://www.gamasutra.com/features/20010815/shelley_01.htm (accessed November 7, 2004).

Smith, Harvey. "The Future of Game Design: Moving beyond Deus Ex and Other Dated Paradigms." IGDA, 2001. Available at http://www.igda.org/articles/hsmith_future.php (accessed November 7, 2004).

Smith, Harvey. "Orthogonal Unit Differentiation." Paper presented at the Game Developers' Conference, San José, Calif., March 4–8, 2003. Available at http://www.gdconf.com/archives/2003/Smith_Harvey.ppt (accessed November 7, 2004).

Suber, Peter. *The Paradox of Self-Amendment: A Study of Law, Logic, Omnipotence, and Change*. Bern: Peter Lang Publishing 1990. Available at http://www.earlham.edu/~peters/writing/psa/index.htm (accessed November 7, 2004).

Suits, Bernard. *The Grasshopper: Games, Life and Utopia*. Toronto: University of Toronto Press, 1978.

Suits, Bernard. "Tricky Triad: Games, Play, and Sport." In *Philosophic Inquiry in Sport*, 2nd ed., edited by William J. Morgan and Klaus V. Meier, 16–22. Champaign, Ill.: Human Kinetics, 1995.

Sutton-Smith, Brian. *The Ambiguity of Play*. Cambridge, Mass.: Harvard University Press, 1997.

Tacitus, Cornelius. *Dialogus. Agricola. Germania*. London: William Heinemann, [98 AD] 1914.

The Tech. "ChessMate. White to Move and Checkmate in Two." *The Tech* (Cambridge, Mass.), February 21, 2003, p. 8.

Tosca, Susana. "The Quest Problem in Computer Games." In *Proceedings of the First International Conference on Technologies for Interactive Digital Storytelling and Entertainment TIDSE '03*, edited by Stefan Göbel et al. Darmstadt: Fraunhofer IRB Verlag 2003. Available at http://www.itu.dk/people/tosca/quest.htm (accessed November 7, 2004).

Tronstad, Ragnhild. "Semiotic and Non-Semiotic MUD Performance." Paper presented at COSIGN, Amsterdam, September 10–12, 2001. Available at http://www.cosignconference.org/cosign2001/papers/Tronstad.pdf (accessed November 7, 2004).

Waldrop, M. Mitchell. *Complexity—The Emerging Science at the Edge of Order and Chaos*. London: Penguin, 1994.

Walker, Jill. "Do You Think You're Part of This? Digital Texts and the Second Person Address." In *Cybertext Yearbook 2000*, edited by Markku Eskelinen and Raine Koskimaa, 34–51. Jyväskylä: Publications of the Research Center for Contemporary Culture, 2001.

Weisstein, Eric W. "Königsberg Bridge Problem." From *MathWorld*—A Wolfram Web Resource, 2004. Available at http://mathworld.wolfram.com/KoenigsbergBridgeProblem.html (accessed November 7, 2004).

Wibroe, Mads, K. K. Nygaard, and Peter Bøgh Andersen. "Games and Stories." In *Virtual Interaction*, edited by Lars Qvortrup, 166–181. London: Springer Verlag, 2001.

Wittgenstein, Ludwig. *Philosophical Investigations*. Oxford: Blackwell, [1953] 2001.

Wolf, Mark J. P., ed. *The Medium of the Video Game*. Austin, Tex.: University of Texas Press, 2001.

Wolfram, Stephen. *A New Kind of Science*. Champaign, Ill.: Wolfram Media, 2002.

Wolfram, Stephen. "Complex Systems Theory." In *Emerging Syntheses in Science: Proceedings of the Founding Workshops of the Santa Fe Institute*. Boston: Addison-Wesley, 1988. Available at http://www.stephenwolfram.com/publications/articles/ca/88-complex/2/text.html (accessed November 7, 2004).

Wright, Talmadge, Eric Boria, and Paul Breidenbach. "Creative Player Actions in FPS Online Video Games." *Game Studies* 2, no. 2 (2002). Available at http://www.gamestudies.org/0202/wright/.

Games

Key to platforms:

Amiga: Commodore Amiga.

Arcade: Arcade game.

Board: Board game.

C64: Commodore 64.

DC: Sega Dreamcast.

GBA: Gameboy Advance.

GC: Nintendo Gamecube.

Mac: Apple Macintosh.

N64: Nintendo 64.

PC: PC, DOS or Windows.

PS: Sony Playstation.

PS2: Sony Playstation 2.

SNES: Super Nintendo.

WWW: Web-based game.

Xbox: Xbox.

Amusement Vision. *Super Monkey Ball 2*. Sega, 2002. (GC)

Anim-X. *Majestic*. Electronic Arts, 2001. (PC)

Anspach, Ralph. *Anti-Monopoly*. 1974. (Board)

Atari. *Pong*. Atari, 1973. (Arcade)

Atari. *Asteroids*. Atari, 1979. (Arcade)

Atari. *Battlezone*. Atari, 1980. (Arcade)

Atari. *Star Wars*. Atari, 1983. (Arcade)

Atari. *Tetris*. Atari, 1986. (Arcade)

Bally Midway. *Rampage*. Bally Midway, 1986. (Arcade)

Blizzard Entertainment. *StarCraft*. Blizzard Entertainment, 1998. (PC)

BlueSky Software. *Risk*. Hasbro Interactive, 1997. (PC)

Blue Byte. *The Settlers*. Strategic Simulations, Inc, 1994. (PC)

Cinemaware. *Defender of the Crown*. Cinemaware, 1986. (Amiga)

Core Design Ltd. *Tomb Raider*. Eidos Interactive, 1996. (PC)

The Counter-Strike Team. *Counter-Strike*. 2000. (PC)

Creative Assembly. *Shogun: Total War*. Electronic Arts, 2000. (PC)

Criterion Studios. *Burnout 2: Point of Impact*. Acclaim, 2002. (PS2)

Crowther, Willie, and Don Woods. *Adventure*. 1976. (Mainframe)

Cyan. *Myst*. Brøderbund, 1993. (Mac)

Data East. *Burger Time*. Bally Midway, 1982. (Arcade)

Denki Limited. *Denki Blocks*. Rage Software, 2001. (GBA)

Digital Illusions. *Battlefield 1942*. Electronic Arts, 2002. (PC)

Electronic Arts. *FIFA 2002*. 2002. (Xbox)

Ensemble Studios. *Age of Empires II*. Microsoft, 1999. (PC)

Exidy. *Death Race*. Exidy, 1976. (Arcade)

Epic MegaGames. *Unreal Tournament*. GT Interactive, 1999. (PC)

Funcom. *The Longest Journey*. IQ Media Nordic, 2000. (PC)

Harmonix. *Frequency*. SCEA, 2001. (PS2)

Harmonix. *Amplitude*. SCEA, 2003. (PS2)

Hasbro Interactive. *Axis & Allies*. Hasbro Interactive, 1998. (PC)

Hitmaker. *Virtua Tennis*. Sega, 2000. (DC)

ID Software. *Quake III Arena*. Electronic Arts, 1999. (PC)

Infocom. *Witness*. Infocom, 1983. (PC)

IO Interactive. *Hitman: Codename 47*. Eidos Interactive, 2000. (PC)

Ion Storm. *Deus Ex*. Eidos Interactive, 2000. (PC)

Juul, Jesper. *Puls in Space*. 1998a. (WWW) Available at http://www.soup.dk/pspace/ (accessed November 7, 2004).

Juul, Jesper. *Game liberation*. Published in the M/C journal, November 2000. (WWW) Available at http://www.jesperjuul.net/gameliberation/ (accessed November 7, 2004).

Konami. *Dance Dance Revolution*. Konami, 2001a. (PS)

Konami. *Metal Gear Solid 2: Sons of Liberty*. Konami, 2001b. (PS2)

Lionhead Studios. *Black & White*. EA Games, 2001. (PC)

Magie, Elizabeth J. *The Landlord's Game*. 1904. (Board)

Mateas, Michael, and Andrew Stern. *Façade*. 2004. (PC)

Maxis. *SimCity*. Brøderbund, 1989. (PC)

Maxis. *The Sims*. Electronic Arts, 2000. (PC)

Maxis. *SimCity 4*. Electronic Arts, 2003. (PC)

Maxis. *The Sims 2*. Electronic Arts, 2004. (PC)

Melbourne House. *The Hobbit*. Melbourne House, 1984. (C64)

Milton Bradley. *Frogger*. 1981. (Board)

Milton Bradley. *Pac-Man*. 1982. (Board)

Milton Bradley. *Berzerk*. 1983. (Board)

Namco. *Galaga*. Namco, 1981. (Arcade)

Namco. *Pac-Man*. Namco, 1980. (Arcade)

Namco. *Tekken 3 Tag Tournament*. Namco, 2000. (PS2)

Namco. *Tekken 4*. Namco, 2002. (PS2)

NaNaOn-Sha. *Vib-Ribbon*. SCEI, 1999. (PS)

Nintendo. *Donkey Kong*. Nintendo, 1981. (Arcade)

Nintendo. *Super Metroid*. Nintendo, 1993. (SNES)

Nintendo. *Super Mario 64*. Nintendo, 1996. (N64)

Nintendo. *Pikmin*. Nintendo, 2001. (GC)

Nintendo. *Super Mario Sunshine*. Nintendo, 2002. (GC)

Nintendo. *The Legend of Zelda: The Wind Waker*. Nintendo, 2003a. (GC)

Nintendo. *WarioWare Inc.: Mega MicroGame$*. Nintendo, 2003b. (GBA)

Nova Game Design. *Axis & Allies*. Milton Bradley, 1984. (Board)

Origin Systems. *Ultima Online*. Origin Systems, 1997. (PC)

Parker Brothers. *Monopoly*. 1936. (Board)

Pazhitnov, Alexey. *Tetris*. Spectrum Holobyte, 1985. (PC)

Planet Moon Studios. *Giants: Citizen Kabuto*. Interplay, 2000. (PC)

Polyphony Digital. *Gran Turismo 3: A-Spec*. SCEA, 2001. (PS2)

Power and Magic. *Top Spin*. Microsoft, 2003. (Xbox)

Remedy. *Max Payne*. Take 2 Interactive, 2001. (PC)

Rockstar Games. *Grand Theft Auto III*. Take-Two Interactive, 2001. (PS2)

Rogue Entertainment. *American McGee's Alice*. Electronic Arts, 2000. (PC)

Russell, Stephen. *Spacewar!* 1961. (PDP–1 mainframe.) Available at http://lcs.www.media.mit.edu/groups/el/projects/spacewar/ (accessed November 7, 2004).

Sales Curve Interactive. *Carmageddon*. Interplay, 1997. (PC)

Sega. *Pengo*. Sega, 1982. (Arcade)

Sega-AM2. *Shenmue*. Sega, 2000. (DC)

Sonic Team. *ChuChu Rocket*. Sega, 2000. (DC)

Peter Suber. *Nomic*. 1982. (Mind game)

Taito. *Space Invaders*. Taito, 1977. (Arcade)

Taito. *Bust-A-Move 4*. Taito, 1998. (PS2)

Three Rings Design. *Puzzle Pirates*. 2003. (WWW) Available at http://www.puzzlepirates.com (accessed November 7, 2004).

Valve Software. *Half-Life*. Sierra, 1998. (PC)

Verant Interactive. *EverQuest*. Sony Online Entertainment, 1999. (PC)

Movies

DeMille, Cecil B. *The Ten Commandments*. 1956.

Cameron, James. *Titanic*. 1997.

Stone, Oliver. *Natural Born Killers*. 1994.

Welles, Orson. *Citizen Kane*. 1941.

Index